A *WESTERN HORSEMAN*

M000316874

# The Horseman's Guide to Tack and Equipment

## Form, Fit and Function

### By Cynthia McFarland

**Edited by Fran Devereux Smith**

# The Horseman's Guide to Tack and Equipment

*Published by*
**WESTERN HORSEMAN** magazine
2112 Montgomery St.
Fort Worth, TX  76107
817-737-6397

www.westernhorseman.com

*Design, Typography, and Production*
**Globe Pequot Press**
Guilford, Connecticut

*Cover Photos by Darrell Dodds*
*Front Cover: Fizzabar Pep DFO; Back Cover: Jazzy Little Guy*
*Horses owned by Ward and Gene Heid, Alvaredo, Texas.*

*Printing*
**Versa Press, Inc.**
East Peoria, Illinois

Manufactured in the United States of America

*First Printing: May 2013*

ISBN 978-0-7627-8626-8

# Contents

# Dedication and Acknowledgments

I remember my delight at discovering *Western Horseman* magazine in my early teens, reveling in page after page devoted to my favorite subject and lifestyle. I'd read the articles, study the photos and then get on my horse and put to use what I'd learned. Some lessons were easier than others; I still remember one especially effective tip on getting a horse to back quickly!

There was both great satisfaction and serendipity when, decades after reading my earliest issue of *Western Horseman,* I sold my first article to the magazine.

Through the years, I've had the privilege as a full-time freelance writer to interview and write about many of the world's top horsemen. It was a distinct honor to write two previous *Western Horseman* books with Chris Cox (*Ride the Journey*), and Martin Black (*Cow-Horse Confidence: A Time-Honored Approach to Stockmanship*). I've known Chris since the mid-1990s and always will be grateful that he asked me to write for him. I count both men as good friends and consider them two of the finest horsemen and educators I've ever had the pleasure of knowing.

When the publishers asked me to write my own *Western Horseman* book, this volume devoted to tack and equipment, I was excited at the opportunity. I also knew that such a book would benefit greatly from the vast experience of lifelong horsemen and women. Some of them I knew long before I began this project; others I had the privilege of meeting directly because of this book. To each of them, I extend a heartfelt and grateful, "Thank you! I couldn't have done it without you."

At the back of the book, you'll find a Resource Guide, which includes contact information for everyone I interviewed while working on this project. I am enormously indebted to the kindness of these individuals who took time out of their own hectic schedules to talk with me at length, sharing their personal expertise and knowledge so that this book could serve as a helpful and informative resource. Their practical insight and experience were invaluable as I wrote each chapter. I appreciate their attention to detail and willingness to work with me to make this book as practical and useful as possible for readers.

I am especially grateful to Patricia McFarland for her enthusiastic support and careful proofreading (and for nurturing my interest in books and reading when I was very young), Fran Smith for her artful and consistent editing, and Ernie King, for trusting me with another *Western Horseman* book.

I also owe a debt of gratitude to all the good horses through the decades in my life—teachers, friends and partners—thank you for the lessons you've taught me, the countless miles and hours we've shared, the trust and devotion you've given. I'm a better person because of you.

Cynthia McFarland

# Introduction

Horses have been my passion for as long as I can remember. In a kindergarten workbook, I found an illustration that embodied all my dreams: a picturesque farm complete with the classic red barn surrounded by pastures with horses, cattle, and sheep. There's a creek, spanned by a narrow bridge, and a gently curving road. I pictured the drivers in those 1960s-era vehicles looking at the farm as they passed—the farm where I vividly imagined myself living.

Growing up in Tucson, I spent long hours reading about horses, drawing them, writing stories about them, taking riding lessons. Eventually, I worked at a local riding stable, thrilled to be paid $2 an hour and able to ride for free at the end of the day. I saved my hard-earned baby-sitting dollars to buy a horse of my own, and a saddle, too. The saddle didn't have to be fancy; I'd be happy with a decent used one. At 13, I fell head-over-horse-crazy-heels for Yuma, a bright sorrel Quarter Horse with a perfect star and two diagonal socks. It took nearly 2 years until I was finally able to buy him, but he was worth the wait.

Yuma's papers revealed his fine bloodlines, but pedigree had nothing to do with why I loved that horse. On his back I felt like I could do anything, heady emotion for a teen-age girl trying to find her way in the world. We jumped every obstacle we could find, worked cows, ran barrels, swam flooded riverbeds. We galloped the arroyos for the sheer bliss of it and explored countless miles of Arizona trails. I rode bareback for 9 months while I worked to pay off that used saddle.

When I bought my first saddle, I knew next to nothing about buying horse gear, or why certain choices would be better than others. I longed for some of the fancy equipment I saw in magazines, but had no reference book like the one you now hold in your hands. Still, I had my horse, so I was on my way.

Yuma had a generous heart, a bold attitude and a definite sense of humor, not to mention a smooth trot I could sit comfortably for miles. He taught me more about horsemanship than all the lessons I took and books I read, and he looked out for me when I didn't know better. He set the bar for the equine partners who would share my life, the latest being Ben (short for Dun Ben Seduced), the trusty red dun Paint gelding who has been my riding buddy since 2003.

When I started this journey so many years ago, what I knew about horses and gear paled in comparison to all I didn't know, but the joy I found in horses as a child has never faded. I still think nothing beats a long trail ride on a good horse. My knowledge of and appreciation for equipment has certainly expanded. I don't compete, so I can't justify some of the tack purchases I'd like to make, but my dun horse looks quite handsome going down the trail in his rawhide hackamore and horsehair mecate.

Today, the framed illustration from that kindergarten workbook hangs in my country home on my own little farm. Every day, when I sit down at the computer to write, I'm thankful for the blessing and a privilege of making a living doing something I love.

In writing this book, I endeavored to bring together solid information, interesting facts and practical advice. I'm well aware that descriptions of tack and terms vary, depending on the region, just as slang words for equipment also differ. My focus is on the use, fit and adjustment of tack, so I trust readers appreciate the differences rather than bog down on them. My goal was to create a tack and equipment guidebook that is useful to riders of all levels. I hope you find it serves that purpose and that your time in the saddle reminds you—in all the best ways—just why you started riding in the first place.

Cynthia McFarland

# 1

# Halters, Leads and Longeing Equipment

When it comes to tack, equipment doesn't get much more basic than the halter and lead rope, but that doesn't make them unimportant. You might be camping in the backcountry with your horses on an overhead picket line or have your horse tied to the trailer at a competitive event. You might be schooling that new yearling colt in his first groundwork lessons, leading a stallion to the breeding area, or tying a seasoned older horse to the hitching post while waiting on the farrier. Whatever the scenario, a strong, dependable halter and lead help ensure your horse's safety and security.

Whether you prefer to use a rope, nylon or leather halter, one of the earliest lessons for any horse is learning to yield to pressure so he is thoroughly broke to the halter.

"There is no substitute for a horse that is really halter-broke and taught to lead well and respond to light pressure," says Pete Melniker of Double Diamond Halter Co., Inc., in Gallatin Gateway, Mont., which has been in business since 1985.

If you have the opportunity to work with a horse from a very young age, you often can avoid the trauma of him ever pulling back and fighting any restraint. Once a horse is older—and stronger—it becomes even more crucial that he doesn't get loose by breaking a halter or lead rope. If this happens even one time, you can be sure the horse tries again. If equipment breaks multiple times, the horse quickly learns that by pulling hard enough, he can get loose, and he continues to test the halter and

lead. Spare your horse and yourself from such frustrating and potentially dangerous situations by using sturdy equipment from the start.

"Really beware of bargain-priced tack," cautions Melniker. "Tools don't break in the toolbox; they break when you're using them. Don't buy the cheapest halter just to save a few bucks. The difference [in price] between a good halter and a better one isn't that much. Look for a halter that is built with quality materials and workmanship, and with correct measurements so that it fits the horse."

## Safety First

Whether you prefer a rope, nylon or leather halter, all three types come in a wide variety of sizes; you can find a halter that provides a good fit for virtually any horse. That good fit helps you communicate to manage your horse. But fit is about more than appearance and control; safety is a big factor:

- A too-small or too-tight halter can interfere with the horse's jaw movement.

- An overly large halter or one adjusted with a loose, sloppy fit doesn't give adequate control when you handle the horse.

- Never leave a halter on a horse when he is loose in a stall or especially when he's turned out in pasture. The halter can get caught on anything, and your horse pays the price.

*Serviceable halters and leads are important anytime horses are tied, no matter the circumstance.*
DARRELL DODDS

*The better the fit of a rope halter, the more effectively the handler can communicate with the horse.*

ROSS HECOX

### Check for Fit

**Rope halters** often are referred to as "cowboy halters" and with good reason. Cowboys likely made some of the earliest rope halters using old reatas or other natural-fiber ropes. Ideally, a rope halter that fits should encapsulate the horse's head:

- The noseband should rest about halfway down the face, between the horse's eyes and his muzzle, with the side knots just below the cheekbones.

- The throatlatch knot should rest deep in the center of the throatlatch, and the ropes should go under and behind both jaws on the way to the poll.

- The knot fastening the halter should be tied correctly and firmly so that

it doesn't slip and the halter become loose over the poll. If that happens, the throatlatch ropes aren't in proper position, and when pressure is applied to the lead, the halter pulls on the halter cheekpieces, instead of behind the horse's jaw. Also, with an incorrectly tied knot, the horse might get loose or the knot might tighten to the point it can't be untied.

- A rope halter offers significant adjustment when you fasten the tail, as compared to a nylon or leather halter, which requires punching additional holes in the crown piece to create a close fit.

- A quality rope halter allows you to adjust the size of the noseband through the fiador knot under the horse's chin.

**Flat halters** are made of nylon or leather, and in the case of a breakaway halter, a combination of both, so the leather crown piece ideally breaks if the halter catches on anything. The side and bottom rings on a flat halter make it easy to snap a horse to a trailer tie, a hot walker, or crossties.

One thing you can do with a nylon or leather halter that you can't do with a rope halter is run a chain through the side rings and over the horse's nose or under his chin to gain more control. Plenty of horsemen, however, say that when a horse needs a chain over his nose to keep all four feet on the ground, he actually needs more handling rather than tougher equipment.

Here are some tips for fitting a flat nylon or leather halter:

- Adjust a flat halter so that the crown piece rests just behind the horse's ears, without sliding backward several inches.

- The noseband should rest about halfway down the face, between the horse's eyes and his muzzle, with both side rings just below the cheekbones.

- Be able to easily slide two or three fingers between the noseband and the horse's head. Some nylon and leather halters have buckles on the noseband or chin straps, which allow for easy adjustment.

- The halter cheek straps should rest parallel to the horse's cheekbones.

- Make sure you can slip three to four fingers under the throatlatch straps in the jaw area.

## Fit Affects Function

**Rope halters** are designed so that when you start to lead a horse forward, he first feels pressure at the back of the jaw and at the poll. This gives the horse no excuse to lift his nose or resist by flinging up his head, which often happens when a horse feels pressure only on the poll. The halter must fit correctly to have the desired effect.

Melniker points out that a rope halter allows greater nose control than a flat type of halter. Many rope halters sport two knots on the noseband portion, but some trainers and clinicians use halters with four noseband knots, citing additional control as the reason. Melniker has sold countless rope halters through the years and doesn't find the extra knots necessary.

"The nose knots don't come into play unless you're backing a horse or you're pulling from the side, and the noseband rolls to the side," he says. "If you're going to back a horse, you can grip the fiador knot with your thumb pointing away from the horse and toward the ground. If you don't get a response this way, just rock your hand left and right a little; as soon as the horse takes a step back, release. You really don't need four knots on the noseband; you can get enough pressure just by rocking a halter with only two knots.

"As far as leading a horse, those knots don't come into play at all because when you pick up on the halter, the horse first feels pressure from the throatlatch loops behind the jaw and on the poll."

**Flat halters** made of nylon or leather, however, are designed so that pressure from the lead is first felt on the head, from the halter crown piece over the poll.

When, for example, backing a horse wearing a flat halter, pressure on the noseband, because of its width, is less concentrated than that on a rope halter noseband. Make the most of any noseband adjustment with a flat halter; a too-loose noseband can function as ineffectively as one that is too tight, numbing a horse to any pressure you apply.

*Don't fasten a rope halter so loosely that pressure isn't properly engaged when a horse is being led.*

KATE BRADLEY

*To properly engage rope halter pressure, be sure the throatlatch ropes are under and behind the horse's jaws on either side.*

DARRELL DODDS

## Rope Halter Construction

Spend a little time browsing through tack shops, catalogs or online resources, and you discover there are more rope halter options than you might imagine.

Rope halters are formed by using a series of double overhand knots and the decorative, but practical fiador knot or an overhand knot under the horse's jaw to form loops for attaching the lead rope. On occasion, the fiador is referred to as a "Theodore" knot, named after hard-riding President Roosevelt, but that usage is simply a corruption of the correct and more commonly used "fiador."

Today's rope halters are made primarily from synthetic materials, which are stronger than natural fibers; the synthetics also are rot- and mildew-resistant, as well as washable. Rope halters can be made of several different types of rope, with the most common materials being nylon and polypropylene.

The overall strength and integrity of a halter depends on the material used and the type of construction. The design and material of the noseband, for example, can make a halter more severe—or less—when used. For example, a thin, single strand over his nose gets a colt's attention more quickly than a wide, soft strand of rope.

The rope used for halter construction typically is one of the following designs:

- Solid braided rope, a continuous braid of multiple strands, can unravel if cut.

- Core-material-with-cover construction is similar to that used in mountain-climbing rope. The core can be twisted or untwisted nylon, polypropylene or polyester, with twisted versions having more ability to stretch under a load or a pull from a horse. The cover can be polyester nylon or polyester. The theory with this type of construction is that the cover withstands abrasion, protecting the core material from wear, which could cause the halter to fail.

- Double-braided rope is especially strong because it is essentially one hollow braided rope encased within another hollow braided rope.

## Other Considerations: Rope

Choosing a specific rope halter, "comes down to what is the right tool for the job," says Melniker. "With a young horse you're schooling, you have more control with a halter made of stiffer rope and of a thinner diameter than what you need for the 'Ol' Dobbin' kids' horse. Nylon, by nature, is going to be stronger than polypropylene, while a double-braid polypropylene is softer than the single-braid nylon."

Since the diameter of the rope used directly affects your level of control and the horse's response, you frequently find trainers using halters made of rope of approximately ¼-inch diameter or just slightly thicker on young horses. For general use on broke horses, many horsemen opt for a halter made of ⁵⁄₁₆-inch, medium-firm rope that is braided polypropylene.

*A braided rawhide noseband can dress up a basic rope halter, just as a horsehair tassel and rawhide can dress up the lead.*

JOHN BRASSEAUX

# MAKE IT WORK FOR YOU

## The Correct Knot

Correctly tying the knot used to fasten a rope halter is key to ensure that your horse remains tied and that you can unfasten the knot. Here's how to tie the knot:

Slip the horse's nose into the noseband and pass the tail end of the halter over the horse's head and behind the poll by putting your right arm over the horse's neck and passing the tail from your left hand under the neck to your right hand. Do not throw the tail from underneath and over the neck as this might cause the horse to throw his head, and the tail could hit his eye.

Pull the tail under and through the loop on the left side of the halter and adjust the halter so it rests in proper position on the horse's head.

To tie the halter, wrap the end of the tail below, not above, the halter loop, circling the tail to the right, toward the back of the horse, and then under the loop toward the front of the horse. Now, again, pull the tail back, away from the eye, running the tail through the loop you just created.

Snug the knot, or half-hitch, to tighten it. Your knot should rest below the end of the halter loop, not above it. If you tie the knot above the loop, it can be difficult—if not impossible—to untie when a horse pulls back.

*Correctly fastening a rope halter is critical. If necessary, to keep the tail from flopping and possibly hitting your horse in the eye, that tail also can be tucked beneath the halter throatlatch rope below the knot.* KATE BRADLEY

Too, some horsemen like to use rope halters, instead of bridles and bits, when making the first few rides on colts. In that case, you might want to look for a halter with metal rings tied into the nose knots, which allow you to attach reins. This design also is helpful if you like to stand a horse in crossties.

Melniker cautions against buying cheaply made halters, simply because of the questionable quality and workmanship. "Inexpensive rope often doesn't have the same quality, and you don't know about the core material or how it's spliced together," he notes. "Also, some of the knots on some poorly made halters are so loose that they can move and affect how the halter fits and functions."

The weakest link with any halter is usually the hardware. One main advantage of using a rope halter and lead, whether it's braided into the halter or attached with a loop to make it removable, is that you avoid the liability of hardware altogether since no metal is involved.

"You can't say a rope halter is unbreakable because anything can break if you put enough force to it," notes Melniker. "But given normal circumstances, it's hard to break one."

## Flat Nylon Halter Construction

Plenty of horsemen, for various reasons, prefer the flat nylon halter. A well-made nylon halter requires no real maintenance or special care, and can last for decades although it's bound to be faded and showing wear when it has been around that long. The main advantages of nylon are strength and durability.

As with rope and leather gear, there are varying degrees of quality when it comes to nylon halters. Consider the following to select a long-lasting nylon halter:

- Look for a quality, heavy-weight nylon halter with box-stitching in areas where the halter is most stressed.

*Ideally, when this type of halter is fastened, the tail of the crown piece should be placed through the buckle keeper.*

ROSS HECOX

- A halter constructed with solid brass hardware and brass eyelets for the buckle holes wears longer than a halter with plated-metal hardware and plain buckle holes.

- Better nylon halters often have a buckle on the chin portion of the noseband, allowing for adjustment.

- A rolled throatlatch with a sewn-in snap for fastening the halter makes it easy to slip the halter on and off a horse's head.

## Other Considerations: Nylon

The flat nylon halter provides a few perks for the horse handler. Some people, for example, like to longe a horse in a nylon halter with a sliding ring across the top of the noseband for ease in changing the horse's direction. Too, because of the flat construction, a nylon halter can remain on a horse's head under the bridle. That makes it simple to tie a horse along

the trail or to the stock trailer when taking a break from working cattle.

Although a nylon halter is extremely durable, it, too, can fail. However, when a quality nylon halter breaks, in nearly every case, it does so because the hardware fails.

## Leather Halter Construction

It's hard to beat the appearance of a quality leather halter. Many outfits use leather halters exclusively on their breeding stallions and show horses. In certain facets of the equine world, such as Thoroughbred breeding and racing, it's a deep-rooted tradition to use leather halters on all horses. Consider these points about leather halter construction:

- Look for products crafted of premium leather.

- Bargain-priced halters tend to be made from lower-grade leather, the less desirable parts of the hide, such as the thin hide toward the belly. Even a halter of excellent workmanship can't hold up when made with inferior leather or hardware.

- Check the stitching. For longest life, buy a leather halter sewn with synthetic thread. Natural-fiber threads, such as cotton and linen, rot with time, especially when exposed to the elements.

- Opt for brass or stainless-steel hardware. Both have earned reputations for durability, as well as good looks. Inexpensive halters often are made with nickel or inferior plated metals, which can break under pressure, leaving you with a loose horse—or worse.

## Other Considerations: Leather

Some horsemen might shy away from a leather halter because of the initial expense, but as with most leather goods, if you buy quality and take care of the halter, you can expect it to last for many years. The old adage definitely applies: You get what you pay for. In many cases, spending just $10 more gets you a much better halter that lasts two to three times longer than less expensive options.

*No matter how fancy or plain a leather halter, quality materials and hardware ensure that the halter does its job for a long time, which somewhat justifies the initial expense.*

DARRELL DODDS

One advantage of leather is that a halter can be repaired—to a point. If your yearling colt pulls back when tied and breaks the crown piece of his leather halter, that section easily can be replaced. If your horse's shenanigans break the halter in several places, however, the halter might not be worth repairing.

Once you're faced with replacing three pieces—and that might or might not include hardware—you're probably better off buying a new halter. In some cases, the leather actually can be weakened by additional repair stitching. If a halter is dry-rotted or brittle, a tack shop might decline the repair job altogether because of safety reasons. No amount of repair or tender, loving care can restore leather once it deteriorates to that point.

*Quality counts when purchasing a leather halter—and any desired trim—and proper care contributes to both lasting for several years.*
ROSS HECOX

*Initially more expensive to purchase than a rope or nylon halter, a leather halter is durable and, if necessary, can be repaired although not always.*
ROSS HECOX

## Leather Care

Unlike nylon and rope options, a leather halter requires basic maintenance. Do these things to get the longest life out of your leather purchase:

- Clean leather thoroughly several times a year with saddle soap or a water-based leather cleaner.

- Look for ripped stitches that need to be replaced and cracks or tears that need to be repaired.

- After cleaning a halter, hang it to dry for at least 48 hours or until completely dry before oiling it. If you use saddle soap that contains glycerin, you might not even need to oil the halter since glycerin works to preserve the leather.

- Pure neatsfoot oil, which can darken light leather, is a good choice for lubricating a leather halter. Either submerge a halter in a bucket of oil or apply the oil with a paintbrush or cloth.

- Make sure the leather is totally dry before applying any oil. If moisture remains inside the leather when you apply oil, the halter starts to dry-rot, which breaks down stitching and fibers. Typically, that halter looks fine, but it has been compromised; the halter ultimately fails at some point—usually when you least expect it.

- If you must store a leather halter for any length of time, never put it in a plastic bag or container. Leather needs to breathe. Plastic also causes brass hardware to oxidize. A climate-controlled area is the best place for leather tack when not in use. Then you can avoid the dryness that sucks moisture out of leather and eventually makes it brittle, as well as the humidity that causes leather to mold and mildew.

*Lead materials vary, as do the convenient snaps sometimes used on the leads.*

KATE BRADLEY

## Lead Construction

Whether you refer to it as a lead, lead line, lead rope, or lead shank, you benefit from having one that is strong and has the proper weight and feel when working with your horse. A good working length for a lead is anywhere from 10 to 15 feet, but as Melniker says, "There's no ideal length; it all depends on what a person wants to do. We sell a lot of 12-foot lead ropes. These are good for groundwork and also if you're tying a horse

# MAKE IT WORK FOR YOU

## The Quick-Release Knot

A quick-release knot can be used with any type of halter and lead to tie a horse. One quick pull of the lead-rope tail can release the knot quickly—but only when the tail has not been pulled through the knot loop as shown in the third step of the illustration. However, many horsemen pull the tail through the loop because, when that isn't done, a horse playing with the tail often releases the knot—and himself.

*This simple knot works as a quick-release knot only when the tail is not pulled through the loop, as shown in the third step at right.*

DWAYNE BRECH

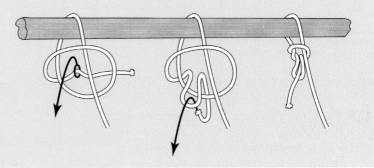

# GOTCHA!

## Turn 'em Loose "Naked"

The actual word "halter" is of German origin and means "that by which something is held." Considering that most basic meaning, a halter can do its job only if it stays securely on the horse's head. Because of this, there is no foolproof halter guaranteed 100-percent safe to leave on a horse when he's turned out to pasture. You need only to see the horrific aftermath of a horse that hooked his halter on a gate-hinge bolt or a corral latch, or even snagged a hind foot in a too-loose throatlatch strap, to realize such tragedies can be avoided. A horse with his head caught does one of two things: He fights until he gets free or fights until he can't fight any more. Either scenario can end disastrously.

Halters are made specifically to withstand pressure, and it takes a lot of pressure to break a well-made halter, especially one constructed of rope or nylon. Despite the marketing hype on the breakaway halter, which typically features a leather crown piece that is supposed to break away if the halter gets hung on something, you never can be sure the leather breaks before the horse gets hurt.

Your best bet? Work with your horse so that he's easy to catch, and turn him out naked—without a halter of any kind. Horses can get into enough trouble without leaving something manmade on their heads when they're loose.

*When a loose horse isn't wearing a halter, he can't get it hung on anything in the pasture.*

ROSS HECOX

high. If you're just tying a horse or tying in the trailer, you might need only a 10-foot lead, but if you're going to longe [a horse], you need at least 24 feet."

Horsemen favor different materials for specific reasons:

- Cotton, polypropylene, nylon, polyester and a combination of nylon and polyester are popular choices.

- Nylon and the nylon-polyester combination are considered the strongest.

- Nylon double-braided yacht rope is flexible and durable.

- Arborist rope, often referred to as "tree line," is a popular choice of clinicians and horsemen, who like the fact that the rope has plenty of feel in hand but maintains its shape and doesn't stretch.

- A hollow-braided rope of spun nylon is strong, but feels like soft mohair in hand.

Different types of lead materials have their own pros and cons:

- Cotton is soft and thick, but absorbs water, shrinks and isn't as strong as synthetic materials.

- Polypropylene comes in many colors and doesn't shrink, but is ultraviolet-sensitive, which means poly lead ropes eventually get stiff because of exposure to sunlight and dirt.

- Nylon is strong, but is probably the worst when it comes to rope burns. Two types of nylon are used in the horse industry. Monofilament is known as the slicker and the "hotter" of the two. Spun nylon is fuzzy like cotton and is preferred around horses, as spun nylon does not cause burns as quickly as the monofilament.

Leads can be constructed in a variety of ways, as set out below:

- Solid-braided rope is just as described. The drawback with this construction: This rope is braided back through itself, so if it gets nicked or partially cut, the integrity of the whole lead is compromised.

- Double-braided rope is especially strong because it is essentially one braided rope within another braided rope.

- Hollow-braided rope has no core in the center and is easily spliced.

- A multiple-strand twisted rope usually consists of three strands twisted around one another under pressure. Be aware that without a swivel being attached, a twisted rope can untwist when used on a highline.

- Core-material-with-cover rope has an inner core that might be twisted or untwisted nylon or polypropylene, with the twisted core having less ability to expand under pressure. The cover can be polyester or nylon.

*A loop at the end of the lead coupled with the fiador loops make it easy to attach a lead to a rope halter and later remove the lead.*
COURTESY DOUBLE DIAMOND HALTER CO.

*For a permanent attachment, the lead can be put through the halter loops with the rope then braided back through itself.*
COURTESY DOUBLE DIAMOND HALTER CO.

*This removable lead-rope knot has been popularized by clinician Buck Brannaman.*
COURTESY DOUBLE DIAMOND HALTER CO.

## Other Considerations: The Lead

If you choose a lead rope that attaches to a rope halter by a sheet-bend knot or by a removable loop, or if the lead is spliced directly to the halter, there is no hardware to break. However, some people like the convenience of a bolt snap, bull snap or quick-release snap. Some companies put a metal "thimble" in the eye of the lead rope, which functions much like the burner on a lariat and helps the lead last longer and also helps keep the eye open.

"When rope is tested for breaking strength, it's on a straight line, but putting a knot in it changes things," says Melniker. "You can have rope that has 3,000-pound tensile strength, but putting a knot in it decreases the tensile strength because you're bending those fibers. Buy rope that is manufactured by a reputable rope company to guarantee the quality. If you spend a little extra money, you may be out a little cash, but if the product fails, you will have neither the money nor the product, and you or your horse may get hurt."

## The Longeing Cavesson

An English longeing, or lungeing, caves-son is made specifically for the purpose of exercising or schooling a horse as the animal moves around you in a circle while on a longe line. Made of leather or, in some cases, nylon, the longeing cavesson:

- is designed to fit more snugly than a standard halter, so the longeing cavesson doesn't twist and move around on the horse's head.

- has a metal-reinforced, padded noseband with a stationary ring at the top point of the noseband.

- allows you to attach the longe line to the ring so a horse can change directions on the circle without being stopped to reattach the line, which is typical when using the side rings of a standard nylon or leather halter to longe a horse.

## The Longe Line

No matter if you attach a longe line to a traditional halter or a cavesson, a longe line:

*Many people use the halter, rather than a longeing cavesson, to work a horse on the longe line.*
ROSS HECOX

- can be made of cotton, nylon web or polypropylene, or a combination of fibers.

- can burn your hand, as can any rope attached to a fast-moving horse, but a cotton line doesn't do as much damage as nylon before you turn the line loose.

- should be at least 24 feet in length so your horse doesn't have to work in too small a circle, which can put unnecessary stress on tendons, joints, and bones, especially in young horses.

# EXPERT TIP

## Longeing in a Rope Halter

Although you might think a rope halter ineffective for longeing, multiple American Quarter Horse Association world champion Mike Major came up with a modified design. He's used this design since around 1990 for training horses at his Flying A Ranch (Gene Autry's old place), in Fowler, Colorado.

Major always has liked the traditional rope halter with the fiador knot tied under the chin, but found that when used for longeing, this halter has the same shortcomings as a nylon or leather halter with a stationary ring at the bottom of the noseband.

"I see horses that have been longed a lot in a rope halter carrying their faces turned to the outside. The longe line is pulling the horse to the inside, but it's actually pushing his nose to the outside. When the horse's nose is pushed to the outside, it drives the inside shoulder down and makes the horse pick up the outside shoulder. He often cross-fires in the back," explains Major, a longtime rancher.

Major found a solution by adding a ring about 1½ inch in diameter to the section of rope halter under the horse's chin. Because the ring is not stationary, it can slide back and forth along the chin section and partway up the noseband to below the cheek knots on either side of the halter.

"When I put pressure on the horse's face, I want his nose to turn into the pressure, not for him to counterbalance and push away from it," he explains. "The horse's nose should follow the arc of the circle; it's natural for the horse to do this. With the halter I made, you can keep the inside shoulder picked up and get the horse to really arc his body so that his nose and hip are bent to the inside of the circle.

"The main reason I made this halter was because I did a lot

*Although a traditionalist prefers a halter without hardware, the snap is convenient, and the ring helps keep the horse from dropping an inside shoulder when being longed.*
JOHN BRASSEAUX

of flexing with colts. The sliding ring helps them understand quickly, so they don't second-guess what I'm asking. This also starts softening the neck. We always should be trying to find ways to make it easier for the horse to understand what we're asking him to do."

When longeing a horse in this halter, Major finds that not only does the horse arc his body correctly with his nose to the inside of the circle, but also that the sliding ring means the handler doesn't have to stop the horse and reattach the longe line when he wants to change directions. The ring also makes it easy to attach the horse to a hot walker or trailer tie, if necessary.

# 2
# Saddle Construction

Saddles have come a long, long way since someone first thought of strapping a piece of animal hide or cloth to the horse's back for a more comfortable ride.

Without delving into a detailed history of the saddle, it is known that the Chinese, Persians and Assyrians already were horseback 2,000 to 3,000 years before Christ walked the earth. The Chinese had been using horses in harness as early as 4000 B.C. although it's not known for certain that they first invented the saddle. Some historians believe the Assyrians might have come up with the first actual saddle with metal stirrups, while others credit the Sarmatians, a group of people of Iranian heritage, who lived by the Black Sea and were known to be skilled horsemen.

Today's Western saddle traces its early roots back to the Moors of North Africa. When those Moors invaded Spain in the 700s, they were riding saddles distinguished by long stirrups, high forks and cantles.

The Spanish later adapted this Moorish style to create their Spanish war saddles, which became known as the saddles of the knights and the Crusaders. When the Spanish conquistadors landed in the New World, they brought those saddles, as well as horses and donkeys. The first vaquero-type saddles evolved from these early Spanish saddles, eventually developing into the Western stock saddle ridden today. In fact, this saddle was long known as a Spanish saddle, in acknowledgment of its origins.

Two major styles of stock saddles developed in the early days of the working cowboy in North America: the Texican and the Californio. Popular east of the Rockies and up into Canada, the Texican had a swell fork; heavy, square skirts; and double rigging, suited for hard-and-fast roping with the rope tied to the horn. Found along the Pacific coast, in the Great Basin and the Northwest, the Californio-style was a lighter-weight saddle, often featuring elaborate decorative tooling. The saddle, designed for dally roping, had a slick fork, round skirts, and centerfire rigging.

Saddle styles continue to vary according to region and use, but all are built with the same basic components. Although this book is dedicated to the fit and function of gear and equipment, a basic understanding of saddle construction is helpful. This chapter looks at the "ingredients" of the saddle, while Chapter 3 focuses on how various types of saddles function for different uses, and Chapter 4 details saddle fit.

## The Saddletree

In a custom saddle, every piece of leather is designed and cut for that particular saddle. With a factory-made, assembly-line saddle, pieces are precut and then attached to the saddle during production. Not every saddle is put together in the exact same order of construction, but no matter where and how a saddle is made, the tree always is the starting point. It creates the foundation of the saddle, determines the size, and defines the shape of the bars, seat, swells, horn and cantle.

The bars of the tree are the part that contacts the horse. The bars create the loading surface meant to evenly distribute weight across the horse's back. Trees and saddle fit are discussed in greater detail in Chapter 4 but, for now, a few brief thoughts suffice:

*Even in today's technological world, saddlemaking remains a time-honored profession, and fine craftsmanship is respected and appreciated.*

ROSS HECOX

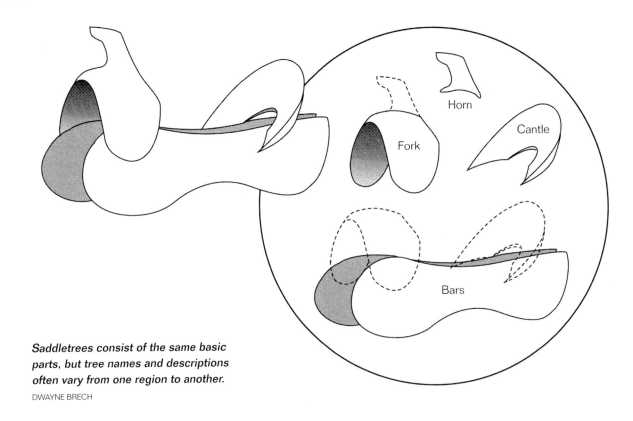

*Saddletrees consist of the same basic parts, but tree names and descriptions often vary from one region to another.*

DWAYNE BRECH

*A finished saddle reflects the shape of the tree.*

KATE BRADLEY

- Traditionally made of soft woods, such as pine or Douglas fir, or a light hardwood, such as poplar, trees then are covered with rawhide for additional strength. The entire tree might be varnished or have a synthetic coating, such as fiberglass.

- Some trees are made entirely of synthetic materials. Although purists might find the idea of a synthetic tree blasphemous, such trees have found a practical use in lightweight saddles, such as those designed for barrel racing and trail riding.

Mention tree sizes and you open the proverbial can of worms. Custom treemakers and saddlemakers refer to specific measurements, not such tree descriptions as "regular," "full-Quarter Horse," "semi-Quarter Horse" or "Arabian." In addition, a custom maker measures the tree across the back of the fork, while factory-made saddles are measured across the front of the fork. This obviously results in significantly different measurements.

"Styles of trees are very regional, so the same tree might have different names in different areas," explains Bret Collier of Big Bend Saddlery in Alpine, Texas. "In some circles, any tree without swells is known as a Wade tree. In actuality, there are many varieties of slick-fork trees, such as a Homestead, 3B, Cliff Wade, or Ray Hunt. There are very subtle differences in all these trees based on swell width and thickness (swell stock).

"The name really only tells you the shape of the swell; the names are the patterns on which the swells are built," adds Collier. "You can make the swell more narrow or more wide, and it has an altogether different look. Measurements of trees are more important than names."

- Saddletree measurements vary when it comes to gullet width and height, bar width, and the pitch of the bars, and these are what determine how the tree fits a horse's back.

- Pitch of the bars ranges from steep (at 86 degrees) to flat (94 degrees), with 90 degrees being common.

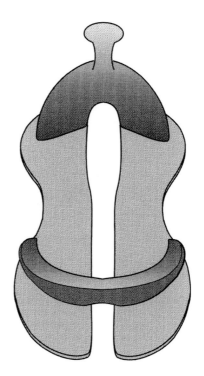

A-fork or slick-fork

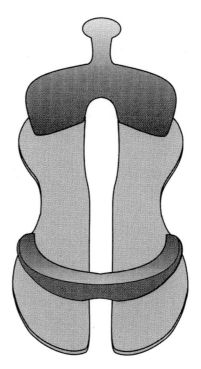

Swell-fork

*The fork shapes the front of a saddle, and these two fork designs are so-named for obvious reasons.*
DWAYNE BRECH

*No matter if a saddle is an old-time collectible or a contemporary model, basic components serve the same purposes in either style.*

ROSS HECOX

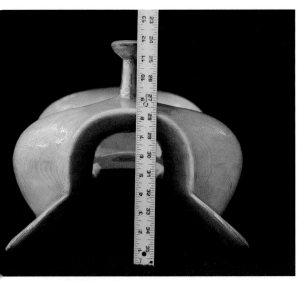

The finished appearances of saddles built on swell-fork trees can vary greatly, so actual tree measurements are important considerations.

DARRELL DODDS

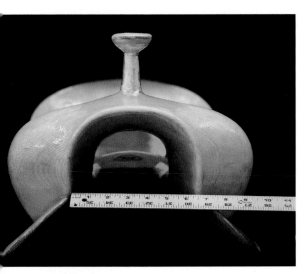

Gullet width, as well as its height, and bar width and pitch ultimately determine how well a saddletree fits a horse's back.

DARRELL DODDS

- It's a misconception that height and width of gullet determine how low or high the saddle sits on the horse. Bar width and pitch are crucial, but often overlooked, parts of the equation. For example, a Thoroughbred-type, high-withered horse typically needs more steeply pitched bars and less width than a broad, flat-backed Quarter Horse that requires a flatter pitch and more width.

## Rigging Styles and Placement

If the tree is the foundation block of any saddle, the rigging is the next most important piece of construction. **Rigging** refers to the arrangement of rings and hardware that provides the method by which the saddle is secured to the horse. Many Western saddles are double-rigged, meaning they have riggings for both front and back cinches. A single-rigged saddle has a rigging position for only a front cinch. There are three basic rigging styles:

- **Ring rigging,** also referred to as double rigging, has rings attached to leather plates, which are screwed directly into the saddletree. The front and rear rings are attached with separate pieces of leather. A ring rigging is strong and also easy to repair if it breaks or wears out, but is bulkier under the rider's leg and can interfere somewhat with free stirrup movement.

- **Flat-plate rigging,** also referred to as drop-plate rigging, debuted in the early 1900s and is a rigging style in which both front and back rings are attached to one large single piece of leather that wraps around the whole side of the saddle and all the way back to the cantle. Flat-plate rigging offers the same basic strength as the ring style, but with somewhat less bulk under the rider's leg and almost as much stirrup movement as with an in-skirt style. The flat-plate rig adds a little weight to the saddle, but because of the way the rigging hangs low, some riders think that helps the saddle ride a bit better.

- **In-skirt rigging** became popular in the second half of the 1900s, but some in-skirt riggings were seen in saddle catalogs in the early part of that century. This style features rigging rings or plates attached directly to the saddle skirts, either built into or onto the skirts. Built-in in-skirt rigging has layers of leather sewn and riveted to the skirt, while built-on rigging is attached to the skirt surface and isn't as strong as built-in. In-skirt rigging is growing in popularity because there's less bulk under the rider's legs, plus free stirrup movement.

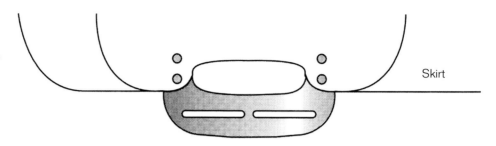

*In-skirt rigging, such as this three-way style, is built into the saddle skirts.*

DWAYNE BRECH

Skirt

The drawback: Each stirrup leather constantly slides over the rigging, so if and when the rigging wears out, it's a more expensive repair than that for the ring rigging.

**Rigging placement** refers to the position of the rigging rings or plates. Although the rear rigging always is located directly below the cantle, the position of the front rigging varies, with names of the various positions based on the rigging's distance from the low points of the bars front to back, as Ken Tipton of Tip's Saddlery in Winnemucca, Nev., describes it.

When cowboys roping cattle started tying hard and fast to their horns, the ropers found that the backs of their saddles tipped up. To remedy this problem, the cowboys came up with the idea of adding a back cinch, which gave birth to two new rigging positions in the last half of the 1800s—the three-quarter and seven-eighths positions. Here are brief descriptions of each rigging position:

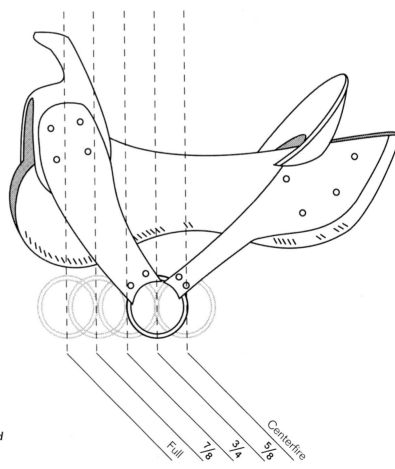

*Placement for front rigging varies from the forward full position to the appropriately named centerfire position.*

DWAYNE BRECH

Full   7/8   3/4   5/8   Centerfire

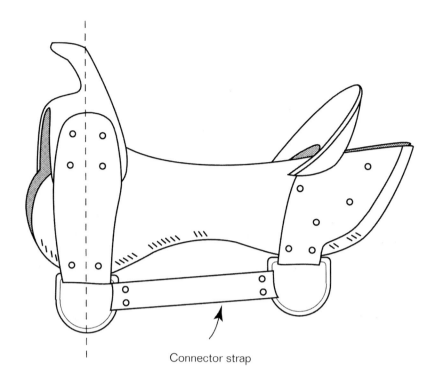

Connector strap

- **Full rigging,** also known as full-double rigging, which is the most forward of all positions, places the front ring under the center of the saddle fork. Saddles of early Spanish explorers had full riggings. Roping saddles generally have full-double riggings to withstand the torque and pressure caused by heavy livestock on the end of a rope.

- **Centerfire rigging** takes its name from the fact that it is situated halfway between the fork and cantle, basically in the center of the saddle. The Spanish eventually replaced their early full riggings with centerfire riggings. Because of the position, a saddle with centerfire rigging can be only single-rigged. Although used on the U.S. Army McClellan saddle, centerfire rigging is not widely used today.

- **Three-quarter rigging** is positioned half the distance between full and centerfire positions, or three-quarters of the way from the cantle to the fork.

- **Seven-eighths rigging** is halfway between full and three-quarter positions, or seven-eighths of the way from cantle to fork.

When buying a custom saddle, you can request any type of rigging placement, but the majority of factory-made saddles today come with either a seven-eighths or full-double rigging. Some saddles have adjustable in-skirt rigging, which can be set in more than one position.

Contrary to what some people think, setting the rigging back just makes the cinch fall farther back around the horse's body; the saddle doesn't actually move forward on a horse. Using a three-quarter or seven-eighths rigging position moves the cinch from right behind the horse's elbow, so there's more spring in the horse's ribs, and the cinch is less likely to gall the horse.

## The Ground Seat

Although the bars of the tree are all about the horse, the ground seat of a saddle is all about the rider. As the name implies, the ground seat, the foundation of the seat itself, is where the seat is shaped to fit a rider. At the customer's request, a saddlemaker might do something unique with the ground seat, but otherwise it follows a standard shape for that particular style of saddle. Basic ground-seat considerations follow:

- In a traditional wooden tree, the saddlemaker forms the ground seat using leather, a metal strainer plate, synthetic materials, or a combination of all these things.

- In a synthetic tree, and in some trees that incorporate both wood and fiberglass, the ground seat already is molded into the tree.

- The type of saddle determines the amount of materials used; for example, there is much less leather in the ground seat of a barrel-racing saddle than in a roping saddle.

- If the ground seat is not properly formed and completely smooth, it can result in an uncomfortable ride, like having a tiny, but annoying, piece of gravel in your boot.

## Fenders

Fenders didn't appear on the Western saddle until sometime around the 1870s. The shape and style of fender varies, depending on the type of saddle, and can be plain leather or feature elaborate stamping and/or tooling. There are different methods for attaching the fenders to the saddletree.

- The standard method is to attach the fender to a complete stirrup leather that fits around and over the bar of the tree on either side of the saddle. This attachment breaks in slowly, but lasts a long time.

- To create less bulk under the rider's leg, some makers attach the stirrup leather to the tree and then only to the top of the fender. This method breaks in faster

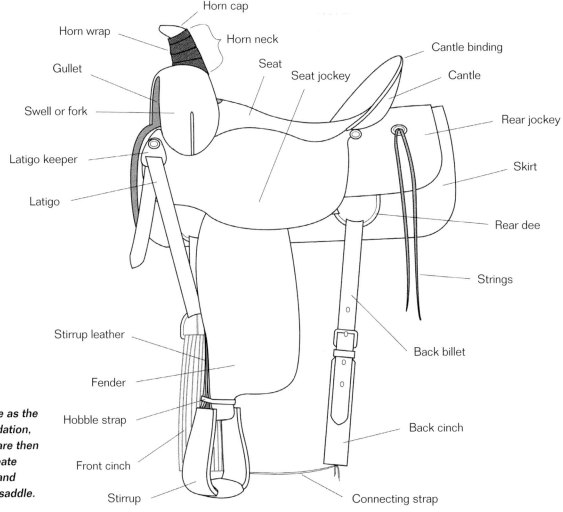

*With the tree as the saddle foundation, many parts are then added to create a complete and serviceable saddle.*

DWAYNE BRECH

than the standard method, but isn't as long-lasting.

- On most quality saddles, the fenders are twisted before they're attached to the saddle so the stirrups hang at a 90-degree angle for a comfortable ride.

## Saddle Skirts

Skirts first showed up on stock saddles around the 1860s. The saddle skirts are attached to the tree with nails, and sometimes screws, placed in such a way that they never come in contact with the horse. Both practicality and eye-appeal factor into the saddle-skirt equation:

- In order to be functional, skirts have to be only as big as the bars of the tree.

- The more skirt material, the more weight added to the saddle, which explains why barrel-racing saddle skirts are round and barely extend beyond the saddletree.

- Skirt shape determines the basic shape of the saddle—round, semi-round, square, or old-time square. In the 1800s, square skirts became so popular in Texas that they often were referred to as Texas skirts. Rounded skirts were so synonymous with California vaqueros that everyone knew a California skirt was round.

- The length of the skirt has more to do with construction and appearance than how the saddle actually fits the horse.

- Saddles traditionally were made so that saddle strings of sturdy oil-tanned leather bound the skirts to the tree. Saddle strings got in the way of roping, so some makers began using solid screw-type conchas in place of the saddle strings.

## Saddle Lining

Covering the underside of the skirt and tree, the saddle lining adds a layer of cushion and protection. Sheepskin, also referred to as woolskin, traditionally has been used, but synthetic linings now available sometimes are hard to distinguish from the real thing:

- **Sheepskin** offers good padding, absorbs moisture, doesn't mat down quickly, and is long-lasting.

- **Synthetic lining** promotes moisture, rather than absorbs it, is hotter than natural sheepskin, mats down quickly, and is not as long-lasting as real sheepskin.

## The Saddle Horn

Before vaqueros invented the saddle horn, they tied roped livestock to the saddle-rigging rings, hardly a convenient option. Carved from the same wood as the tree, the first saddle horns were developed in the early 1800s. Steel horns were introduced later in the 1880s to replace the wooden horns, which frequently broke when tying off cattle. Horn materials and construction vary:

- Horns today are made of metal, wood or synthetic materials, and are bolted into the trees, covered with rawhide and then leather.

- Other than the Wade tree, which typically has a fork made of hardwood laminations allowing the fork and horn to be made as one integral unit, the majority of modern saddle horns have bases of brass or bronze.

*Fine tooling dresses up any saddle, and makers display their best at gatherings and exhibitions.*
KATE BRADLEY

### The Swell Cover

The leather covering the saddle swells, also known as the fork or pommel, protects the tree and is often only a single layer of leather with no padding or extra leather between it and the tree. Depending on the saddle style, the maker might "pretty up" the swell cover with stamping and/or tooling.

### The Seat

Spanish saddles in the 1700s had little in the way of actual seats; the seat was nothing more than triangular section of leather attached to the top of the tree bars. Today, the seat is typically the biggest and most expensive piece of leather, and always one of the last pieces put in place when building a saddle. The seat also is the hardest to fit because it must conform to the swells, where the cantle attaches to the bars and also to the skirt shape. Nonetheless, saddle-seat options abound:

- Cowhide is hardly the only saddle-seat option; saddlemakers often use different

*Although this saddle seat can be considered more plain than fancy, the wear marks indicate that the saddle provides a comfortable ride.*
KATE BRADLEY

leathers for the seat, including such exotics as ostrich, alligator, and stingray.

- Seat styles can be rough-out or smooth leather, inlaid or padded.

- Padded seats have material, such as foam rubber, added between the tree and the top layer of leather. The main benefit is a softer ride, but typically a working cowboy doesn't ride a padded seat because it wears more quickly than an unpadded one, and if he's caught in a rainstorm, the padded seat stays wet far longer than a regular leather seat.

### Cantle Back and Binding

The cantle might be either the original straight style, also known as a pencil roll, or can be a rolled cantle, often described as a Cheyenne roll because it debuted in Frank Meanea's saddle shop in that Wyoming town. This wider cantle design has a rolled back edge, which makes a convenient handhold. No matter the style, the cantle is functional and can be decorative:

- The cantle back is covered with smooth leather and can feature intricate tooling, can be plain and functional, or can be somewhere between.

- The cantle binding holds everything in place where the seat and the back panels of the skirts come together.

*This vintage saddle features eye-catching trim around the gullet and on the traditional straight-style cantle, as well as decorative corner plates.*
ROSS HECOX

*This cantle design often is referred to as a Cheyenne roll, thanks to early saddlemaker Frank Meanea of Cheyenne, Wyoming.*

ROSS HECOX

- Binding can be a solid piece of leather, a leather overlay with a leather edge, leather with a rawhide edge, rawhide, or a rope roll possibly sewn with contrasting colored rawhide or leather lacing.

## Stirrups

Although the earliest stirrups were made of metal, by the 1700s the Spanish were cutting stirrups from solid pieces of wood. Steamed, bent wooden stirrups began showing up in the 1860s. Blevins buckles became popular as they allow a rider to quickly and easily adjust and change stirrups. Today's stirrups come in a variety of styles and materials, including:

- steamed and bent oak wrapped with outer bands of metal for strength.

- other hardwoods with lacquer finishes and leather treads.

- aluminum, either polished or engraved, also with leather treads.

- a metal base, such as iron, available with or without leather, and/or rawhide coverings and treads.

- a polymer base covered with leather and/or rawhide.

*A ranch cowboy might prefer to have metal covering his stirrups for durability and the wide tread for comfort.*

KATE BRADLEY

Saddle style, region and use impact the stirrup design chosen by a particular rider:

- A heavy, 3-inch deep stirrup offers security but is easy to get out of quickly, which is why calf ropers favor this style.

*Just as with other Western gear, stirrups often are personalized with brands, initials and/or names.*

KATE BRADLEY

*Narrow-tread stirrups can provide secure footholds for fast-paced stops and turns when sorting or cutting cattle.*

DARRELL DODDS

- A narrow stirrup, such as an oxbow, offers good "hold" for the foot and is better to use than a wide stirrup when breaking colts that might buck.

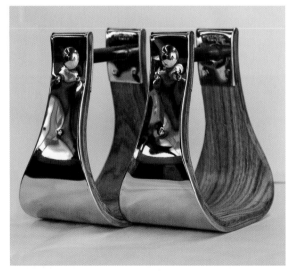

*Although not commonly used to cover stirrups, copper overlay makes an attractive addition to this pair of stirrups.*

DARRELL DODDS

- Sleek and lightweight, aluminum stirrups are a favorite of barrel racers.

- Fancy, engraved metal stirrups offer flash in the show ring.

- Comfort and security are the goals for trail riders, who opt for a variety of stirrup materials and designs.

Region and use also influence whether or not a rider has tapaderos on his stirrups. In addition to being decorative, tapaderos provide multipurpose protective coverings over the stirrup fronts that:

- prevent brush or branches from poking through the stirrup, potentially causing a wreck.

- save the rider's feet from cacti and thorny brush.

- help keep feet warmer than they would be in open stirrups during cold weather.

- prevent a young or inexperienced rider from running a foot through a stirrup.

## What Exactly is Hermann Oak Leather?

You've likely seen advertisements promoting saddles and other tack made with "Hermann oak" leather. That's frequently used to designate high quality, but some people don't realize the term simply refers to leather tanned by the Hermann Oak Leather Company in St. Louis, Missouri.

The company was started in 1881 by founder Louis Charles Hermann and made a reputation for turning out quality leather, especially when using the vegetable-tanning process, which utilizes the tannin found in tree bark. Although this process takes one month, compared to one day when hides are tanned by the chrome, or chemical, method, vegetable-tanning produces firm, strong leather well-suited for carving and shaping. So, no matter what kind of saddle you ride or where you bought it, if it's made with Hermann oak leather, at least now you know where the hides were tanned.

# MAKE IT WORK FOR YOU

## Turn Those Stirrups

When you buy a well-made saddle, the stirrup leathers usually are pretwisted, or turned, so the stirrups hang at a 90-degree angle to the fender. If the stirrups hang parallel to the fender, solve the problem by turning the stirrups. Doing so makes it easy to slip your boot into a stirrup, and your knees can thank you after a few hours of riding. Here's how to turn your stirrups:

Clean and oil the saddle fenders to make them more pliable.

With the saddle sitting on a rack, insert a sturdy broomstick or similar object through first one stirrup and then the other, so that both fenders angle toward the back of your saddle. Some people prefer using a 2x4 or even a piece of pipe through the stirrups.

When you aren't using the saddle, leave the broomstick in place for as long as it takes to make the fenders, leathers and stirrups stay in the correct turned-back position.

*A broomstick is a handy tool for turning stirrups that haven't been pretwisted to stay in a comfortable riding position.*
KATE BRADLEY

# EXPERT TIP

## Saddle-Shopping Insights

Ken Tipton of Tip's Saddlery, Winnemucca, Nev., shares valuable insights on what to look for when shopping, whether you're buying new or hunting for a quality used saddle:

Check with other riders doing the same type of riding you do and ask what brand of saddle each is using and how well it's working.

Research the reputation of the brand or the saddlemaker you're considering.

When examining a saddle, look at the overall craftsmanship and the lines of the saddle. There should be a snug fit—no gaps—every place the points of the saddle meet. A word of caution: When visiting a custom shop, show the saddlemaker respect by asking him or her to help you properly examine the saddle's construction. That person has spent many hours making sure all the pieces lay neatly, so don't start pulling up the stirrup leathers or picking up the seat jockey without asking first.

Examine the seat and sit in it to get an idea of how you'll feel after spending a few hours in the saddle. A well-made seat shouldn't be a straight line to the cantle. The seat should have some shape to it and a good, narrow pocket where you sit.

Have the stirrups been turned so that they hang at 90-degree angles to the fenders? If not, and the stirrups are parallel to the fenders, you want to turn them for a more comfortable ride if you buy this particular saddle. (See "Make it Work for You" on page 33.)

Look underneath a used saddle and examine the lining. If the sheepskin is matted and shows even wear, that is usually the sign of a well-fitting saddle. If the lining is excessively worn, you always can have it replaced, but proceed with caution if the lining shows uneven wear, as this might signify fit problems with this particular saddle.

Compare apples to apples when looking at saddle prices. Realize that although a custom saddle, in most cases, costs significantly more up front than a factory-made one, the custom saddle generally holds its value much longer. It's not unusual for a good custom saddle from a known maker to hold or even increase in value after 10 or 15 years.

Beware of a good-looking saddle with a cheap price tag. The adage is usually true: You get what you pay for. A top quality custom saddle usually has around $1,500 in materials alone and anywhere from 40 to 400 hours of labor, depending on the amount and style of tooling.

Don't buy a saddle for only one specific horse. A well-made saddle is meant to last much longer than the horse you ride now, so ideally you should buy a saddle you can use on multiple horses for years to come. The saddle industry has gotten far better at building saddles to fit a variety of horses.

*The more saddles you scrutinize and examine, the better you can become at recognizing quality materials and craftsmanship—no matter how new or used a saddle might be.*
KATE BRADLEY

## Q & A: Considering the Industry

A visit with Bret Collier of Big Bend Saddlery in Texas and Nevadan Ken Tipton of Tip's Saddlery shines the light on just what has changed about saddlemaking—as well as what hasn't. Collier has been in the business since 1978, while Tipton has been making saddles since 1972.

**Have you seen any significant changes in saddle construction?**

**Tipton:** "I think each step of the construction process has become better. We have better quality hardware to work with, and the trees available today are better quality and fit horses better. Treemakers have had to work harder to get trees to fit a great variety of horses because the horses have changed. Fifty to sixty years ago, horses on the same ranch, and even from a general region, were of similar conformation. With the advent of artificial insemination, it has become very common for someone, say in Nevada, to breed his mare to a stallion in, say, Texas, so you now have a variety of horses' backs."

**Collier:** "The most notable changes have been the use of synthetic trees, synthetic threads and assembly-line production. Our saddles really are made the same way they always have been except that we've changed to nylon thread instead of flax because nylon holds up longer. The top-of-the-line custom saddles are made from American leather, and I prefer American hides because I think they have the best tanning process, which means firmer leather with less stretch. The quality of the leather makes a big difference in how long a saddle will last."

**Generally speaking, would you say saddles are better made now than in the past?**

**Collier:** "The world is shrinking because of technology, and there's more sharing of information between saddlemakers, so I think that is a help. We're making better trees now, but I don't think the leather is as good as the leather we used to get. The hides today come from plumper animals that are butchered at a young age. I think the tannery process is faster than it used to be, and this means the leather isn't as easy to cut. Also, there are more assembly-made saddles today than bench-made custom saddles. There are people who make their livings in a saddle today, but generally speaking, saddles now are used most often as a hobby, not day in and day out, so they don't have to be as good as they did when people were using horses as the main means of transportation."

**Tipton:** "It's ironic that saddles today are better made than ever although plenty of saddles out there aren't very good. Years ago, everyone needed a saddle and often wore it out. The saddlemaker's job was to turn out saddles and get them out the door. Don't get me wrong; there were a lot of really well-made saddles, but they were functional items and everyone needed one."

**What about trends in the saddlemaking industry?**

**Tipton:** "In the 40 years I've been in the industry, I have seen the business grow and grow. The trend I see, as far as custom saddlemakers go, is that there are more really good saddlemakers today than there have ever been. There are some tremendous craftsmen, and the artistic value today is over the top. I can't recall any old saddles on which the tooling was as masterfully done as it is today. Shows like the Elko, (Nev.), cowboy poetry gathering, Trappings of the American West, and ranch rodeos with vendor booths have brought together top artists and craftsmen, who borrow and share ideas. These shows serve as inspiration, and all those artists getting together have allowed the people in the saddle business to step up their craft."

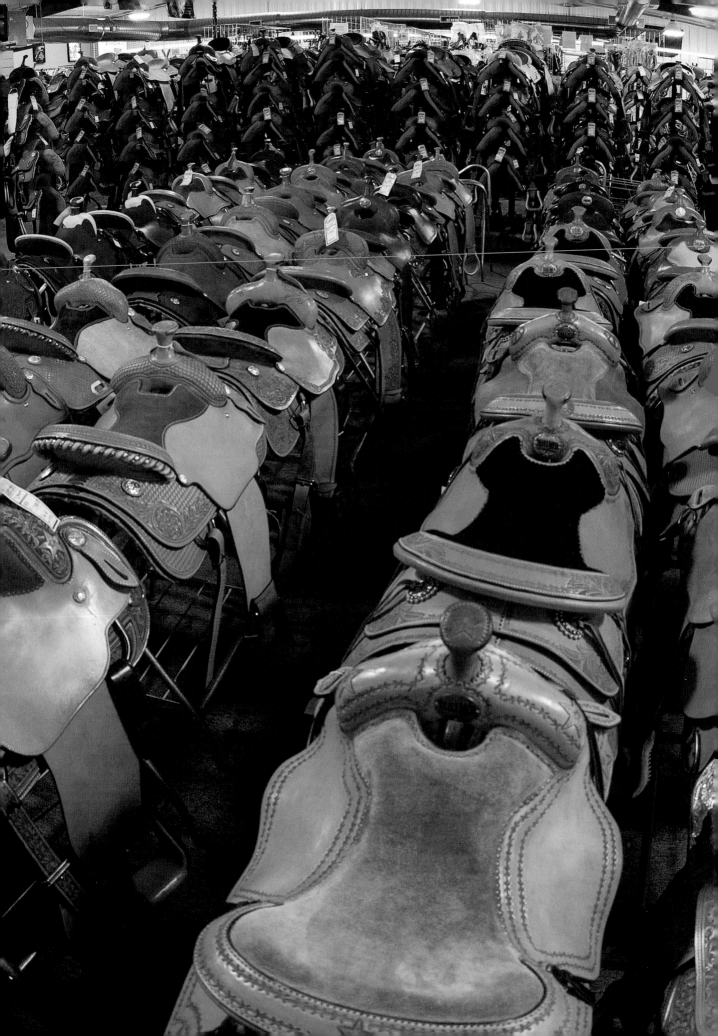

# 3

# A Saddle for Every Job

Today's riders talk about saddle brands and saddlemakers just as they discuss horse breeds and bloodlines, but this hasn't always been the case. The first "branded" saddles made an appearance somewhere in the mid-1850s, thanks to the Visalia Stock Saddle Company, Hamley and Co. and Hermann H. Heiser. Not until nearly a century later did the saddle industry began marketing a wide variety of saddles strategically made for specific disciplines and activities.

Saddlemakers and manufacturers in the 21st century are able to offer the best of both worlds: products that are rich in history, tradition and craftsmanship, and built with the finest materials available. The industry caters to rider preference in practically every aspect of saddle design. The end results are almost unlimited options of saddle styles and designs, no matter what kind of riding you do. If you can't find exactly what you want in a ready-made saddle, you always can order a custom saddle crafted to your exact specifications.

Representatives from prominent saddle companies have been asked how saddle styles differ in design, as well as what riders look for when they need saddles for specific tasks. Robb Thomas is vice president of sales and marketing at Circle Y in Yoakum, Texas, and Webb Fortenberry is quality control manager at Cactus Saddlery, located in

*An abundance of saddle choices, both new and used, await the savvy shopper.*

DARRELL DODDS

*A ranch hand's choice of saddle might vary from region to region, but comfort and suitability for the work at hand always play into the decision.*

KATE BRADLEY

- **horn:** 3- to 3½-inch horn with generally a 2½- to 3-inch cap for roping

- **cantle:** 3½ to 4 inches; steeper angle than that on a roping saddle

- **seat:** pocket with high ground rise to provide secure seat

- **fender and stirrup placement:** slightly forward of perpendicular

- **rigging:** flat-plate most popular

## Roping Saddles

When it comes to roping, not all saddles are equal, and riders don't always look for similar things. Roping saddles are some of the heaviest and most sturdy of all stock saddles, but a ranch cowboy roping full-grown cattle for doctoring on the range, or dragging calves to the branding fire, wants slightly different things in his saddle than a competitive calf or team roper. Saddle horns are basically similar, and most riders want a narrow ground seat. Ranch-, calf- and team-roping saddles have differences and similarities.

**Ranch-roping saddles** can vary from one region to the next, but share similar characteristics:

- **swells or fork:** large enough to hold heavy cattle for long period of time; bigger and heavier than those in competitive roping saddles

*Ranch ropers, particularly those in buckaroo country, prefer saddles somewhat different than those used by rodeo cowboys.*

KATE BRADLEY

Greenville, Texas. Circle Y has been making saddles since 1960 while Cactus Saddlery has been in the business since 2002. Their comments detail differences and similarities among Western saddle styles.

## All-Around Ranch Saddle

Comfort and function are at the top of the list for riders who spend large portions of the day working horseback. Skirt style often depends on region, and many riders now look for saddles with somewhat small skirts. Less leather means a lighter load for the horse toting that saddle—and rider—all day. In some respects, ranch-hand preferences are similar; in others, not so much:

- **swells or fork:** big swells popular with riders seeking secure seat; A-fork still a preference for others

- **horn:** somewhat short, around 3 inches, with flat, 2½- to 3-inch cap

- **cantle:** 3½ to 5 inches for secure seat and all-day riding support; steeply upright or angled back, depending on rider preference

- **seat:** more ground rise in front to create deep, comfortable pocket for riding long hours

- **fender and stirrup placement:** straight down or slightly forward for deep seat in saddle

- **rigging:** full-double

**Calf-roping saddles,** designed for quick dismounts that help ensure fast times in arena competition, usually have the following characteristics:

- **swells or fork:** somewhat lower and smaller than found in ranch saddle, for calf roper to ride up, in the front of saddle; lower swells for quick dismount

- **horn:** flat with generally a 2½- to 3-inch-diameter horn cap

- **cantle:** 3 to 3½ inches; angled back to aid in quick dismount

- **seat:** varies, especially if saddle is based on an endorsee's style; slightly more ground rise to push the rider back toward the cantle or a flatter seat, depending on rider preference

- **fender and stirrup placement:** straight down so roper can use stirrups to stand in a centered, balanced position

- **rigging:** full-double

**Team-roping saddles,** used for header and heeler to dally their ropes and hold a steer, rather than dismount and tie one, typically feature the following:

- **swells or fork:** somewhat lower and smaller than those in ranch saddle to allow header to lean forward without swells getting in the way

*When a professional competitor endorses a saddle, it's designed with his preferences in mind—in this case, those of Trevor Brazile, multiple-world-champion rodeo cowboy.*

COURTESY CACTUS SADDLERY

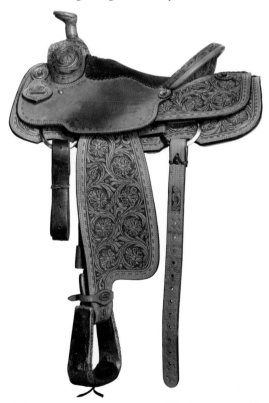

*Although not wrapped, this saddle horn can hold a dally, and the wide-tread stirrups help a roper maintain a balanced, correct position.*

ROSS HECOX

- **horn:** somewhat short, about 3 inches; flat with generally a 2½- to 3-inch cap

- **cantle:** 3 to 4 inches high; steeply upright or angled back, depending on rider preference

- **seat:** varies, especially if a saddle is based on an endorsee's style; slightly more ground rise to push rider toward cantle or a flat seat, depending on rider preference

- **fender and stirrup placement:** straight down so roper can use stirrups to stand in a centered, balanced position

- **rigging:** full-double popular with team ropers, as with ranch and calf ropers

## Cutting Saddles

A cutter wants to move with the horse, but still maintain a solid seat throughout a variety of sharp turns, stops and starts, so the saddle must provide both security and freedom of movement. Cutters often buy roomier saddles than ropers or reiners; it's not unusual for an average-sized rider to cut in a 16- to 17-inch saddle. The horn, perhaps, is one of a cutting saddle's distinctive features:

- **swells or fork:** typically bigger than those on a roping or barrel-racing saddle to help rider maintain position

- **horn:** 3½ to 4 inches; thin and narrow to offer good handhold

- **cantle:** typically 3½ to 4 inches high with steep angle to offer rider a secure seat

- **seat:** from flat to slight rise in ground seat to keep rider centered and stable in saddle-seat pocket

- **fender and stirrup placement:** lightweight; of thinner leather and smaller size than those on ranch or roping saddles to allow rider better feel of horse; generous stirrup movement allowing rider's legs to hang straight down when sorting cattle and forward when cutting a cow

- **rigging:** full-double, in-skirt rigging

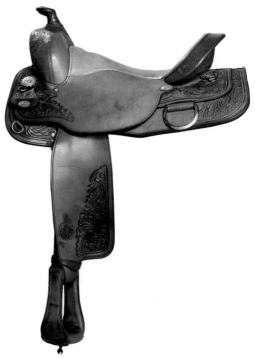

*This saddle has design features that cutters prefer—a tall horn, free-swinging stirrup leathers and a seat pocket to help the rider feel secure during this fast-paced event.*

ROSS HECOX

*Although an older, used model, this saddle has the low horn with forward tilt that reiners like and enough rise in the ground seat for rider stability when stopping and turning.*

ROSS HECOX

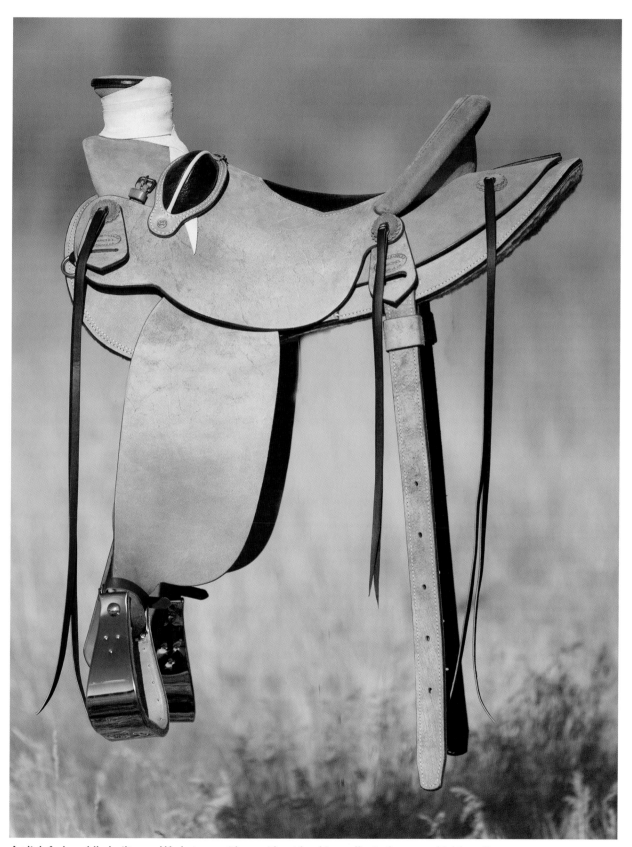

*A slick-fork saddle built on a Wade tree, with or without bucking rolls, is the proverbial favorite among buckaroos in such areas as the Great Basin.*

DARRELL DODDS

### Reining Saddles

Riding a reining pattern requires the rider to maintain a deep seat while moving with the horse through a variety of maneuvers. It's common for a reiner to want a slightly larger seat, to adjust position and stay with the horse's center of gravity. Reining saddles often have a butterfly-shaped skirts with flowing curves to the design. Many, but not all, reiners ride without back cinches and share other preferences:

- **swells or fork:** some swell, but not as much as that in reined cow-horse saddle

- **horn:** fairly short at 2½ to 3 inches; smaller structure and cap than a cutting saddle horn; slight forward tilt for ease when rider leans forward with horse's movement

- **cantle:** 3 to 3½ inches; angled back more than upright; typically with a Cheyenne roll rather than a vintage style

- **seat:** substantial rise in ground seat with pocket for security during sliding stops and for centered position during rollbacks and spins

- **fender and stirrup placement:** free-swinging for forward foot position when necessary, as during sliding stops

- **rigging:** full-double, in-skirt rigging popular

### Reined Cow-Horse Saddles

Reining and reined cow-horse saddles have strong similarities, but the cattle factor in the cow-horse event adds another dimension. Unlike a reiner, the reined-cow-horse rider can grab the horn and brace against it when working cattle—definitely helpful when a "squirrely" heifer makes the horse work for every point. Skirts are somewhat more squared than those on reining saddles, and back cinches are common in cow-horse events, as are other characteristics:

- **swells or fork:** slightly higher with more swell than typical on a reining saddle

- **horn:** about 3 inches; slightly taller and stouter than reining-saddle horn;

*This cow-horse saddle seat is a bit flatter than that usually found in a cutting or reining saddle, and the horn has been wrapped so the rider can rope if necessary.*

ROSS HECOX

possibly a modified dally-post horn for roping, but smaller cap than on a roping saddle

- **cantle:** about 4 inches high; angled back

- **seat:** somewhat flat, firm ground seat; not as deep a pocket as that on reining saddle

- **fender and stirrup placement:** slim in shape and free-moving; sometimes with slightly forward set as compared to that of a reining saddle, for ease of movement and a centered position during cow work

- **rigging:** in-skirt, full-double rigging

### Barrel-Racing Saddles

In a sport where mere fractions of a second determine placing and prize money, every ounce counts when it comes to saddle weight.

*The tall horn and deep seat help a barrel racer feel confident throughout a fast run, and round skirts typically are preferred to minimize weight.*
ROSS HECOX

Because of their light weight and ability to flex, synthetic trees tend to show up more frequently in barrel racing than in any other discipline, although some saddles still have wooden trees. Rider preference can vary significantly, so there is a good variety in saddle design when it comes to swells and cantles. Taller, more substantial swells might help a rider stay down in the seat when a horse makes a turn, but not every rider wants that much front end on a saddle. Although some riders think a tall cantle helps put them up and over the horse's back for a faster run, other barrel racers opt for a low cantle design. Despite such differences, barrel-racing saddles are designed with speed—and security—in mind:

- **swells or fork:** from tall, thick swells to less bulk in the front end, depending on rider preference

- **horn:** 3½ to 4 inches; slight forward tilt so as to stay out of the rider's way, but easy to grip when leaving turn at third barrel and heading home

- **cantle:** 3 to 5 inches high, depending on rider preference; more steep than angled back

- **seat:** from a flat seat to a deep pocket, depending on rider preference

- **fender and stirrup placement:** fenders not overly long; placement for rider to be in balanced, centered position or with feet just slightly ahead; sometimes tied forward so rider's feet don't fall to rear and behind horse's movement

- **rigging:** drop-down, in-skirt rigging popular

## Trail and Recreational-Riding Saddles

When it comes to trail riding, it's all about comfort—for both horse and rider. "The ideal trail saddle is like riding your recliner on your horse down the trail," says Thomas. A trail rider wants to be able to ride at any easy pace for hours at a time, so the saddle should be durable, as well as comfortable. Since women make up a majority of trail riders, these saddles tend to be more lightweight than, for example, an all-around ranch saddle, and typically weigh from 20 to 30 pounds. Here are other things recreational riders like in their saddles:

- **swells or fork:** ample to provide security and support when riding uphill and downhill

- **horn:** 3 to 3½ inches high and of varying thicknesses; usually with a slight forward tilt

- **cantle:** 3 to 5 inches in height; low and angled back to high, steep design, depending on rider preference

- **seat:** often padded; deep pocket and enough rise from the ground seat to front end to keep rider back in the saddle; often of soft, supple, glove-tanned leather requiring no break-in period

- **fender and stirrup placement:** slightly forward placement for deep seat back toward cantle

- **swells or fork:** often a rounded pommel design or Western-style front end

- **horn:** typically no horn

- **cantle:** 4 to 4½ inches high; more steep and upright than angled back

- **seat:** padding for comfort; from flat to deep pocket, depending on rider preference

- **fender and stirrup placement:** free-moving to allow rider position over horse's center of gravity when negotiating hills

- **rigging:** drop-down, in-skirt popular

## Equitation and Show Saddles

A Western stock saddle used for showing is nothing like that found on the range. Show saddle skirts come in a variety of shapes, and although the tree can be similar to that of a working saddle, an equitation or show saddle typically features significant—and often elaborate—leather tooling and silver work, from mild decoration to serious bling. Although the amount and type of silver and the type of leather and tooling directly affect price, construction remains similar:

*No matter what type of riding a person enjoys, saddle choice is all about personal preference and comfort.*

KATE BRADLEY

- **rigging:** in-skirt rigging popular; some three-way in-skirt riggings with full, seven-eighths or three-quarter positions to accommodate trail horses of different sizes and shapes

### Endurance

Endurance saddles borrow from the design of the stock saddle, but are lightweight and meant for long rides, in which much of the time is spent at a ground-covering trot. Saddles are typically close-contact with little skirting; the shape of the saddle closely follows that of the tree. Rider preference comes into play with cantle design, as some believe a taller cantle helps fight back fatigue. Again, despite differences in opinion, endurance riders generally share some preferences:

*Show saddles of finely tooled leather often display dazzling silverwork to help catch a judge's eye.*

DARRELL DODDS

# GOTCHA

## Beware of Broken or Damaged Saddle Trees

When looking at a used saddle, carefully inspect the integrity of the tree as best you can, even if the saddle exterior looks fine.

"On a concrete surface, stand the saddle up with the horn against the floor and push down firmly on the cantle. There should be no give at all. If there is any give, this is indicative of a weakened tree. It may be cracked, damaged, or weakened in some way, so steer clear of this saddle," says Webb Fortenberry of Cactus Saddlery in Texas.

"On an older wooden tree, the rawhide covering can come loose and if this happens, the tree looses support. You won't know what's wrong unless you actually tear down the saddle to inspect the tree, so it's best just to avoid a saddle if there's any sign the rawhide covering has loosened."

While inspecting a saddle, you also want to check for symmetry. With the horn facing the ground, hold the cantle in one hand and evaluate the underside of a saddle. Tilt the saddle away from you and then toward you while assessing the symmetry of the panels. Any significant deviation might indicate problems with the tree or inferior workmanship.

*Even though a used saddle might look serviceable, it always should be checked for tree damage.* KATE BRADLEY

- **swells or fork:** moderate to mild with slope blending smoothly into front of saddle

- **horn:** 2½ to 3 inches; similar in height and style to a reining horn, but more for looks than practicality; typically stainless steel or silver; usually with slightly forward tilt

- **cantle:** 3 to 3½-inches high; generally a Cheyenne roll, often oversized for appearance's sake

- **seat:** padded with a lot of ground rise to keep rider in proper position

- **fender and stirrup placement:** hung for center balance so rider's legs hang straight down

- **rigging:** in-skirt rigging preferred

## Treeless Saddles

Riders either love them or hate them, but a segment of the horse industry looks for treeless saddles, and some manufacturers have risen to the occasion. For example, a treeless saddle put on the market in the mid-2000s has the appearance of a traditional Western stock saddle with a cutout skirt shape. Although having wooden swells and

cantle, the saddle has no bars; instead, wool felt skirts and neoprene filler mold to the horse's back and help distribute the weight of saddle and rider.

*This treeless trail saddle provides close contact, yet accommodates hard-to-fit horses and allows the rider ample leg freedom.*

COURTESY CIRCLE Y OF YOAKUM

**45**

The seat rides like a 1-inch-thick pad; any contours felt are from the horse itself. Because there's no restriction from tree bars, the saddle is much easier to fit than a traditional one and can accommodate a vast assortment of riding stock, making this a good option for hard-to-fit horses. Typically lightweight, treeless saddles weigh about 20 pounds.

"Since around 2005, there's been a big push for a more natural, treeless saddle offering more freedom for the horse and close contact for the rider. It was big in the endurance world, but it's taken a long time to get to the Western world," says Thomas. "We had experience in this area and saw it as an opportunity. Now we make a trail-riding treeless saddle and a treeless barrel-racing saddle."

- **swells or fork:** no bars to attach to wooden swells, so swells actually farther down horse's side than with traditional saddle; accommodating fit for horse's anatomical structure yet offers rider security

- **horn:** 3 to 3½ inches high

- **cantle:** 4- to 5-inch-high; angled back

- **seat:** very deep pocket as no tree bars; only ground rise in seat a result of horse's back shape

- **fender and stirrup placement:** slightly forward placement to keep legs slightly in front of rider

- **rigging:** in-skirt popular

## Australian Stock Saddle

When *The Man From Snowy River* hit the big screen, American riders became enamored of the movie's hero and his unforgettable, dramatic downhill ride. The movie gave Australian Colin Dangaard an idea: Why not sell Australian stock saddles in America? He advertised the saddles with the marketing slogan, "Ride like the man from Snowy River," and sold out immediately. That was 1979. Since then, his Australian Stock Saddle Co. has sold thousands of saddles to riders looking for durable, lightweight saddles that are both comfortable and secure.

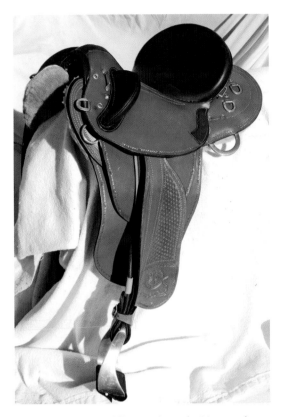

*This Australian saddle weighs only 20 pounds, has an adjustable tree, and features "poleys" up front for a secure seat.*

COURTESY AUSTRALIAN STOCK SADDLE CO.

Built on a wooden and aluminum tree similar to that found in a full-tree English saddle, the Australian-style stock saddle had been made for dangerous riding at high speed over rough country, just as the movie depicted. Originally, the saddle looked much like a big dresssage saddle, but riders soon found that this style did little to help them stay in their seats. In the late 1800s, Aussie saddlemakers started adding "poleys" to the front of the saddles. These knee pads, or rolls, help a rider stay firmly in the saddle and soon became standard design. Aussie riders tend to sit against the base of the cantle at slow speeds, but ride in forward position with the thighs against the poleys when traveling fast.

"Like all other saddles, the Aussie stock saddle has gone through a transition," says Dangaard. "The new modern Aussie saddle has a swing fender and has skeepskin on the underside instead of the traditional animal hair stuffing; it also sits closer to the horse. The swinging fender is very forgiving on the knees," he adds, "and is vital for going downhill or racing cross-country. If an Aussie saddle fits you properly, you don't have sore knees or a sore back."

- **swells or fork:** 4½-inch knee pads, or poleys, instead of Western-style swells; security for staying in saddle, but not restrictive to taking a forward position and traveling at speed

- **horn:** new models with or without horn; horn about about 3 inches tall; at a 45-degree angle forward to stay out of the way when rider leans forward

- **cantle:** 4 to 5 inches high; fairly steep and upright

- **seat:** plenty of ground rise for rider to sit securely at back of saddle

- **fender and stirrup placement:** forward position as with dressage saddle, but free-swinging to allow easy leg movement

- **rigging:** in-skirt, big-dee rigging similar to full-double rigging

## Q & A: Current Industry Considerations

Two saddle company representatives, Robb Thomas of Circle Y and Webb Fortenberry of Cactus Saddlery, discuss contemporary considerations in the saddle industry.

**Is there a good example of how saddles continue to change to meet riders' demands?**

**Thomas:** "In the world of team roping, for example, times are so fast and competitive. There's a lot happening in just a few seconds. Team ropers want saddles that put them in the proper position in the saddle from the beginning of the run. This way the riders can stand up, throw and dally, all without having to leave their seats. We're seeing a trend for smaller seat sizes among team ropers, with 14- to 14½-inch seats common. Most team ropers want the saddle fit to be snug so they don't have to struggle to get to the front of the saddle to make their throws and dally."

**Fortenberry:** "We've changed the look and stucture of our team-roping saddle to get the riders into position to make their throws and make their runs without worrying about where they are in their saddles. We want to give the riders every possible competitive advantage. Team ropers want a slightly higher cantle [around 3 to 4 inches] so they're more secure in the saddle when leaving the box. The higher, straighter cantles make it easier for them to keep position so they don't get rocked back. Both team ropers and calf ropers want a flatter front portion of the seat with a small pocket. This allows them to be more aggressive and hustle so they can get to the front of the saddle quickly."

**How has modern technology impacted the saddlemaking industry when it comes to materials?**

**Thomas:** "We've been making our patented flexible trees since the early 1990s. They're used in barrel and trail saddles, but not in our roping, reining, cutting or other saddles. Some flexible trees are made of molded rubber, but ours are made of both wood and synthetic materials; the swells and cantle are wood, while the bars are synthetic. This makes the saddle very lightweight and also allows a little flex in the front and back of the bar tips. This helps in barrel racing when a horse is shutting down to make a turn. The tree is designed to flex as the horse's shoulder angles and his body contracts while going through the turn."

**Fortenberry:** "Modern technology has given us the ability to be very consistent throughout the entire saddlemaking process. From trees to the leather-tanning process all the way to the hardware, the whole process is more accurate and consistent today."

**What are the most common mistakes consumers make when choosing their saddles?**

**Thomas:** "I think people often misinterpret the horse's body shape and type. Most seem to think the horse is bigger than he really is. People tend to want a wider saddle to make it fit and that's not necessarily the case. A lot of people are dead-set on getting a big gullet width, but it takes a lot more than that to fit a horse's back.

"You also need to do your homework before buying a saddle. Many consumers don't want to spend a lot of money, so they shop on the Internet, and a lot of those saddles don't fit. This is an investment in your entertainment and relaxation, so make sure you understand what you're buying and that it suits you and your horse."

# EXPERT TIP

## If the Saddle Fits, Ride It

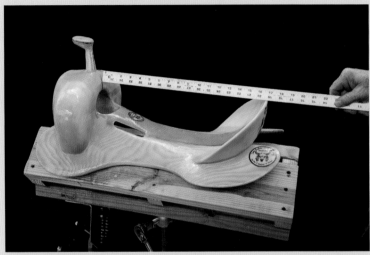

*Seat size is measured from the base of the horn to the top center position of the cantle.*

DARRELL DODDS

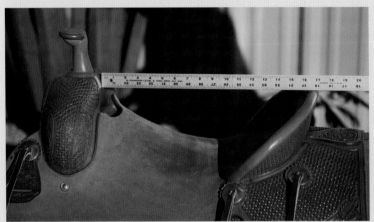

*Two people of the same height and weight might not be comfortable riding in a given saddle-seat measurement because their bodies aren't structured alike.*

DARRELL DODDS

Saddles are sold with a published seat size measured in ½-inch increments, starting at 12 inches for a child's saddle and ranging up to 18 inches. Seat size is the distance from the base of the horn to the top center position of the cantle. Anything larger than 18 inches typically is a special order, since most saddle companies don't keep extra-large sizes in stock.

Finding a saddle that fits isn't as simple as one-plus-one-equals-two. You can't assume a small adult needs a 14-inch seat, while a large adult must have a 16½-inch seat. A lot of personal preference is involved. Saddle shopping is a bit like shopping for boots; some people want them snug, while others prefer a roomier fit.

"There's no way to say that a certain size person is going to fit a specific size saddle. Two people might weigh the same, but need different sizes, depending on their builds and what they're using the saddles for," notes Webb Fortenberry of Cactus Saddlery.

"If you have a 210-pound man who stands 6 feet, 4 inches, he's probably going to be lanky, and might need a 14½-inch seat, whereas a 210-pound man who is only 5 feet, 7 inches has bigger legs and probably needs a 15½-inch seat. Saddle fit has a lot to do with a person's size and lower body build, in particular, the length of his legs."

Of course, when it comes to fit, personal preference is most important. Not all team ropers want snug seats, and not all trail riders want low, rolled-back cantles.

**Fortenberry:** "You can't go by just visuals; it's about more than just how a saddle looks. You need to inspect the leather, the rig and the underside of the saddle to make sure it's well-made and will last. You want to take the time to work with a reputable dealer or saddlemaker, and don't be afraid to ask questions. Let them know what you want to do with the saddle and be sure to sit in it; you should feel comfortable."

When sitting in a saddle, as a general rule of thumb, there should be:

* about 4 inches from the front of your body to the horn.

* at least one finger's width between your thighs and the swells for a snug seat fit.

* at least two fingers' width between thighs and swells for a roomy seat fit.

* enough room for your behind to rest against the bottom of the cantle without feeling as though you're pushed back, pressing against it.

Keep in mind: Seat size is just one aspect of how a saddle fits the rider. Other factors that affect fit are the fork angle and style, cantle slope and "dish," and seat slope and depth:

* A saddle with wide swells, originally known as "bucking rolls" because they were designed to help a cowboy maintain his seat on a bucking horse, or a saddle with undercut swells that angle back slightly can help a rider stay in the saddle. On the other hand, a slick A-fork has virtually no swells, so basically there's a smaller front end to the saddle.

* A deep saddle pocket with a fairly steep slope to the ground seat helps keep a rider in one position, but a shallow, flatter seat allows more movement.

* A tall cantle with a steep, upright angle offers more security and back support than a low cantle that angles back. Although a barrel racer might want a tall, steep cantle, a roper or reiner typically wants a shorter cantle with a milder, less upright angle.

* A cantle with significant dish, or recessed portion carved out of the lower face of the front of the cantle, offers more comfort and security than a saddle with little or no dish. Dish can be as deep as 1½ to 2 inches, or much less.

*Bucking rolls are an easy after-market add-on for those who prefer using them on an A-fork saddle; if not, they're just as easy to remove.*
DARRELL DODDS

# 4

# The Importance of Saddle Fit

When the saddle fits properly, that's one less obstacle in the way of the horse's opportunity to succeed, whatever the type of riding. Some exceptional horses have enough heart and athletic ability to perform well despite problems caused by improper saddle fit. Yet, in time, chronic pain eventually can hinder performance, sometimes even altering or ending the horse's career.

To better understand how saddle fit either enhances or interferes with the horse's natural movement, consider the construction of the equine back. It is made up of three sections: the thoracic area, 18 vertebrae to which the ribs attach, forming the horse's trunk; the lumbar region of six vertebrae; and the sacral region, the final five vertebrae of the spine, which are naturally fused together. The Arabian is the one breed that differs, as Arabs have 17 ribs and five lumbar bones.

The region where the lumbar vertebrae connect with the sacral vertebrae is known as the lumbar-sacral junction, or the horse's croup. Flexibility here is vital for performance and collection. Movement and performance are negatively affected when a horse experiences chronic pain in the lumbar-sacral junction.

The longest muscle in the horse's entire body, the *longissimus dorsi,* runs the entire length of the back. The longissimus dorsi originates at the first three sacral bones just above the tail and goes all the way to the base of the neck, to the last four cervical vertebrae. The saddle rests on this main muscle.

When a saddle doesn't fit properly, the longissimus dorsi tightens and constricts in an effort to protect the spinal column. When this major muscle becomes tight, the horse starts using his hind legs differently to avoid discomfort. As the lower back locks, that compromises normal movement of the stifle, hocks and hips. Because driving his body forward with his hind legs becomes painful, the horse avoids engaging his hindquarters and begins to move without bringing his hind legs deep beneath his body. These actions combine to increase the amount of weight put on the horse's front end, which, in turn, can lead to lameness issues and muscular damage.

However, saddle fit isn't the only thing that can cause these problems; significant conformational flaws can do the same. A horse with camped-out hind legs, an angular "goose" rump, a short hip, straight or shrunken shoulders, upright pasterns and/or other conformation issues has poor quality of movement, whether under saddle or not.

The horse experiencing back pain—whatever the source—often tries to avoid or reduce that pain by dropping his back and raising his head and neck. A frustrated rider might then experiment with different bits, martingales or tie-downs in an effort to lower the horse's head—without realizing these things don't address the true cause of the problem. Improper saddle fit can cause:

• objection to being saddled.

*A saddle that fits well complements a horse's athletic abilities, rather than diminishing his performance.*

KATE BRADLEY

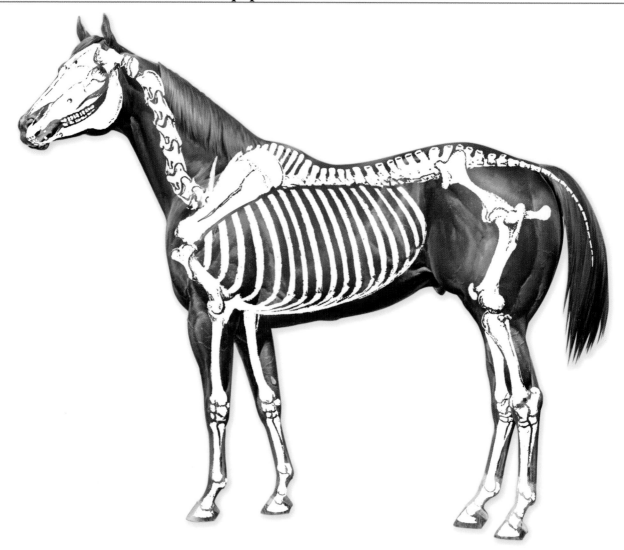

*Eighteen thoracic vertebrae connect to the horse's ribs, followed by the lumbar and sacral vertebrae, which join at the horse's croup.*

COURTESY AMERICAN QUARTER HORSE ASSOCIATION

- sensitivity to being brushed or touched in the back area.

- tail-swishing.

- pinning the ears.

- tossing the head.

- slowness in warming up or relaxing.

- reluctance or refusal to change leads.

- lack of extension in the gaits.

- excessive concussion or choppy movement.

- an inability to use the back and hindquarters properly.

- muscle atrophy or lack of development, despite exercise.

- restriction of the respiratory system.

- uneven hoof wear.

## Proper Fit

If the top of the saddle is for the rider, the bottom of the saddle is all about the horse. Since the tree is the foundation of the saddle, this is where proper fit begins. Saddle-fitting goals ensure the horse's comfort:

- The bars of the tree should follow the contours of the horse's back, making as much contact as possible.

- There should be enough gullet space for the horse's spine, so that when the rider is mounted, the underside of the saddle clears the entire length of the spine.

- The saddle should be properly placed in the "pocket" on the horse's back, neither too far forward nor too far back, so the horse's stride is not impeded.

## Common Fit Problems

Today's riders are more aware and more concerned about saddle fit than ever before. Saddle-fitting clinics and information presented at horse expos and equine events are among the reasons. If the tree doesn't fit the horse's back, the problem might be due to one or more flaws. Common saddle-fitting problems include bridging, tree-rock, an ill-fitting gullet, bar angle and/or flare.

**Bridging.** Picture a short bridge over a creek or ravine. Both ends are firmly grounded, but there's air under the center of the bridge. A saddle that "bridges" does much the same thing. The front and back parts of the tree bars make contact with a horse's back, but there's no contact in the centers of the bars.

One cause of bridging is placing the saddle too far forward. Another common reason is conformation; a horse with a large amount of spinal or ribcage curvature is likely to have problems with a bridged tree fit. This often can be remedied by using a saddle pad that fills areas with a lack of surface contact at the centers of the bars; otherwise, bridging problems continue:

- Instead of distributing the rider's weight uniformly, bridging creates greater pressure on the points of the bars that do touch the horse.

- In time, this pressure can cause soreness and can even cause the horse to shorten his stride.

**Rocking.** When a tree has too much bend in the shape of the bars, the tree rocks back and forth on the horse's back. The opposite of bridging, tree-rock means the centers of the bars make contact with the horse's back before the front and back parts of the bars touch the horse. As with bridging, rocking creates problems:

- Instead of distributing the rider's weight uniformly, tree-rock concentrates pressure in a small area, typically the middle of the horse's back, often causing pain.

- When the cinch is tightened without a rider in the saddle, the back of the saddle often tilts upward.

- When a rider mounts, the pressure is increased at the center and front of the saddle. This pressure becomes even greater and more concentrated on an even smaller area when the horse is ridden in a collected frame.

**Gullet Width.** Many riding horses today are more substantial than horses of the past. For example, it's not uncommon to see well-made roping horses weighing 1,200 to 1,300 pounds. Breeders targeting specific bloodlines might think of athletic ability, overall conformation, mind and disposition while giving less consideration to back shape. The modern tendency among many stock horses is breeding for a shorter, more compact athletic frame, and as a result, many horses have low or poorly developed withers and rounder, more wide-sprung ribcages.

"These conformational traits, and the problems that arise from them, have given rise to requests for wider gullets in saddles, wider than at any time in history," says Jeremiah Watt of Watt Bros. Saddles in Coalinga, California.

"I see firsthand the fitting issues created by having an excess of gullet width as a very common trend with today's riders. They see gullet width as a sort of magical cure to problems they have encountered in the past. They are lead to believe that if they just get more gullet width, then the horse's shoulders are freed up, and all the other issues in turn usually are taken care of, when in fact the opposite may be safer," explains Watt, who has been making custom trees and building saddles since 1977. "Less of our front-end fitting problems are cured by gullet width than are cured by addressing the issues of angle over the front end."

A saddle might have a wide gullet, but the bars still must have the correct angles for a horse. The measurement at the back of the fork determines the distance from bar to bar.

- If the gullet is too narrow, the lower portion of the bars makes contact with the horse's back, but not the top portion. With a too-narrow gullet, all the weight is carried along the bottom edges of the saddletree against the horse's rib cage.

- If the gullet is too wide, there is an excess of pressure along the upper inside edges of the saddletree, especially through the gullet and handhold areas. At the same time, there is little or no pressure along the bottom edges of the tree near the rigging of the saddle.

"The real underlying problem is far more often one of overall angle, and not a gullet issue at all," says Watt. "If you don't change the angles of the bars and only change the width of the gullet, the tree falls down lower on the horse's back. More of the horse's back fits up inside the gullet of the saddletree, which means more weight is carried on the upper inside edges of the tree bars. The entire

*When the gullet is too narrow, pressure primarily rests on the bottom edges of the tree, where only the lower portions of the bars make contact with that horse.*

DARRELL DODDS

bar has less contact with the horse's back, when ideally what you want is to maximize contact along the center line of the tree bars from end to end."

**Bar angle and flare.** A horse is an amazing collection of curves, angles and flowing lines, so it stands to reason that the tree must have contours of its own. In order to fit the back, the bars must have both angle and flare, which is where the skills of the treemaker and the saddlemaker come into play. Fitting the saddle to the horse involves making sure that the angle and flare work with a horse's particular back shape—not against it.

**Angle** refers to the portion of the bars from the center of the saddle swell down and under both sides of the left and right bars. If the angle isn't compatible with the slope of the horse's shoulders and back, a saddle doesn't fit properly. The angle over the horse's wither is of primary concern:

- A round-backed horse with low or "mutton" withers needs a wider angle to the bars; 93 degrees is common.

- A horse with more prominent withers, taller than the hip, and a high spine

*A gullet too wide creates more pressure where the upper inside edges of the saddletree rest on a horse's back, but little or no pressure along the bottom tree edges.*

DARRELL DODDS

usually needs a narrower bar angle; 90 degrees is common.

- When the angles of the bars are too narrow, the bottoms of the bars dig into the horse's back.

- When the bar angle is too wide, the saddle rides too low on the back, possibly even making contact with the withers and spine, which definitely causes discomfort.

**Flare** refers to the curvature seen in the saddletree bars, which allows the bars to rise up and over the horse's shoulders, and conversely to rise up over the horse's loin, in a gentle, constant sweeping curve. Flare can be seen at the front and rear of the bars and, ideally, should cause slightly diminished contact at the ends of the bars:

- If there isn't enough flare to the bars at the tree front, the bars can press into a horse's shoulders, restricting free movement and possibly causing saddle sores on the horse.

- If there isn't enough flare to the bars at a tree's back end, the bars can dig into the back, particularly with the added weight of a rider, causing discomfort and possibly even sores.

The angles of the saddletree bars are important factors in contouring a tree that comfortably fits a horse's shape.

DARRELL DODDS

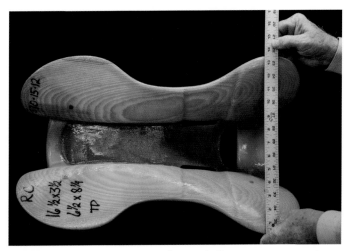

Saddletree fit is a composite of not only linear measurements, but also the angles and flares of the tree, which accommodate the curves of in a horse's body.

DARRELL DODDS

"If you feel under the front edge of the tree, there should be light contact from that leading edge of the bar over the end of the shoulders. I want the tree close—not pushing into the horse—but close," says Watt. "On the tail-end of the tree, I want the end of the tree to rise just about one-quarter inch above the horse. This is because you don't want the saddle to rock forward if you rope something."

## Check for Saddle Fit

There are different ways of checking to see how a saddle fits. Some horsemen advise dusting the underside of the saddletree with baby powder before placing it on the horse, and then lifting the saddle to check the pattern left on the back. Other riders check for even sweat patterns under the saddle, believing dry patches are a sign of poor fit.

One way to do a quick barnyard assessment of fit is to place your saddle on the horse's back with no pad and without fastening the cinches. Of course, the saddle must be placed in the correct position on the horse's back to start. (See "Gotcha!" on page 60.) Then walk the horse and watch to see what the saddle does. It's not a bad idea to have someone else walk the horse while you walk at the horse's side where you can keep an eye on the saddle.

If the saddle stays in place and doesn't move while the horse is walking, this is a good sign. If the saddle "walks" its way down the horse's back, this is a strong indication of poor fit. In this case, have your helper stop the horse before the saddle hits the ground or a horse bucks it off.

At Martin Saddlery in Greenville, Texas, Brad Vance likes to get a baseline on saddle fit by checking for even bar pressure and contact. To do this, he places a saddle on the horse's back in proper position, but without a pad and without fastening the cinch.

"The front concha is located at the front of the bars of the tree. When the saddle is in the correct position, this concha should be right behind the horse's scapula," says Vance, who is vice president of sales at Martin Saddlery and has competed for years in team roping, calf roping and cutting.

"With your palm down, knuckles up, slide your hand up and under the skirt and underneath the bars. Feel for even bar pressure front to back and top to bottom. If you feel more or less pressure on the back of your hand in any area, this tells you the weight of the saddle [and rider, once he or she mounts] is not evenly distributed. You want flat, even bar coverage. If you don't have it with this saddle, you would try a saddle with a slightly different bar pattern and/or maybe even a wider gullet."

"It's hard to evaluate how much of the tree's bars are contacting the horse's back in the middle," says Watt, who uses the "pillowcase" test to check for contact.

"Lay a pillowcase folded in half lengthwise over the horse's back," says Watt. "Put the saddle on the horse's back in the proper position and do up the cinches lightly. Reach up under the fender and gently pull on the pillowcase. Ideally, it should not pull out easily, and that tells you there's good contact by the bars through the middle. If the pillowcase pulls free easily, you basically have a bridge fit; you can adjust this by how you pad the horse.

"Then do the test again and cinch up tight, like you're going to ride. If you can still pull out the pillowcase easily, this tells you that you have a pretty big gap, as much as a quarter-inch or more. Even with a bridging fit, you're going to get a closer fit once you're mounted and the horse is collected because the bars are going to have more contact, not less."

It's worth mentioning that each of these tests looks at saddle fit only while the horse

*One quick assessment of saddle fit involves positioning a saddle on a horse, but without using a pad or fastening the cinch.*

DARRELL DODDS

*A pillowcase can be used to check for bridging, where the saddletree bars should have contact in the middle of a horse's back.*

KATE BRADLEY

is standing still. The tests are static measurements and can't take into consideration the weight of the rider or the movement of a horse and movement of rider together.

## Conformation and Saddle Fit

It's safe to say that most people shopping for a horse aren't focused on how well—or how poorly—a saddle fits his back. Most of the attention is on breed, color, markings, bloodlines, disposition, athletic ability, and performance history. A shopper obviously considers conformation, but not necessarily in relation to saddle fit. The savvy horseman, however, takes a long, hard look at conformation before loading that new horse into the trailer and taking him home.

"There are some horses that are never meant to be ridden because they don't have the conformation for saddles to stay in the middle of their backs," says Watt. "People may blame saddle fit, but it's really the horse's conformation."

## Q & A: Conformation Affects Saddle Fit

Brad Vance of Martin Saddlery and tree- and saddlemaker Jeremiah Watt of Watt Bros. Saddles weigh in on how various points of conformation directly impact saddle fit. Ideally, for example, a horse's withers should be level with or slightly higher than his croup, which is the highest point of his rump, but equine conformation isn't always ideal.

**Ideally, a horse's withers should be level with or slightly higher than his croup. How does the height of the hips as compared with the withers affect saddle fit?**

**Vance:** "What we look for is 'form to function.' The horse has to be balanced in order for the saddle to fit optimally and for the horse to perform and stay sound. A horse that is built downhill is typically harder to fit and because of his shape is going to force more pressure at the front of the saddle than at the back. A horse with this downhill conformation often needs a shim or wedge added to the padding to support the front of the saddle. Supporting the front of the saddle on a downhill horse can help the saddle ride level and help prevent it from digging into the back of the horse's shoulders."

**Watt:** "A 'downhill' horse [one whose withers are lower than his hip] always is going to carry more weight on his front end and has much more trouble staying sound. If the horse is downhill, this almost guarantees a steep shoulder, short, steep pasterns and being toed out behind, which are just more physical attributes working against the horse. The person owning this horse often has expectations this horse can never attain. There is nothing I can add to a tree to make up for serious conformational shortages. This horse can have problems even if you ride him bareback."

**What are the main saddle-fit considerations in respect to a horse's shoulders, and his comfort?**

**Vance:** "While all horses are individuals, typically today's more athletic performance-bred horses have deep, long sloping shoulders. No matter if your horse has straight up-and-down shoulders or long sloping shoulders, the saddle should not interfere with the movement of the shoulders or impede the horse's natural stride."

**Watt:** "Ideally, there should be several inches of smooth muscle at the end of the shoulder blades, not a thin layer or a deep pocket behind the shoulders. If a horse has a really pronounced end to his shoulder blades, that makes him hard to fit."

### How do the shapes of the ribcage and back impact saddle fit?

**Vance:** "Saddle fit is a combination of many factors. The saddle's gullet width and bar angle and how they relate to your horse's back are ultimately the most important, no matter what type of tree or saddle you are looking for. Your goal should be to achieve as even a fit as possible, without interfering with your horse's natural range of motion."

**Watt:** "It's much harder to fit a heavily-muscled horse that has well-sprung ribs because the muscling is actually higher than the spine. Xenophon referenced this as 'double-backed,' meaning rounded and flat-backed, while a 'single-backed' horse has a prominent spine line and ribs that fall off at a steeper angle."

### Beyond Conformation

Conformation isn't the only factor affecting how the saddle fits—or doesn't. The horse's age, feeding program, how often or hard he's worked, and choice of pad or blanket also can impact saddle fit.

"It's crucial that the saddle fits well from the start because you can change a horse's back through poor fit," adds Vance. "If you look at most healthy coming-2-year-olds and even stallions that haven't been ridden, you see full round backs with healthy muscle and not much wither, especially with Quarter Horses. Over time, as those young horses are trained, and if there are issues with saddle fit, they can develop muscle atrophy and more prominent withers than they might have had normally. Keeping the horse's back muscles strong and healthy from the beginning with good saddle fit can help a horse stay sound and have a longer-lasting career under saddle."

Horses' backs also change as they age. You can't assume the saddle that fits fine when the horse is a 4-year-old still fits correctly when that horse is 14. An owner who has the same horse for the animal's entire riding lifetime might use several saddles through the years.

Many horses today are fatter than they should be, but owners often don't think about how those excess pounds can change the way the saddle fits. A horse with a body score of 9, described as "extremely fat," likely is harder to fit than a horse with a score of a "moderate" 5 or "moderately fleshy" 6. When you pull an out-of-shape horse with a big grass belly off pasture and start riding regularly, the horse can lose as much as 100 to 200 pounds as he gets fit. A hard-working horse tends to lose weight first in the wither area, which definitely can change the way the saddle fits.

The type of pad or blanket used also can affect how a saddle fits—and not always in a good way. (More details about saddle pads are in Chapter 6.)

"I don't have any control of the quality of gear they [customers] put under my saddles," says Watt. "It might be a pad they should have given to their Border Collie 10 years ago. Conformation, how the horse is fed, the pad or blanket...these are all things that affect how well a saddle fits, but nobody ever consults the saddlemaker about them."

### Tree Design

Here's a brief look back at the saddletree, where a suitable fit starts. Tree design took a serious turn for the better in the late 1800s when a handful of California-based treemakers—including Antonio "Chapo" Martinez, Ricardo Mattle and Aleck Taylor—began making trees with wider and better-defined bars. The goal was to more evenly distribute pressure on the horse's back. Continued improvements in tree design came about in the next century, thanks to Bill Hubbard of Visalia Stock Saddle Co. in California and Walt Youngman of Hamley & Co. in Oregon.

"The family tree that we treemakers have fallen from has a common root for most of us, going back to Hamley & Co. and Walt Youngman," says Watt. "Walt gets credit

*One reason for the Wade tree's popularity is that it fits a variety of horses, primarily because a great deal of bar surface area can make contact with a horse's back.*

JOHN WILLEMSMA

for coming up with the Wade tree around 1940. After Walt died, Dale Harwood really took over the homemade tree industry. Dale helped other treemakers, including Bob Severe and Todd McGiffin, with templates and patterns. Without Dale, there would be very little of a handmade tree business. He's also helped several tree factories."

From the mid-1940s through the mid-1970s, a proliferation of different trees hit the market, thanks to the endorsements of professional cowboys and popular horsemen, such as Toots Mansfield, Chuck Sheppard and Buster Welch, to name only a few.

"They were changing the fork to get a front end they liked and often not even changing it that much, but giving the tree a different name," Watt explains. "If you lay one tree pattern on top of another, you would see there isn't a lot of difference.

"Trendsetting can make manifest changes. Ray Hunt did this in the natural horsemanship world by making the Wade tree popular, and Buster Welch did it by coming out with the cutting-horse saddletree. What Buster Welch did was as different as coming from another planet back then, but today nobody heads to the cutting arena with a saddle that isn't one of his, or a facsimile thereof."

Watt believes the Wade tree is one of the most popular trees today, and one reason is that it fits a wide range of horses.

"The Wade offers more opportunities to put more square inches of tree bar on the horse's back, and it's mathematically proven that the more square inches of surface I can put on a horse's back, the better off he'll be," says Watt. "The thickness of wood to build the bars is critical, starting with a block of wood seven inches wide and three inches thick in order to attain the right amount of both rock and twist. The Wade, when properly made, has a fork made of hardwood laminations, allowing the fork and horn to be made as one integral unit. The idea behind the Wade tree design is to put the horn as close to the horse's back as possible, which reduces leverage on the horse's shoulders when roping."

## Tree Sizes

Through time, trial and error, and modern technology, tree design has been modified and adjusted to better fit today's horses. Make no mistake: Horses of the 21st century are markedly different from horses 200,

Saddletrees might have changed through the years to accommodate equine changes, but one thing remains the same: There are no industry-wide standards or specifications for sizing saddletrees.

DARRELL DODDS

100, even 50 years ago. Horses today are commonly bred for specific athletic disciplines instead of for all-around purposes. If a certain bloodline has success in the show pen or arena, owners follow that line and change their breeding programs. Trends in bloodlines within a breed and the crossing of different breeds have led to noticeable differences in conformation and size in horses. Saddlemakers have done their best to adjust trees to accommodate the changes in back shapes and angles.

The challenge for consumers is knowing what to look for when shopping for a saddle, and learning enough about conformation to make wise decisions with regard to the saddle and saddletree. This holds true whether buying one of the many well-made factory saddles or one that is handmade.

It might sound like common sense to think a big stout horse needs a tree with what is described as "full Quarter-Horse" bars. There's just one problem with this line of thinking—and it's a big one: There are no industry-wide standards or specifications for tree sizes. What one manufacturer markets as full Quarter-Horse bars isn't necessarily the same in a saddle produced by another company. These are generic terms for which there are no standard rules of measurement.

"Anybody who's ever bought a horse has heard—but may not understand—the terms 'semi-Quarter-Horse' bars and 'full Quarter-Horse' bars. There are no benchmarks for

# GOTCHA!

## Position Your Saddle Well

Your saddle should rest in the natural pocket just behind your horse's scapula. Most riders feel confident they put their saddles in the correct place on their horses' backs, yet in reality many riders put saddles too far forward or too far back. It's a simple mistake, but can create big problems in time. Incorrect saddle placement can lead to chronic pain, as well as inhibit your horse's natural range of motion.

Place the saddle too far forward and the scapula actually can hit the front bars of the tree. Your horse then tries to avoid discomfort by compromising his stride. Instead of moving forward straight and true, he might swing his front legs outward so that his scapula doesn't hit the tree. This altered stride doesn't have the same propulsion as the natural movement; it also causes the horse to land harder, putting more pressure on heels, feet, joints and muscles. In addition, placing a saddle too far forward puts the bulk of the weight on the rearmost tips of the tree bars.

"The horse's back is designed to carry a tree in a specific place determined by his conformation. I believe more people place a saddle too far back these days than vice versa," observes saddlemaker Jeremiah Watt of Watt Bros Saddles in Coalinga, California. "The benefit of placing a saddle by accident a little too far forward is that the natural gait of the horse's shoulders gently pushes the average tree back into its rightful position—but not if the saddle is too far back. I want the front tip of a good saddletree bar to lay over the end of the scapula, not behind it."

If the saddletree has appropriate flare at the ends of the bars, the tree doesn't interfere with the movement of the horse's scapulae.

*A well-positioned saddle improves comfort for a horse, but discomfort from incorrect saddle placement can lead to an altered stride and other problems.*

DARRELL DODDS

those terms," says Watt. "It may be my opinion alone that the entire saddle industry would be improved at every level if we developed a consistent set of terms with regard to the trees, as well as a baseline for such things as angularity, etc. I am not asking for a ruling body controlling saddletree design. What I am looking for is the beginnings of some congruency between what the factory trees do and [what] those of us who build trees by hand do. In truth, I think the factory saddles would benefit the most from this process, especially at the retail level of their product. I think the more mystery we can take out of the saddletree and fit process, the better off all of us are as an end result."

"Unfortunately, the consumer in the saddle industry uses terms like full Quarter-Horse and semi-Quarter-Horse bars, but there's no governing body controlling those sizes, so each saddle company is left to its own marketing as to what tree will be best for them," notes Robb Thomas at Circle Y. "We try not to use those terms. We use 'medium,' 'wide' and 'extra-wide.' In our trees, a medium may be equal to semi- Quarter-Horse bars, but our wide may be different from another company's full Quarter-Horse bars. It's very subjective, which is why today we do more saddle-fitting clinics."

"If a saddle doesn't fit your horse, that doesn't mean the company doesn't build a good saddle. It means the saddle doesn't fit your horse. All companies build a variety of saddletree widths," adds Thomas. "There is no cost to geometry. Just because a saddle price is expensive doesn't mean it will fit your horse better than a less expensive saddle. Your horse's back and the geometry of the tree have to match. This can happen in a $500 saddle or a $10,000 saddle."

Thomas points out that although 100-percent bar contact is ideal, it's not absolutely necessary for good saddle fit.

"The heavier the rider, or the longer a person rides, the more that increases the need for more surface contact," says Thomas. "If a person rides sparingly, or if he isn't very heavy, he can get away with less surface contact. With that said, I believe 80-percent-plus contact is necessary for a saddle to be considered 'good' saddle fit."

Bottom line: Whether you earn a living working horseback, train young horses, compete often or occasionally, or simply trail ride for pleasure, saddle fit is a crucial part of the equation. Even the most athletic, good-minded horse can be hampered by improper fit, and for the horse with conformation issues, poor fit only adds to his problems.

## MAKE IT WORK FOR YOU

### Banish Saddle Squeaks

The occasional gentle creak of a comfortable saddle is almost like music when you're heading down the trail, but if your saddle squeaks and groans to the point of annoyance, it's time to take action. Some riders actually dunk the entire saddle in a barrel of neatsfoot oil and then hang it to dry for a few days, but you don't have to go to such extremes.

In most cases, the noise comes from fender friction as the fenders rub against the seat jockeys and skirts. You usually can solve the problem in a few minutes with a container of talcum or baby powder.

- Place the saddle upside down and sprinkle a generous amount of powder deep between the undersides of the seat jockeys and the fenders, as well as between the fenders and the skirts

- Turn the saddle right-side-up, lift and shake the saddle to remove excess powder. Use a towel or cloth to wipe off any visible powder.

- One treatment might be enough, but repeat as necessary if squeak returns.

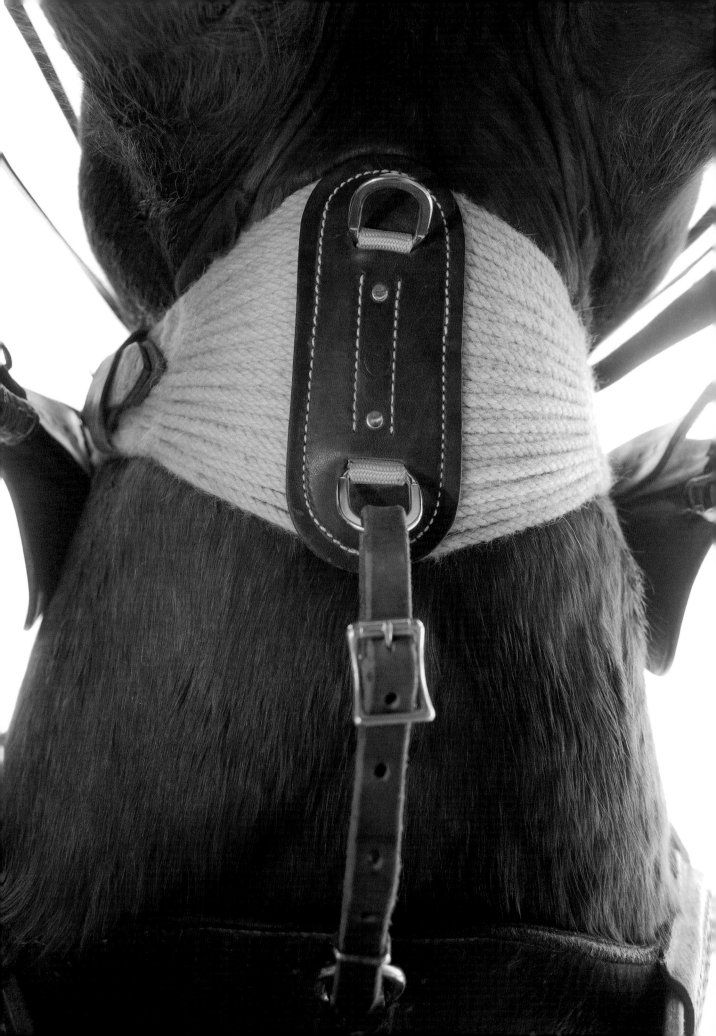

# 5
# Cinches

When Assyrian warriors rode into battle around 700 B.C., historians say the warriors did so mounted on horses with decorative saddle cloths held in place by belly straps of some sort. Although nobody is sure what those Middle Eastern horsemen called that primitive girth, today's Western riders refer to the same piece of equipment as a "cinch," a derivation of the Spanish word *cincha.*

Cinch is one of those clever, multipurpose words that manages to be both a noun and a verb. A cinch keeps a saddle in place, and a rider cinches down—or up—when he tightens this piece of equipment.

Although there are a number of cinch materials from which to chose, there are only two cinch shapes: straight and roper.

- With a **straight cinch,** no matter the material, the entire cinch is the same width.

- A **roper cinch** is contoured to be wider in the middle, providing more surface area to absorb pressure and help stabilize the saddle.

## Plenty of Choices

Whether you opt for a cinch of natural or synthetic materials—or a combination of the two—there are valid reasons for those choices. Synthetic materials are resistant to rot and typically last longer than natural materials. Although natural-fiber cinches flex and fit well, they also absorb moisture and bacteria, so are harder to disinfect and can rot in time if not kept clean.

**Felt** cinches usually are backed with nylon. This makes for a long-lasting cinch, but since there is no give, or stretch, with nylon, you must be careful not to overtighten the cinch. The felt lining can come from several sources, including wool, synthetic and plant fibers, with the fibers pressed together under heat. Felt cinches:

- feel soft and flexible against the horse.

- naturally shape to the horse without pinching.

- can be helpful with a sensitive- or tender-skinned horse.

- don't hold heat.

- repel moisture by wicking it away from the horse's back.

- are quick to show wear.

- become magnets for burrs, hair and dirt, which stick easily, especially as cinch edges become "fluffy" with wear.

- are not easy to clean.

*The felt cinch lining is soft next to the horse, and the nylon-web backing is durable.*

*No matter how you look at it, a saddle cinch is an important piece of equipment.*

*Although comfortable for a sensitive-skinned horse, a fleece cinch requires watchful maintenance to keep it soft and free from burrs.*
DARRELL DODDS

**Fleece** cinches, also referred to as "fuzzy" cinches, usually are made of nylon backed with fleece material, wool or synthetic, or a combination of the two. These cinches:

- are durable, but also soft against the horse, and provide cushioning.

- can be helpful for a sensitive- or tender-skinned horse.

- often seem harder than some other materials to tighten snugly.

- can be hard to clean, especially if the fleece nap is long.

- attract burrs, hair and dirt, which stick easily to the fleece.

- become stiff and hard when dirty, so require extra care to keep clean.

**Neoprene** (foam) cinches first became popular in the 1990s. Manufacturers have since designed thin neoprene cinches, as well as cinches of perforated neoprene. Riders seem either to love or hate this material for a variety of reasons, as neoprene:

- is easy to hose clean and disinfect, which is helpful in a training barn when one cinch is used on multiple horses.

- doesn't absorb water and dries quickly.

*Few cinch materials are as easy to clean and disinfect as synthetic neoprene.*
DARRELL DODDS

- doesn't attract dirt, stickers, burrs or hair.

- is durable and holds up well under use.

- stays flexible in a wide temperature range and is weather-resistant.

- can be hot against the horse and can make him sweat more.

- tends to pull on the horse's hair.

- can be torn or snagged by sharp or rough surfaces.

- dries and cracks after long use, allowing dirt and bacteria into the cracks.

- tends to grip the horse so it's easy to tighten the cinch too much.

- can sore a thin-skinned horse.

- used for a thin, ¼-inch cinch doesn't seem as comfortable to a horse as a ½-inch-thick neoprene cinch.

- can be perforated, in some cases, to increase airflow, but holes are small and can clog with sweat, hair and dirt.

**Leather** is routinely used for Western back cinches although leather front cinches aren't nearly as common in the Western world as they are on English saddles. Those who ride with leather cinches, however, tend to swear by them. Some of the most popular cinches have leather bodies with synthetic coverings or linings. Leather cinches:

- can be strong and durable.

- are naturally flexible and conform well to the horse's shape.

- don't tend to sore a horse easily.

- have some stretch and elasticity.

- are not easily overtightened.

- can be easy to clean and disinfect when combined with a synthetic cover or lining.

*A leather cinch offers the pluses of any such gear and requires the same type of routine maintenance.*

COURTESY COW HORSE SUPPLY

*Channels in flexible high-tech foam help provide cooling air circulation underneath this wide roper-style cinch.*

COURTESY WEAVER LEATHER

- breathe better than nylon or other synthetics, but not as well as natural mohair.

- require maintenance and must be cleaned and oiled, just as with a saddle.

## String or Corded Cinches

The traditional choice of many horsemen, a corded string cinch breathes well and doesn't trap heat against the horse's skin. A natural-fiber string cinch has elasticity not found in synthetics, which makes it easier for the horse's lungs to expand while he works.

String, or corded, cinches are made in either one layer of 14 to 17 strands or two layers of 27 to 31 strands. The benefits of the double layer are additional strength and cushioned comfort for the horse, with similar breathability of the single layer. A string cinch has a centerpiece, or crossbar, meant to keep the individual strands from twisting or tangling. It's especially important to keep a string cinch clean. Cleaning the cinch with a stiff brush or currycomb helps remove the dirt and dried sweat that can rub and gall a horse.

String cinches can be made of several different materials, including cotton, mohair, mohair blends, alpaca and even horsehair.

**Cotton** cinches are an industry staple. Generally these natural-fiber cinches:

- are the least expensive, but also have the shortest lifespan.

- harden with use and become stiff.

- often have nickel-plated hardware, which rusts with time.

- last longer when combined with a synthetic, such as rayon.

- cost less than pure mohair cinches.

**Mohair-blend** cinches, using natural and/or synthetic fibers for the blend, typically:

- last longer than cotton string cinches.

- lose some elasticity if blended fibers are synthetics, such as nylon or rayon.

- breathe well.

- easily can be curried or brushed clean.

**Mohair** cinches, made from angora goat hair, the traditional choice of many horsemen:

- must be at least 95-percent pure mohair to be labeled as such.

*String or corded cinches remain a favorite among traditionalists and often have horsehair shu-flies attached.*

DARRELL DODDS

- are tan in color, originally due to goat urine, although today's mohair cinches are dyed tan—no goat urine required.

- feel soft and comfortable against the horse's body.

- are durable and long-lasting.

- have plenty of stretch.

- breathe well.

- are easy to clean by currying or brushing.

**Alpaca** fiber, which comes from the long-haired South American animal known by the same name and somewhat akin to the llama:

- is softer than mohair.

- comes in many different colors and has a nice sheen.

- has slightly more stretch than mohair.

- breathes well.

- cleans easily by currying or brushing.

**Horsehair** cinches are favored by riders who like a traditional vaquero cinch. Made of woven and/or braided horse mane hair, cinches come in a variety of natural colors. A horsehair "shu-fly" sometimes is attached to the center of a cinch to discourage flies along a horse's midline.

The saddled horse's hair that packs into the cinch helps pad it with time and should not be removed. Springtime, when a horse is shedding, is ideal to start using a new horsehair cinch. This type cinch shouldn't be soaked in water although, if especially dirty, it can be hosed, taking care not to remove the padded hair, and then hung straight to dry. Horsehair cinches generally:

- grip horses well and help prevent saddle slippage, so don't have to be fastened so tightly as some cinches.

- tend to be wide, which better helps distribute pressure.

- have natural smooth edges that guard against chafing and soring.

- are very long-lasting.

- breathe well and don't build heat underneath.

- don't promote the spread of bacteria or fungus.

- catch burrs and stickers, so must be checked with each use.

- can stretch when new or wet, so might need to be retightened when in a downpour or after a horse has sweated significantly.

- can mold or mildew if stored without good air circulation. In a humid region, a climate-controlled environment is best for storage.

## Back Cinches

Texas cowboys generally are credited as being the first to add back, or flank, cinches to their saddles, sometime after the mid-1850s. Because roping cattle and tying hard and fast to the horn caused the back of a saddle to rock upward, cowboys came up with the back cinch, a development that also resulted in the creation of the three-quarter and seven-eighths saddle-rigging positions.

Although back cinches don't have near the variety in materials and contructions as front cinches, there are several width options. A back cinch is made of leather and can range anywhere from 1½ inches to 6 inches wide.

*Keys to back-cinch success include proper adjustment and a secure strap hobbling the back cinch to the front cinch.*

COURTESY COW HORSE SUPPLY

*A multitude of cinches are available in a variety of sizes, styles, and materials.*

DARRELL DODDS

- Ropers tend to use heavy, wide back cinches because their horses need this support when stout cows or steers are on the end of the ropes.

- When a calf-roping horse must stop and then pull backward, a firm, wide back cinch helps hold down the back of the saddle.

- Working cowboys tend to favor narrower back cinches, with 3½ inches the standard, because that's not as hot on horses working all day.

*Much like the leather attached to it, saddle hardware plays an important role in equipment integrity and serviceability.*

KATE BRADLEY

## Cinch Hardware

Although there isn't a great amount of metal hardware on a cinch, those buckles and D-rings, typically attached to the body of the cinch, are crucial for integrity and function. In the past a rider usually tied off the cinch with a latigo knot of some sort, but the vast majority of people today use buckles with tongues to cinch horses, and either method is fine.

Look through a well-stocked tack room and most older cinches have round rings. That is simply because they were easy to manufacture, observes Brad Loesch of Cow Horse Supply in Springtown, Texas. Today, there is a large selection of buckles and D-rings, especially on string cinches. The most common

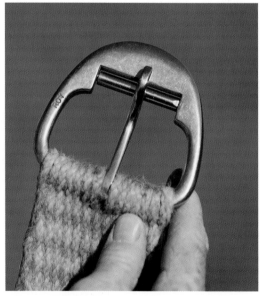

*The easy-to-fasten single-roller cinch buckle is popular among performance riders.*

DARRELL DODDS

is a modified A-frame buckle, and although many riders are adamant about the styles they prefer, it's all personal preference.

"A round buckle may let a latigo turn or pull, while an A-frame keeps the latigo a little more centered and true," says Loesch. "People who aren't saddling a lot of horses every day may not be as choosy, but performance horse riders tend to go for a buckle that's going to let them cinch and uncinch quickly."

Materials include stainless steel, brass, and chrome- or nickel-plated steel. Plated-steel hardware often is found on less expensive cinches, and if you question whether cinch hardware is stainless or plated, just run a magnet over it.

"A magnet does not stick to stainless steel or brass, but it does stick to steel plate and that's how you can tell," explains Loesch. "If it's chrome-plated or nickel-plated steel, over time the plating flecks off and rusts with use. Lesser quality hardware is not as strong as stainless or brass, and it also gets rough and is harder on the leather when the plating wears off the hardware."

Made of either flat or rounded metal, buckles come in two basic styles: single-roller or double-roller, which became popular in the early 2000s. Tongues can be either straight or contoured. Much of this is simply personal preference, but there are differences:

- A **flat buckle** typically is rounded at the top and allows you to either tie a cinch or use the buckle tongue to tighten the cinch.

- A **single-roller buckle** comes in a modified A-frame, or is flat but rounded at the top. Popular among performance riders, this buckle is easy to cinch.

- A **double-roller** functions like a pulley system in that the latigo runs through the top roller and then down and through a bottom roller. Not much strength is needed as the rollers make it easy to pull the cinch snug, but be careful not to overtighten the cinch.

## Latigos and Off-Billets

Most riders today use latigos on the left side to tighten the cinch and off-billets on the right, but some horsemen still prefer to use latigos on both sides.

Made of a short, heavy piece of doubled leather or nylon with holes punched along the length, the off-billet is attached to the right cinch ring. Made of a long, single piece of leather or nylon, the latigo attaches to the left cinch ring (and to the right when used there) with a section of leather laced through three holes at its top. Depending on rider preference, the saddle can be cinched either by tying the latigo on the cinch ring or by using the cinch-buckle tongue through holes in the latigo.

When it comes to these essential latigos and billets, the choice of materials is leather or nylon, and construction is either the single-ply or doubled-and-stitched, which many horsemen prefer. Although there are only a few options available, strong opinions exist.

**Leather** is preferred by some horsemen, who would never use nylon latigos or off-billets even if given a wagonload of them. The traditional leather used in latigos is "Indian-tanned" with burgundy alum and:

- has give and stretches, so isn't as easy to overtighten as nylon.

- is more expensive than nylon gear.

- wears much faster than nylon, and the holes tend to enlarge.

- should be replaced when cracked or frayed before moisture gets in and breaks down the fibers.

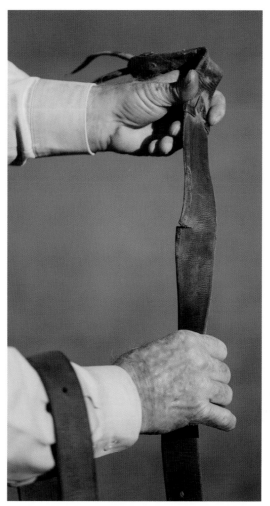

*A sound latigo is critical for a successful ride, so routine checks for wear are important.*
DARRELL DODDS

- has slick edges, which are much smoother against the horse.

**Nylon** latigos and billets are preferred by others, especially those who frequently ride in wet conditions and like the durability of nylon, which:

- is less expensive than leather.

- has no give or stretch, so is easy to overtighten.

- also has rougher edges than leather, which can rub a horse.

- is sturdy and typically lasts longer than leather latigos and billets.

*Although traditionalists prefer leather latigos, others prefer less expensive, but durable nylon latigos, particularly when riding in wet conditions.*

KATE BRADLEY

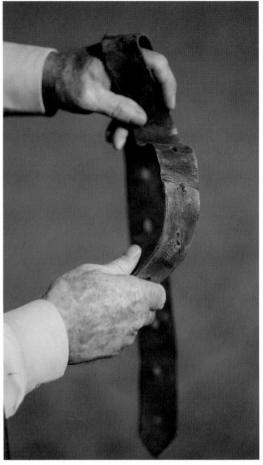

*Even though an off-billet might appear sturdier than a latigo, the off-billet can fail to do its job, just as a latigo can.*

DARRELL DODDS

Whatever the type cinch, it should be long enough that there isn't much latigo or off-billet rubbing against the horse's sides. A good rule of thumb is to have no more and preferably less than a hand's width of latigo touching the horse when the cinch is tight.

"You also want to check your Blevins buckles [on the stirrup leathers]," adds Loesch. "They can rub on your latigo, and if they have sharp edges, they not only can damage the latigo, but also cause it to fail. That will cause a wreck and sure get you pitched off."

The best cinch in the world doesn't do any good when the latigo or off-billet fails. Because they typically aren't removed from the saddle until it's time to replace them, they're easy to overlook. Take a minute to examine your latigo and off-billet for any signs of damage or weakness every time you saddle a horse. After all, this equipment keeps the saddle on your horse, so isn't a place to cut corners.

## Adjusting the Cinch

Lay the cinch out straight and measure from the rings or buckles at either end to determine the size. When choosing a cinch, make sure it is long enough and is adjusted so that the buckles don't fall in the elbow region right behind the horse's front leg.

"It's easy to gall a horse in this area, so you want to see both buckles higher up on the horse's sides, not right behind the front legs," says Molly Wagner of Weaver Leather, based in Mount Hope, Ohio.

Your cinch also has two small D-rings sewn into the centerpiece or crossbar. Even if you never attach a breast collar, martingale, tie-down or cinch hobble to these rings, which is why they exist, the centerpiece serves as an easy way to check and see if your cinch is even and balanced.

When the cinch is tight, be sure these rings are centered under the horse's midline. If the rings are lopsided, this immediately tells you pressure on the cinch is unequal. You need to adjust your off-billet and/or latigo to change and center the cinch.

Likewise, when you cinch your saddle and the top of the cinch is just an inch or two below the bottom of your pad on one side, the cinch adjustment probably is set too low on the other side, or the cinch is too long.

After tightening your cinch, also check to see if you can slip your fingers under the cinch below the buckle. As a general rule of thumb, you should be able to easily slip two or three fingers under the cinch here. If you can't—or if it's a very snug fit—your cinch probably is too tight.

*No matter the length of the ride, the front cinch should be long enough that the hardware doesn't rub a horse behind the front legs.*

KATE BRADLEY

# EXPERT TIP

## Sticking with a Classic

At the Diamond S Ranch outside Wickenburg, Ariz., it isn't unusual for Lee Smith to spend 30 hours or more a week in the saddle. Lee and her husband, Mark, run a cow-calf operation and raise Quarter Horses; in addition, Lee travels the country conducting clinics and demonstrations.

Whether she's dragging calves to the fire for branding or teaching a horsemanship clinic far from home, Smith hasn't strayed far from her cowgirl roots when choosing a cinch.

"I'm pretty simple and a little old-fashioned when it comes to cinches. I'm a mohair girl myself," says Smith. "We ride in Wade saddles and use mohair roping cinches. Roping cinches are our everyday using gear when teaching clinics and working on the ranch. We do have a few cutting saddles, and we use regular straight cinches on them, but they're always made of mohair.

"They breathe well and the natural fibers wick better. Mohair doesn't build up a lot of heat like neoprene can," adds Smith. "They [mohair cinches] work well in this country and are easy to clean. I just run a curry or hard plastic brush over the cinch to keep the salt from building up. I find, if I just keep them curried, that works well. I do this pretty much every time I ride when I'm at the ranch. If I'm doing clinics and the cinch won't get real salty or dirty, I may not do it every time."

Smith has tried just about every type of cinch material through the years, including cotton, felt, fleece, neoprene and more.

"I know the neoprene cinches are easy to hose off, but they get hot, and I think they tend to pull hair," she notes. "I've found the fuzzy cinches gather more stickers and in our country, as hot as it is, when you ride a lot, you can hardly curry them out when they get dirty. Then the fibers lose the ability to soften up. I went back to mohair because I can use a regular curry or brush on them; that softens and pulls up the fibers. I can't remember the last time I had a fungal situation from a cinch, and we ride a lot of horses."

There comes a point when currying no longer softens the cinch fibers. Smith says that's when it's time to replace the cinch because the fibers have soaked up so much sweat that the salt works its way deeply into the fibers, making them stiff. "A mohair cinch should be flexible and feel soft to the touch; when the fibers start to get inflexible, then you run the risk of soring a horse."

When it comes to hardware, Smith has tried different types of rollers and buckles through the years. "I prefer the round rings, and I like a cinch with a buckle on both sides. I also like a latigo on both sides of my saddle so I can keep the cinch centered."

Smith says if you aren't spending long hours in the saddle, you might be able to get away with equipment that you couldn't use when working horseback all day. But she compares a saddle and cinch to a good work shoe.

"You can wear just about any pair of shoes for an hour, but when you have to be in them all day, you want something that fits and is comfortable."

## Q&A: Cinch Questions Answered

Horsemen have some definite opinions about cinches, but questions also abound. A chat with Molly Wagner of Weaver Leather and Brad Loesch of Cow Horse Supply provides answers from industry experts, who also happen to spend plenty of time in their saddles. Wagner, who has ridden since 1992 and competes in reining, is the national sales manager for Weaver Leather, which has been in business since 1972. Loesch regularly travels and competes in steer wrestling in the Professional Rodeo Cowboys Association.

His father, Doug Loesch, managed Ryan's Western Stores in the late '60s and early '70s, and also worked with Pott's Longhorn and M. L. Leddy's. With this experience, he started Cow Horse Supply in 1992, and after his unexpected passing in 1996, Brad took over the business.

### Do riders need different cinches for various sports and activities?

**Wagner:** "Some people think a roping cinch can get in the way of the horse's front end crossing over, so that's why performance riders in reined cow horse, reining and cutting don't use it. Performance people and trail riders typically ride in a straight cinch. Both ropers and barrel racers like a cinch that has a straight front edge and is contoured on the back edge. It gives more coverage and support for the horse during speed events when there is a lot of pulling, jerking and fast turns."

**Loesch:** "Some people think if they're not swinging a rope, they don't need a roper cinch, but to me, that's a fallacy. I think you need the cinch that best fits your animal to hold the saddle in place. It's all about the horse. You want to spread that pressure, and a roper cinch distributes pressure over a wide area. Think of having a tight rubber band around your wrist; a wide one doesn't hurt as much as a thin one. It's the same concept."

### How do I know what size cinch my horse needs?

**Wagner:** "There's no definite way to tell. You can't say, 'If you have a 15-hand horse that weighs 1,000 pounds, this is the size cinch you need.' If the flat part of the ring is in any of the folds or creases behind the horse's elbow, this means your cinch is too short. Cinch sizes come in 2-inch increments, and most stock-horse breeds fall into the 28-inch-to-36-inch size range. Typically, if your saddle has a drop rigging, you will drop at least one cinch size."

**Loesch:** "Some people like to ride with short cinches. Traditionally, if a horse is very deep and big-barreled, he's going to take a longer cinch. A horse can be very tall, but if he's not very wide between the front legs, you would

*Even though a cowboy might not swap cinches when he swaps horses, he's always careful to adjust the cinch to the horse and usually checks the cinch routinely throughout the day.*

ROSS HECOX

# "GOTCHA"

## Back-Cinch Safety Check

Many riders show a lack of concern about back cinches they never exhibit with their front cinches. To be effective, a back cinch should make contact with the horse's belly; otherwise, it's only for looks and even can cause problems. Working cowboys generally ride with snug back cinches, yet many trail riders have a bad habit of riding with inches of space between their cinches and their horses' bellies. This is unwise, not to mention dangerous. There's risk of a serious wreck if a branch gets caught between the back cinch and a horse's body. A horse kicking at flies or just negotiating a steep trail can get a back foot caught in a loose cinch with disastrous results.

"If you've ever seen a horse stick a back leg through a back cinch, it's not a pretty sight," says Brad Loesch of Cow Horse Supply, Springtown, Texas.

Eliminate the risk and make it a point to ride with the back cinch against your horse's belly. There should be no daylight between horse and cinch.

Don't ride with a back cinch unless there's a cinch hobble attaching it to the back D-ring on the front cinch. Check to see that the hobble is tightened properly so that the cinch can't swing backward.

"Every time you ride, check the cinch hobble for integrity and make sure it's adjusted so the cinch can't swing back into the flank area. This gets overlooked a lot," cautions Loesch. "Even with a broke horse, all heck breaks loose if that happens. A lot of good cowboys have been dumped off broke horses when that cinch hobble breaks."

Finally, make it an inviolable rule that your back cinch always is fastened last and undone first. All it takes is one time—undoing the front cinch and starting to pull off the saddle with the back cinch still tight—to realize how much damage even a quiet horse can do to a good saddle. Follow the rule: "Back cinch on last and off first," and you never have to learn this lesson the hard way.

A note of caution: If you've been riding with a loose back cinch—or no back cinch—give your horse plenty of chances to react to a snug back cinch without you on his back. Tack up, check your cinch hobble, and then longe or work him in a round pen to gauge his reaction. Make sure he's accustomed to that back cinch before you mount.

*The too-loose back cinch and breast-collar strap to the center of the cinch should be adjusted properly for safety, and the back-cinch hobble strap should be checked routinely.*

DARRELL DODDS

need a shorter cinch [if using a roper cinch], to prevent rubbing and to keep from having too much width behind the legs. Ideally, you want the cinch rings or buckles to have straight up-and-down pull off the dees of the saddle, not to rest on the curve of the horse's barrel."

**I want to make sure my saddle stays put, but how can I guard against over-tightening my cinch?**

**Wagner:** "With any cinch, you don't want to totally cinch down the horse at one time. Make it snug and then walk out to where you're going to ride. Then check the cinch again and retighten it before you mount up."

**Loesch:** "I like to use a cinch that has the give of natural materials, because they are harder to overtighten than synthetic materials. A common mistake made by amateur riders is leaving an overtight cinch on the horse too long, while most cowboys rely on good-fitting saddles—not tight cinches—to stay in the middle of their horses. You only want to have the cinch tight enough for performance for a short time. You see working cowboys, when they get to the cows and have to rope, step down and tighten their cinches for that job. If you have a horse saddled 14 to 15 hours a day, that's when you can get into problems if the cinch isn't right. That won't be as important for someone who is riding only an hour or so."

**With so many options available, how do I know I'm choosing the right cinch material?**

**Wagner:** "It's all strictly personal preference and up to each individual. You have to take into account what type of riding you do and what type of climate you're in. If you're in a really hot climate, you're probably going to want to steer clear of the black neoprene and look for a synthetic material that is vented or allows airflow, or a natural fiber, such as mohair, for its breathability. Then you have to look at fit and function. If you're going to be riding for short periods of time—more performance-type riding—and want to be able to rinse off and keep your cinch clean, a

*A cinch and the latigo that fastens it can be made from natural or synthetic materials.*

KATE BRADLEY

synthetic cinch works better. If you're going to be riding for long periods of time, something more breathable, like mohair, is going to work better for you. You also need to listen to your horses and see what's working for them."

**Loesch:** "I think about fit, feel and function; if the horse doesn't feel good, it's not the right cinch for him. Those reinforced nylon cinches have zero give. As they get old, they become hard and narrow. You want a cinch with give and flex that can help spread the pressure. That's why I like a roper cinch because, to me, a straight string cinch gets narrow and firms up once I tighten it. With a roper, you cover more surface area, and the more area you cover with the cinch, the less you need to overtighten. You have less chance of soring the horse and less roll of the saddle."

# 6
# Saddle Pads

Horse owners in the market for saddle pads find a wealth of options in materials, design and price points, but all saddle pads are not created equal and marketing jargon can be confusing. Being aware of the pros and cons of different materials can help you make an informed decision when choosing a pad.

Cushioning and cooling are the two main purposes of an effective pad. No matter how fancy or pricey the pad, the material is what makes it effective and comfortable — or not. A good pad:

- provides a protective cushion between horse and saddle.

- helps with minor saddle-fit issues by filling slight gaps to improve contact with the horse's back and distribute pressure.

- alleviates areas of concentrated pressure.

- helps prevent the saddle from slipping or rolling.

- can help to cool the horse's back by drawing away moisture and heat.

## Saddle Fit Essential

You can put a $225 pad under your saddle, but if the saddle doesn't fit the horse, you end up with — at best — a temporary fix. Ultimately, proper saddle fit is the most important factor; choice of pad should be secondary.

"The main purpose of the pad is to complement the fit of the saddle. A common mistake with saddle pads is thinking that a pad can correct equipment that does not fit," says Don Doran of Animal Dynamics near Ocala, Fla., which focuses on equine-performance consultation and equine-sports therapy. An equine-sports massage therapist since 1989, Doran's work takes him around the country. He routinely sees muscular problems and diminished performance resulting from saddles that don't fit correctly or are placed improperly on the horse.

"When you walk into a tack room and someone has 10 different pads, most of the time what's going on is he is trying different pads to fix saddle problems," Doran notes. "A poor-fitting saddle is going to create a problem no matter what pad you use. There's not a pad out there that's going to make an ill-fitting saddle work. Changing to a different type of pad might give your horse some short-term relief from the ill-fitting saddle, but you have not eliminated the problem — you have just shifted the location of the pressure."

If the tree is too narrow for a horse, a pad only makes things more snug and increases pressure points. Imagine wearing thick wool socks in boots a size too small. If the tree is too wide for the horse, trying to make up the difference with extra padding can make the saddle unstable and likely to roll. To keep everything in place, you have to cinch down too tightly, which makes the horse uncomfortable and can sore him.

As covered in Chapter 4, when a saddle fits properly, there is maximum bar contact with the horse's

*A 100-percent pure wool Navajo remains an industry classic, no matter if it's used alone or tops the latest the most innovative high-tech material.*

DARRELL DODDS

*A saddle pad or blanket should complement the fit of the saddle, and together they should allow a horse to perform at his best.*
JENNIFER DENISON

horse's back, not concentrated contact on a few pressure points. A pad should be used to enhance saddle fit so the horse can perform to his full capabilities.

"I don't want to 'shim' the saddle; I want to 'shim' the horse," Doran explains. "Let's say the saddle is sinking because of muscle atrophy in the shoulders, and you try to build up this area with a pad or inserts. This just shifts the weight to the back of the bars. We should use the pad to lift the saddle off the horse's back and keep the seat level. If the seat isn't level, it throws off the balance of the saddle, and that throws off the rider's balance. We've found that if you use a properly constructed [correct design, high density and adequate thickness] wool felt pad and use only that pad on one horse, the pad begins to custom-contour to that horse and the underside of that horse's saddle."

In the world of saddle pads, "pressure" is considered a "four-letter word," but as Doran points out, "There's no pad in the world that doesn't have some pressure when you add a saddle and rider. The key is that you have the proper fit with the saddle so you don't have extreme pressure in any one spot."

The reason he prefers wool felt: When the pad is fresh and not worn, it doesn't compress and, therefore, spreads the pressure across a larger area, rather than concentrating pressure as some materials can do.

## Pad Shape and Design

Although saddle pads come in a number of materials, there are several standard designs and shapes, allowing the rider to choose one best-suited to a particular horse's conformation.

**Straight pads** with no additional shaping, padding or built-up areas, and in a basic rectangular shape:

- are good for wide, round-backed, mutton-withered horses, as well as those with average withers.

- require a break-in period to fit the horse's back.

- slip more than contoured pads.

*The basic rectangular pad has no additional padding or contouring, so a break-in period generally helps it shape to fit a horse's back.*
DARRELL DODDS

**Contoured pads,** made to fit and follow the natural shape of the horse's back:

- don't tend to put pressure on the withers.

- are seamless at the top in higher-end models for best fit.

*Because a contoured pad is designed to follow the shape of a horse's back, this type of pad requires no breaking-in period.*
DARRELL DODDS

- work well on a wide range of horses of all sizes.

- help keep a saddle in place and help prevent saddle slippage.

- are designed to improve overall saddle fit and help to hold the saddle in correct position.

- don't require breaking in, as with straight pads.

- can work well for horses with more prominent withers.

**Cutout** pads, meant to relieve pressure on the withers and/or spine in the areas cut out of the pad:

- can be helpful for especially high-withered horses.

- are round or rectangular in shape.

*The cutout portion of a pad can help relieve pressure on a specific area, such as the withers, and/or, in some cases, allow the rider to have close leg contact.*
DARRELL DODDS

- also can be cut out in the rider's leg area to offer close contact.

**Round pads,** designed to be used with rounded saddle skirts, such as those on barrel-racing saddles:

- are smaller and weigh less than traditional rectangular pads.

- can be useful on short-backed horses when rectangular pads might be too long to fit the horse.

- typically are available in the same materials as other pads.

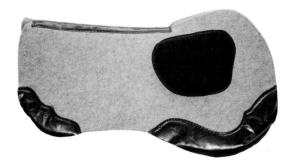

*This design—with or without the adjustable padding—is a favorite among barrel racers as the pad shape complements round saddle skirts.*
DARRELL DODDS

**Built-up pads** that have additional padding or cushioning in different areas to help with specific fit and comfort issues:

- help relieve pressure in specific areas, depending on where padding is increased.

*Pads slipped into individual pockets can shim specific areas with additional cushioning to help accommodate specific fit problems and increase comfort.*
DARRELL DODDS

- help distribute pressure more evenly across the back.

- can help with older horses lacking definition or muscle tone behind the shoulders.

- also can help raise the saddles on horses having prominent withers.

- can help saddles fit sway-backed horses when build-up is in the center of pad.

## Pad Materials

The type and duration of riding you do can influence pad choice. If you pack into the backcountry or ride across thousands of acres to push cattle into better grazing, you're horseback for long hours at a time. In those situations, the last thing you want is a saddle pad made of material that holds heat and moisture. Instead, you want a pad that keeps the horse's back as cool and comfortable as possible by wicking away moisture. If you ride for only a short period, say less than an hour, you probably can get away with using a material that doesn't wick, but that's not the ideal.

Below are the pros and cons of the various materials used in making saddle pads.

**Wool felt** has been the traditional saddle pad choice of many horsemen for years, and computerized pressure-testing has shown this material to be superior in several respects. Made of compressed wool and typically available in thicknesses from ½ inch to 1 inch, wool felt pads earn high scores for cooling and for wicking away moisture. The more dense the wool, the better it can disperse pressure from the weight of saddle and rider.

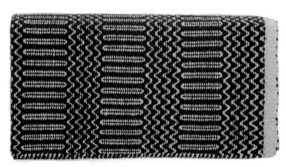

*The double-weave synthetic blend, available in many color schemes and relatively inexpensive, remains a popular choice for many.*
DARRELL DODDS

*A felt pad might be made of natural wool or synthetic fiber, and can be plain or "needled" with tiny holes made during construction.*
DARRELL DODDS

Needled felt can be identified by the tiny holes made by needles during construction, but pressed industrial felt lacks these needle marks. Both types of felt are created through a process that combines heat, steam and pressure to lock the wool fibers together. Wool felt is graded and numbered. Without getting too scientific, the commercial felt industry recognizes more than a dozen grade specifications based on compression ratings and tensile strength. A wool pad made of F10 or F11 felt is considered superior.

Bear in mind that a wool felt pad is a disposable item and takes a beating doing its job and protecting your horse's back. In time, the pad compresses and no longer provides effective protection. A wool felt pad is intended to be replaced when it wears out; the frequency of replacement depends on how much you ride. Wool felt:

- is firm, but pliable.

- naturally is flame-resistant.

- molds naturally to the horse's back, just as the top of the pad conforms to the saddle's underside.

- offers good shock-absorption.

- doesn't collapse or "bottom out."

- disperses pressure and helps prevent pressure points.

- wicks away moisture from the horse, absorbing as much as three times its weight in water.

- is breathable.

- dissipates heat and doesn't hold it against the horse.

- can help with saddle fit.

**Synthetic felt** pads are made from synthetic fibers, such as polyester and polypropylene; they also might be blends of wool and synthetic. These pads, usually made of "needled" synthetic felt, offer many of the same benefits of wool felt, but typically cost less. Synthetic felt:

- is pliable and molds easily to the horse's back.

- offers good shock-absorption and helps prevent pressure points.

- can help with saddle fit.

- is less expensive than 100-percent wool felt.

- isn't as breathable as natural wool felt.

- is hotter than wool felt typically is.

**Fleece**, widely used for saddle pads, is available in both natural wool fleece and, more commonly, synthetics, with wool fleece being the highest quality and most expensive, and synthetic fleece more economically priced. Fleece pads:

- are soft and provide good cushioning.

- wick moisture from horses when fleece is made of wool.

*This pad has it all—a woven wool blanket top, wool felt center and Merino wool fleece lining, plus a gel-pad insert.*

DARRELL DODDS

- conform to horses' backs best when fleece is made of wool.

- are slightly more durable and longer-lasting when made of synthetic fleece.

- compact down with time.

- are warmer when made of synthetic materials.

- attract burrs, stickers, and dirt.

- become harder to clean with age.

**Neoprene** was invented in 1930 by scientists at DuPont Laboratories and first marketed under the name "duprene." A type of synthetic rubber, neoprene, also known as polychloroprene, first became popular in the equine world in the 1990s. Neoprene sometimes is referred to as a closed-cell foam because it returns to its original shape after compression, but does have some qualities different from foam. Neoprene traditionally has been made using a petroleum-based technique, but recently a more environmentally friendly, limestone-based process has become available. As saddle pad material, neoprene:

- requires little maintenance.

- is easy to clean and dries quickly, making it convenient to use on multiple horses.

- maintains flexibility in a wide range of temperatures.

- is very durable with a long lifespan.

- grips the horse and provides "tackiness" to prevent saddle slippage.

- offers a cushioning effect, but can't disperse pressure like a wool felt pad.

- is waterproof, so doesn't absorb sweat or moisture.

- comes in perforated and waffle-bottom styles intended to increase air circulation, but hair, sweat and combined weight of saddle and rider can negate that benefit.

## MAKE IT WORK FOR YOU

### Extend Pad Life with Proper Care

"It's hard to give a timeline on how long a pad can last because it depends on how much you use it and how well you care for it. If you let dirt and moisture build up on a pad, that's going to limit the lifespan," says Erin Goss of Professional's Choice.

"You don't want to wash a Western pad in a washing machine. People used to recommend taking pads to a car wash; a regular garden hose with a pressure nozzle is fine, but not a pressure washer," notes Goss.

"With an all-natural fiber pad, we recommend hand-washing or hosing it with a pressure nozzle. You can use a small amount of a mild soap or horse shampoo, if needed. Always use cold water and rinse until the pad is completely clean; then let the pad air-dry. When drying, place it on a fence bottom-side up, so the underneath can air out. This is especially important if it's wool or felt."

To get the longest life out of a pad, read the care tag when you buy it and follow recommendations. If you no longer have the tag, call the company's customer service line to answer any care questions you might have.

*No matter the preferred type of pad or blanket, routine cleaning helps ensure that it lasts for as many saddlings as possible.* KATE BRADLEY

- absorbs and holds heat.

- is not breathable.

- has been known to create frictional heat, which can sore a horse.

**Closed-cell** and **open-cell foam** are made of polyurethane, and both are used as saddle pad material. The foam is poured into a mold to create the desired shape and then typically is encased in another material. Both types of foam are essentially plastics with gas-filled cells, or bubbles.

With open-cell foam, the cell walls are interconnected, making the product relatively soft and porous with a grainy or sponge-like appearance. Submerged in a bucket of water, open-cell foam fills with water. On the other hand, the cells in closed-cell foam aren't interconnected, making the product more dense with a fine grain and smoother appearance. Closed-cell foam dunked in a bucket of water doesn't absorb any water.

Here are examples of both types of foam. Imagine you're spending a week moving cattle down to lower pasture and plan to be sleeping out along the way. Before settling into your bedroll each night, you might put a piece of canvas or a camping mat on the ground to keep moisture from getting through to your bedroll. That camping mat that helps keep your bedding dry is made of closed-cell foam. You might choose to top that mat with a thin foam rubber mattress made of open-cell foam. If a rainstorm pops up, however, the foam rubber mattress can become soggy, but the camping mat sheds the water. Your bedroll, of course, is another matter.

**Closed-cell foam,** which is more dense and finer-grained than the open-cell material:

- is firm, durable and long-lasting.

- provides good shock-absorption and has a cushioning effect.

- helps support and evenly distribute weight.

- molds to a horse's back and improves contact.

- helps prevent the saddle from slipping.

- is easy to clean and dries quickly.

- helps to prevent spread of skin problems when a pad is used on multiple horses.

- is not breathable.

- cannot wick moisture as a wool pad does.

- absorbs and holds heat, and has been known to create frictional heat, which can sore a horse.

**Open-cell foam** is spongy and absorbs liquids, and also:

- is flexible and lightweight.

- doesn't attract dirt.

- is more breathable than the dense closed-cell foam.

- doesn't slip.

- has a long lifespan.

- provides good shock-absorption.

- helps disperse pressure.

- returns to its original shape after use.

- helps support and evenly distribute weight.

- molds to a horse's back.

- doesn't compress, so doesn't bottom out as some foam products do.

- helps disperse heat.

- cannot wick moisture away from the horse as a wool pad does.

**Gel-insert** pads can be made of a variety of materials. Plastic or vinyl pockets, or inserts, within the pad layers are filled with a gel substance similar in consistency to gelatin. The inserts typically are placed in the pad to improve contact between the saddletree bars and the horse's back. Gel insert pads:

- are intended to improve shock-absorption.

- are designed to improve comfort and fit.

- offer a cushioning effect, but can't disperse pressure as do wool felt pads.

- are meant to conform to horses' backs.

- add weight to pads.

- are not breathable.

- can compress with time.

- absorb and hold heat.

- cannot wick moisture away from the horse as do wool felt pads.

- tend to bottom out after more than a short ride.

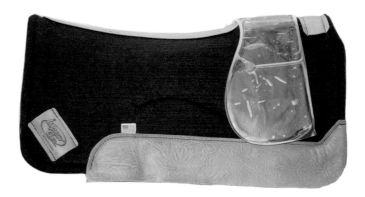

*Gel inserts can be used in a pad to improve contact between the tree bars and the horse's back, and increase comfort.*

DARRELL DODDS

*Equine conformation, the type of riding, the amount of time spent horseback, as well as cost, factor into saddle-pad selection.*
DARRELL DODDS

pad. Some pads are definitely made for high-performance situations, and help absorb shock, dissipate energy, and evenly distribute weight from saddle and rider throughout the core, which bounces back rather than compacts down with use. As the horse is working and his temperature rises, this type pad can actually help the horse retain energy because the pad disperses heat. A slightly thinner core allows for close contact, while one with a thicker core is perfect for a high-impact discipline like team roping, tie-down roping and cutting, as well as for all-day trail riding. When it comes to looks, it's all personal preference. Someone who is showing might want dramatic patterns and colors, while someone running barrels might want lime and purple. We've sold tie-dyed pads to 'tween' riders, but not usually to middle-aged team ropers."

**Doran**: "Whatever type of riding you do and however long you ride, you always want to have a quality saddle and good quality pad on your horse. We've consistently seen that wool felt is the best choice. For most horses, a 1-inch thick wool felt pad is a good choice under a Western saddle. However, if you're covering the pad with a blanket, for example, when showing a horse, then you want a thinner pad underneath the show blanket. If you are competing with your horse, you might need to distinguish between the saddle and pad you need for the daily basic conditioning exercises versus the specialized equipment you need and use for actual competition in your specific equestrian sport."

## Can I just use a blanket, or does my horse need an actual pad?

**Goss:** "A blanket on its own has no real shock-absorption, but a lot of people like the tradition of using a Navajo wool blanket. If they're showing, they can change blankets to match their show outfits. The best bet can be to buy a good base pad, then top it with a blanket or purchase an all-in-one pad with a 100-percent wool Navajo blanket top."

**Doran:** "Some people just use a Navajo blanket and if that's all the horse needs, it's fine, but the wool ones are expensive, so companies make them out of synthetic materials. Those synthetic 'Navajo' blankets aren't going to have the same benefits as real wool ones."

## How much does "you get what you pay for" come into play when buying a pad?

**Goss:** "I think it's huge. Higher-end pads last longer, and those quality materials also impact how the horse feels. We have bought other pads, cut them open to see what was inside and it varied greatly according to price, so price is reflective of the pad quality. There are different price points."

**Doran:** "It comes into play a lot. Good quality wool is expensive. The cheaper pads are generally made of synthetic materials. A lot of those synthetics collapse or bottom out if you press or pinch the pad. But also remember that, whether you are buying a saddle or a pad, sometimes you don't get what you pay for. The price of an item can be used as a general gauge of quality, but in no way does it guarantee good quality, good design and proper fit. I have seen far too many expensive, poorly fitting pieces of equipment. Consumers need to look beyond price when making their selections of saddles and pads. Remember what the pad is there for: to act as a buffer and offer additional cushion between the saddle and the horse's back. Any time you put more than two pounds of pressure per square inch, it shuts down capillary blood flow to that muscle."

(Author's note: One study that tested a number of different types of Western saddle pads, each for 200 hours, found that the more expensive pads tended to hold up better.)

# GOTCHA!

## Is Your Saddle Pad Where it Should Be?

"The mistake a lot of people make with pads is that they put the excess sticking out behind the saddle," says Texas horseman and clinician Craig Cameron. "I want just the opposite. If a pad is going to move any, it's going to slip back, so it's going to look better—and ride better—if I put the excess material toward the front."

For an average-sized horse, he likes a 32-by-36-inch pad, although he notes that some riders prefer smaller pads.

When tacking up, Cameron says it's best to put the pad too far forward, and then slide it back into the right position. This makes the hair lay flat on the horse's back, which is important for comfort.

Concerned about how warm your horse's back gets when the weather is especially hot and steamy? Follow Cameron's tip. "On a really hot day, I wet my horse's back before putting on the pad. The horse is going to sweat anyway, and I think he's going to stay cooler if I wet down the back first, and then put that natural fiber pad on his back."

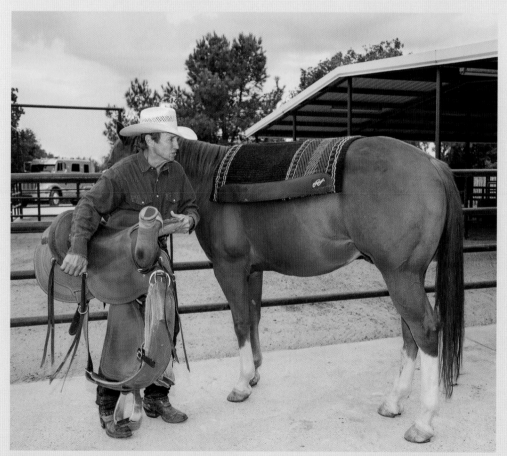

*When a pad is first placed slightly forward on the horse, the pad can slide back into the correct position, which allows the horse's hair to lay flat and smooth.*

DARRELL DODDS

# 7
# Headstalls

When the Plains Indians made bridles, more often than not, there were no steel bits attached. The riders typically looped pieces of thin rawhide or braided buffalo hair around their horses' lower jaws in place of bits. These early American horsemen crafted headstalls using a variety of materials, including horse and buffalo hair and rawhide, as well as tanned leather. Ironically, today's riders still rely on horsehair and rawhide to adorn their headstalls. As for buffalo hair? Not so much.

A headstall is the foundation of any bridle and comes in a variety of styles, ranging widely in materials, craftsmanship, embellishments and, of course, price points.

"People do get bridles and headstalls mixed up," notes Roger Allgeier of Brighton Feed & Saddlery in Brighton, Colorado. "The headstall is what you start with, and after you put everything [headstall, bit and reins] together, then it becomes a bridle."

Roger and Verna Allgeier left a ranch in southern Arizona and headed to Colorado in 1973 to purchase Brighton Feed & Farm Supply, as it was originally known. Clyde Peterson had started the company in 1943, building a respected business that focused on livestock needs of all kinds, and ran the company, located just outside Denver, until 1971. Under the Allgeiers' ownership, the outfit has evolved from a shop with one saddle in stock to include a fine tack and saddle inventory with at least 350 saddles in stock year-round.

Choice of headstall often depends on what's popular at the moment, and also can vary according to discipline and specific regions of the country.

"In the late '70s and '80s, the one-ear headstalls were more prevalent than headstalls with browbands," says Allgeier. "I think Texas horsemanship was a big influence because the one-ears were common in Texas. There was also a southern California influence, but their one-ears were finer, and a lot of them had rolled leather and silver ferrules, which is a silver tube slipped over the rolled leather. That is really a take-off of vaquero horsemanship; they like equipment that is both fine in appearance and fine in quality.

"That vaquero influence kind of collided with the Texas influence with one-ears, and our shop is located in the crossroads of those cultures," he adds. "To the west and northwest [buckaroo country], Wades and slick-forks are common. North to northeast, we see full association 14-inch swells and 5-inch cantles. Further east, there are more roping saddles, and to the south and southwest, a brush country-type saddle that has a 3½- to 4-inch straight-up cantle, a hard seat and modified or roper swells, and tapaderos. I really like this middle area because our customers want a variety of equipment."

Just as with clothing fashions, headstall styles come and go. For example, teardrop-shaped cheekpieces came back in vogue around 2000, and large, flared browbands, once favored by buckaroos, are now seen beyond the Great Basin area. The popularity of cowboy mounted shooting also has revived interest in some of the tack and equipment regularly used from the late 1880s to 1930s.

"Years ago, a lot of front-range cowboys liked the wide, scalloped headstalls with 'silver' spots," recalls Allgeier. "When I started cowboying in the 1960s, we thought that was old-fashioned. We called them 'sheepherder' headstalls because the sheepherders got the leftovers. These headstalls came back in

*The double-ear design, rawhide braiding and hair tassels make this an eye-catching piece of headgear.*

vogue around 2005, but probably in some areas of the country, like Montana, they never went out of style."

## Browband Headstall

Browband-style headstalls, which were popular back in the country's early cowboy era, made a comeback starting in the late 1980s and remain popular.

"Part of the reason for this was the influence of good natural horsemen like Buck Brannaman, the Dorrance brothers and others, who like to start horses in a snaffle and ride them in that until 4 or 5 years old, and then put them in a bridle," Allgeier points out.

The vast majority of headstalls with browbands also have throatlatches, making this style more stable and secure on the horse's head than a one-ear.

"If you ride in a snaffle, a browband headstall is recommended because it's a little more stable on the horse's head when you're

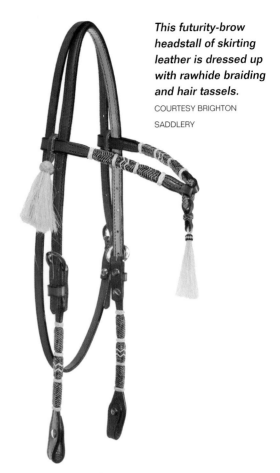

*This futurity-brow headstall of skirting leather is dressed up with rawhide braiding and hair tassels.*

COURTESY BRIGHTON SADDLERY

using direct-rein pressure," says Allgeier. "You don't want the headstall rotating so the snaffle ring slips into the horse's mouth, and we suggest using a curb strap, even with a snaffle bit, just for this reason. When a rider is fairly green, a browband headstall is best, just because it's more secure."

Another plus of the browband-style headstall is ease of repair.

"If the horse steps on a rein, one of the first things to break—besides the rein itself—is the crown piece," says Allgeier. "When the browband is removable, this makes repair and replacement easier."

- Most browbands, no matter their designs, aren't fixed. Instead, they move and slide on the crown piece, so they are easy to adjust, and it's easy to take the headstall apart for cleaning.

- Some trail riders prefer the browband headstalls that are combination halter and headstall, making it easy to tie horses on the trail.

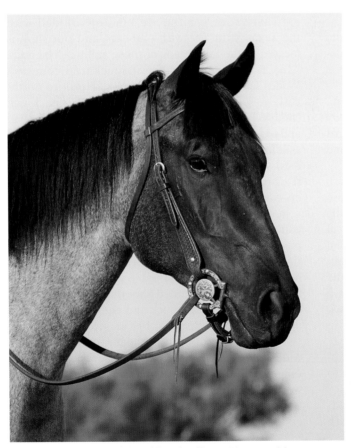

*A browband headstall provides a stable, secure hanger for a snaffle bit.*

ROSS HECOX

- The "futurity brow," a very popular style, features two leather pieces knotted together in the center of the horse's forehead.

- Large, flared buckaroo browbands are back in style, and today's versions often can be fancier than the early originals.

"What a lot of people call a futurity brow was originally a kind of homemade ranch-style browband made with saddle strings or 'whang' leather with blood knots around the crown and throatlatch, then laced or knotted at the center. It was designed by necessity, not because it would look 'cute' at the [All American Quarter Horse] Congress," says Allgeier.

"It's always been a neat style, and then it became fashionable in the heyday of the pleasure-horse classes in the mid-1980s. It was named a futurity brow because a lot of them were seen at the Quarter Horse world show in Oklahoma City and at other big breed shows. The Arabs and Morgans also picked up on it. This style hasn't gone out of vogue and has kind of leaked over into the working headstall. It really accentuates a pretty head."

## One-Ear Headstall

Headstalls with a leather piece around just one ear are commonly used with a variety of bits. One-ear headstalls typically don't have throatlatches although you occasionally find some that do.

Many working cowboys and trainers like one-ears because they are quick and easy to slip on and off, which saves time when you ride a dozen horses or more a day. The fact that a one-ear is easy for a person to put on and off also means it's fairly simple for a horse to inadvertently slip off the headstall. A sweaty horse, dropping his head to rub an itchy spot on his leg, easily can slide a one-ear headstall right off his head when the bridle doesn't have a throatlatch.

There are several different types of one-ear headstalls, such as the:

- **slip-ear,** in which the whole earpiece and crown piece are cut from one piece of leather, but the ear section doesn't move at all.

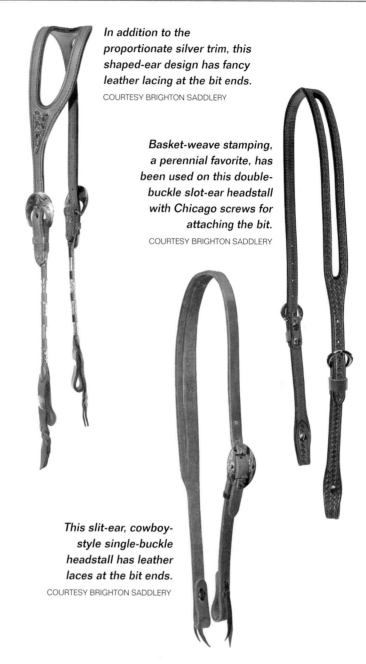

*In addition to the proportionate silver trim, this shaped-ear design has fancy leather lacing at the bit ends.*
COURTESY BRIGHTON SADDLERY

*Basket-weave stamping, a perennial favorite, has been used on this double-buckle slot-ear headstall with Chicago screws for attaching the bit.*
COURTESY BRIGHTON SADDLERY

*This slit-ear, cowboy-style single-buckle headstall has leather laces at the bit ends.*
COURTESY BRIGHTON SADDLERY

- **shaped-ear,** which features a shaped leather piece that fits around the ear. This piece might be part of the crown piece or might be a separate piece that slides onto the crown piece.

- **slot-ear,** which is similar to a shaped ear, except that the slot is long and narrow and is made in one piece with the crown of the headstall.

- **slit-ear,** where the ear goes through a single slice in the crown piece, usually ¾- to 1-inch wide.

A good example of a regional one-ear style is that found in the Texas Panhandle. Some headstalls there have 1-inch-wide crown pieces with two holes strategically punched, one above the horse's ear and the second below that. The cowboys then run a saddle string through the holes and around the horse's ear.

### Double-Ear Headstall

This headstall is found in the same styles as those described in the one-ear section above—but with pieces to accommodate both of the horse's ears.

"The double-ear headstall is more of a show trend than a working style," explains Allgeier. "The fancy silver two-ears are popular in the show ring; they're probably seen more in Western pleasure classes and some reined cow-horse classes in California. If a working cowboy is using a double-ear, it's probably a Southern California trend."

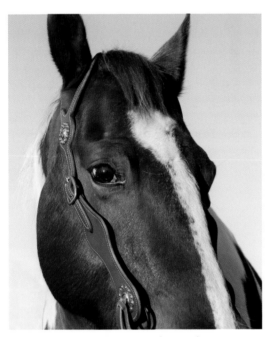

*Although only one earpiece shows, this buckaroo-style headstall is actually a two-ear design.*

COURTESY BRIGHTON SADDLERY

### Leather Construction

Leather, of whatever type, is sold by weight. Headstalls are typically made from 7- to 9-ounce leather, meaning one square foot weighs 7 to 9 ounces. To give you comparisons, most saddles are made of 13- to 15-ounce leathers, while chaps are often made of 4- to 6-ounce leathers.

The durability of a headstall—or any piece of leather tack for that matter—depends on the quality of the leather. Although the craftsmanship might be exceptional, an item doesn't hold up if the material isn't of good quality.

A bit of background about the tanning process sheds light on different types of leather and how they are used to make headstalls. Hides are tanned in one large piece. If a hide is thick enough, it actually provides three "splits," or layers of leather. The three splits serve different purposes:

- The top layer, which is the hair side, eventually becomes smooth during the tanning process. Known as "top grain," this split is the most expensive, strongest of the layers.

- A middle split is suede leather.

- The third, or bottom, layer, if a hide is thick enough to yield three splits, is low-quality suede. As Allgeier says, "This explains why you can buy a $29 suede jacket or a $299 suede jacket."

With the popularity of saddles made with rough-out leather, some companies offer matching headstalls. "These are mostly top-grain leather that is reversed because true suede would be too stretchy for most headstalls," notes Allgeier.

How the hide is tanned also affects the resulting leather and how it is used.

**Harness leather,** which doesn't have a lot of stretch, or give, but is known for its durability:

- typically is thicker, heavier and stronger than skirting leather and latigo.

- might come from the same cowhide, but has had a different solution used during the tanning process than is used to tan skirting leather and latigo.

- is known as "hot stuffed harness" when harness leather has had hot wax pressed into it after tanning to add durability.

- usually is made into heavy, single-ply headstalls, but not always. "You can split it down and then double and stitch it," says Allgeier. "You can also add a latigo backing just to pretty it up and add a little more supple feel."

**Skirting leather,** which is vegetable-tanned and has a shinier finish than harness leather:

- is quite strong, but not as strong as harness leather.

- doesn't have a lot of stretch.

- often is doubled and stitched when made into headstalls, meaning the skirting leather is backed with another piece of skirting or another type of leather or material.

**Latigo leather** is typically chrome-tanned or alum-tanned, and:

- usually is burgundy red in color and can "bleed" onto a light-colored horse.

- is very soft and stretchier than harness or skirting leather.

- isn't as strong or durable as the other two types of leather.

- usually is less expensive than harness or skirting leather.

- has a broken-in, "buttery" feel from the start, but doesn't hold up as well as harness or skirting leather.

**Braided rawhide,** Allgeier explains, has a long history. "Traditionally, the hides from younger animals, such as calves or yearlings, would be used for reins, romals, headstalls and maybe even a bosal, depending on the size of the bosal. Hides from mature cows were typically used for reatas and hobbles. Some imported rawhide may actually be made from split hides."

Braided rawhide is different from harness and latigo leather in several respects. Rawhide:

- is "raw," meaning it's made from a dehaired hide than hasn't been tanned.

*Although both headstall and tie-down noseband are made of leather, such factors as the age of the hides and the tanning process, or lack of one, contribute to obvious differences in the leathers' appearance.*

KATE BRADLEY

After the hair is removed, the hide is scraped down on the flesh side. Old-timers used to make rawhide by leaving the hide in a creek until the hair slid off.

- is beautiful but labor intensive to make into headstalls because of the time required to prepare the strings for braiding. "Some of the best braiding comes out of Mexico and Argentina," notes Allgeier.

- can be among the most expensive headstalls because of the time involved in leather preparation and braid construction.

- probably is most popular for headstall use in Southwestern states.

*No matter the preference—one-ear, double-ear, browband, plain or fancy—or the price point, headstall choices abound.*

DARRELL DODDS

- should not be oiled and must be cared for using solutions specifically made for rawhide. Old-time cowboys often used hard, white kidney fat to keep their rawhide equipment, including reatas, for example, supple.

**Bargain-priced leather** usually can be identified by the price tag, as it's often half the price of quality-tanned and well-made tack. Such bargain leather:

- might be imported water buffalo hide, not cowhide.

- typically is not as durable as higher-quality leather.

- can be dry and more brittle, even more so when new.

## Synthetic Headstalls

Many headstalls are made of leather, but there also are synthetic options appealing to many for various reasons.

"A lot of racehorse trainers like nylon headstalls because of the colors, the cost, and the fact that they're easy to keep clean," says Allgeier. "They often are bought for commercial use, such as for rental dude strings, and by entry-level riders."

Basically, two synthetic materials are used for headstalls—BioThane®, sometimes called artificial leather, and nylon.

**BioThane®** closely resembles leather in appearance, but:

- has been made of polyester webbing with a PVC-type coating.

- comes in different colors, in addition to leather-like black and brown.

- is waterproof, durable and pliable.

- commonly is used to make draft-horse pulling harness because of its great strength.

- wipes clean, is easily washed with soap and water, and can be disinfected.

- doesn't absorb moisture or bacteria.

- does not require the routine care of leather.

- is less expensive than leather.

- does not get hard or brittle in cold weather.

- weighs about 20 percent less than leather.

- is a popular choice among racehorse trainers, endurance and trail riders, and draft-horse owners.

**Nylon** is unlike leather in appearance and:

- is extremely strong and durable.

- requires no routine care or maintenance as with leather.

- easily wipes or washes clean.

- comes in many colors, but can fade in time.

- can fray at the ends and where holes are punched, but fraying easily can be repaired with a propane torch or electric soldering iron.

## Getting Fancy

There are almost endless ways to pretty up a headstall, from the leather itself and the way it is crafted to the addition of embellishments.

"For dressing up a headstall, silver is the number one choice, but the imagination can run wild, especially with barrel racers and the guys roping at the National Finals Rodeo," says Allgeier.

**Silver.** When someone wants a fancy headstall, he or she often turns to silver in the way of conchas, trim, buckles, and narrow, round decorative rings known as ferrules. At Hansen Silver in Oakdale, Calif., owner and silversmith Tim Hansen has been working magic with silver since 1997. As a wholesale manufacturer, he creates silver trim of all kinds, from buckles to saddle corner plates, or as he puts it, "pretty much everything silver that goes on a headstall, saddle and spur strap."

Any "silver" pieces on a headstall are shiny, but that doesn't mean they're actually made of silver. Pricing also can be confusing, according to Hansen, who provided clarification:

- German silver is actually an old name for nickel, or monel, a metal alloy, and is the least expensive silver-type option. German silver doesn't tarnish, but its finish is duller than silver plate or real sterling.

- Stainless steel has plenty of shine, but no actual silver content.

- Silver plate is not technically sterling plate, but rather rhodium. It can be plated over nickel, brass, or other inexpensive metals to keep down costs. In time the plating eventually peels or wears away.

*Silver decor for headgear can be purchased at price points that reflect varying quality, but hand-engraved sterling work always is considered top of the line.*

COURTESY HANSEN SILVER

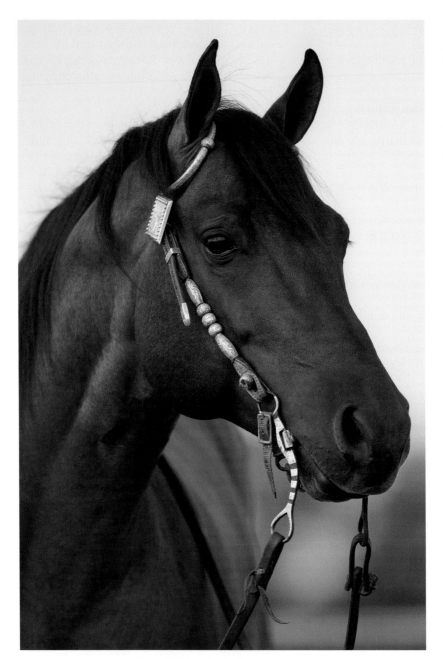

*No matter how good-looking the horse, a headstall with silver trim and decorative ferrules is sure to catch the light and draw even more attention.*
ROSS HECOX

- Sterling overlay is solid sterling silver laid over a nickel back, a popular choice because the item has the strength of nickel, but the quality of real sterling on the top.

- Sterling silver is the highest quality and most expensive, but the disadvantages of sterling silver are that it is soft and bends easily. It also tarnishes, so must be polished.

Many people have a tough time identifying the various materials just by looking. If you can look at the back of the concha or buckle, typically it is stamped by the maker or manufacturer to let you know the content. Price is also a strong indicator of the type of silver used.

"If a headstall has a lot of silver and is only $150, it's obviously not sterling or sterling overlay," says Hansen. "A good sterling overlay bridle will cost $300 to $500, depending on how much metal is on it."

If a shaped-ear headstall has silver trim around the earpiece, you can't look underneath to see what metal has been used, but Hansen says the same type of silver trim typically is used on the entire headstall or saddle.

# EXPERT TIP

## Keep it Basic

At the Pate Ranch in Ryegate, Mont., clinicians and ranchers Curt and Tammy Pate spend plenty of time horseback.

"We raise cattle and our daughter, Mesa, is in the bucking-bull business, so typically we use our horses to work cattle," says Tammy, who grew up rodeoing and roping. "I also trail ride and ranch rope. Here at the ranch, we do rotational grazing, so we're moving cattle. Our whole focus is on keeping the horses calm to keep the cattle calm so they put on weight."

Tammy usually rides with a snaffle bit and browband headstall.

"If I were to use a one-ear headstall, it wouldn't stay as stable as the browband headstall if the horse doesn't follow the feel of the bit. The browband allows there to be a little 'play.' I like a medium-weight stitched, leather headstall, but I don't like Chicago screws to fasten either my bit or my reins because the screws can come undone. If you do use them, check them regularly! I prefer leather ties or leather buttons because they are more reliable.

"On my snaffle bit, I like a rawhide or leather chin strap because I don't like the bounce or sound of a chain strap," she adds. "The chin strap does nothing as far as leverage on a snaffle, but it does keep the bit from sliding through the horse's mouth."

Whenever she's done for the day, Tammy makes sure to buckle the throatlatch on her browband headstall before hanging it up. It takes only a couple seconds to fasten the buckle, and that can prevent the decorative conchas below the browband from sliding off and getting lost.

So, if you check the underside of the buckles and they're stamped "silver plate," the earpiece is likely the same.

Many riders want the quality appearance of sterling but without the maintenance required to keep it looking good.

"When people say, 'I want something that doesn't tarnish,' then they don't want sterling. If someone advertises his silver doesn't tarnish, then it's not sterling," says Hansen. "If you have sterling overlay conchas, 20 years from now, you can polish them up, and they still look new."

If a concha or other piece of silver trim is quite inexpensive, it's likely cast "pot" metal, and there's no telling exactly what it's made of. A good indicator that a concha is cast—meaning it's made by pouring liquid metal into a mold—is to flip over the concha and look at the back.

"If the post on the back of the concha is soldered on, then it's made of higher quality," Hansen notes. "The less expensive ones are cast as one piece."

Although Hansen's business is silver, not leather, when he and wife Marie head to the Denver trade show each January, they always take along completed headstalls to display in their booth, along with individual silver pieces.

"We make up sample headstalls because those really help people to see it all put together, so they can see what the finished product looks like," he says. "It's important to use good quality leather, and you don't want cheap embellishments on a custom headstall or saddle. You want to put quality material on quality material."

**Braiding and lacing.** It's not unusual for a headstall to be embellished with rawhide braiding or lacing. Either can add a distinctive look without making the finished product prohibitively expensive.

"This is very common in buckaroo country," says Allgeier. "Some braiding will add flash, but won't be as expensive as a headstall made totally of braided rawhide."

**Bling.** The trend of headstalls decorated with crystals, or bling, as it's commonly known, hit around 2005. The embellishments run the gamut from just a few crystals for a bit of sparkle to serious flash. Some headstalls even boast high-end Swarovski crystals.

"Bling is really hot with certain riders," says Allgeier, who sells blinged-out headstalls to barrel racers, 4-Hers and women riders of all ages. "You can get conchas with crystals, but often the crystals are attached to the headstall with either glue or prongs.

*Nothing staid or stuffy about horse gear with bling; it's now available in a wide variety of choices.*

DARRELL DODDS

The problem is that they can pop loose if the horse rubs the headstall on something, but most hobby shops sell crystals and glue, so you can replace them pretty easily."

**Inlaid leather.** Another trend in some riding disciplines, including barrel racing, is the inlaid headstall, also known as "inlay."

The craftsman building the headstall uses a wider piece of leather for the foundation and cuts the interior portion down just enough to inlay a different piece of contrasting leather. The inlay often is made of exotic leather, such as alligator, crocodile, lizard, stingray, ostrich, snake or elephant. In some cases, the inlay is "faux exotic," which is cowhide that has been treated to look like exotic leather.

"As many years as I've been in business, I can't tell the imitation ostrich from the real thing," says Allgeier. "You can tell only after the item has been used for a while and the finish wears off."

Hair-on cowhide is also popular for inlay, especially when using colorful speckled or brindle hides.

**Overlaid leather.** Also known as "overlay," this technique allows the maker to create a headstall that appears to be made solely of expensive or exotic leather when, in fact, it is simply a layer of the fancier leather applied over top of the foundation leather.

"There are some headstalls made completely from exotic leather, but these are more expensive than overlaid," says Allgeier. "Most of the time what you see and think are exotics are actually manmade faux exotic leathers. The strap itself is generally real leather, but the top has an artificial or manmade applied exotic finish and dye process."

**Horsehair tassels (shu-flies).** No doubt about it, horsehair tassels, or shu-flies, are fun and colorful ways to liven up a headstall. Depending on size and design, shu-flies can be attached to the browband, throatlatch, sides of the headstall, and even the curb strap.

Made of real horsehair, the tassels come in a range of natural colors and often have braided button accents. Shu-flies likely are

*Silver "spots" have long been considered one of the traditional types of decor for leather horse gear.*
ROSS HECOX

crafted from tail hair since they don't have to be soft and pliable like a mecate, which typically uses mane hair.

"They're sometimes called a 'shu-fly' [or shoo-fly] when they're hanging off the bottom of a throatlatch or a cinch," Allgeier explains. "Some of these can hang down 6 to 8 inches, and they probably have some practicality for shooing away flies, but the shorter ones are just called tassels and are more for looks than function."

## Hardware and Fasteners

There are several fastening methods used to hold the headstall together and to attach the bit, including Chicago screws, string ties or laces, leather buttons and buttonholes, buckles, and snaps.

**Chicago screws,** which can be covered with a decorative concha or button:

- are easy to use and inexpensive to replace.

- can vibrate and loosen with time, but putting a drop of Loctite® or clear fingernail polish can prevent this by making the screw threads "sticky."

*In recent years, retro-style gear reminiscent of the 1920s, '30s, and '40s has experienced a resurgence in popularity.*

COURTESY BRIGHTON SADDLERY

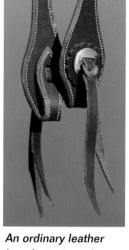

*An ordinary leather lace fastening takes on a different look when backed with leather and a shiny concha.*

DARRELL DODDS

*Here's another way leather braiding can be used to fasten horse gear.*

DARRELL DODDS

**Leather buttons and buttonholes,** which fancy up a headstall, yet serve a practical purpose, can:

- be stylish and exhibit detailed craftsmanship.

- take a little longer to fasten when changing bits or making adjustments.

*A dab of nail polish can help keep a Chicago screw from inadvertently coming loose.*

DARRELL DODDS

**String ties, or laces,** which are easy to find, typically:

- are made of latigo leather because it is soft, stretchy and easy to tie in a knot.

- are easy to use and inexpensive to replace.

- possibly are the first things to break when a horse pulls back or hangs his equipment on something, possibly saving the rest of the headstall from damage.

*Braided buttons with loop closures often are used on rawhide gear.*

DARRELL DODDS

**Buckles,** which here indicates the more serviceable stainless, rather than sterling, have proven:

- strong and durable.

- easy to use and inexpensive to replace.

**Harness snaps,** which can be used instead of other fasteners:

- are quick and easy to use.

- aren't favored by many serious riders because snap movement can distort the bit signal in the horse's mouth.

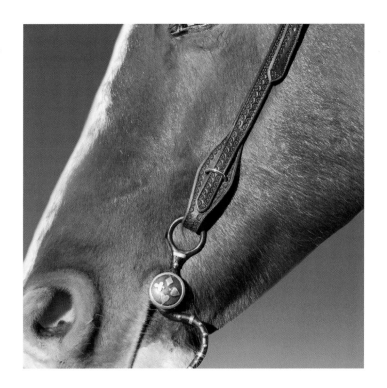

*Convenient quick-change bit ends can be found on several headstall styles.*
COURTESY BRIGHTON SADDLERY

# MAKE IT WORK FOR YOU

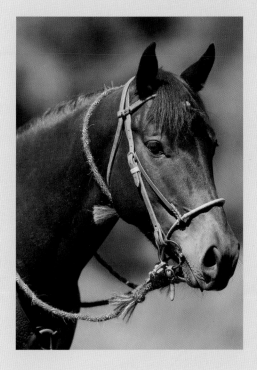

## Nosebands or Cavessons

An English-type bridle has a noseband, also referred to as a cavesson, which is specifically designed to keep the horse's mouth closed. Since Western-style headstalls don't have nosebands, some riders add separate cavessons, or dropped nosebands, to their horses' headgear.

A simple, yet effective piece of equipment, the typical Western noseband has a leather crown, usually about ⅝-inch wide, that adjusts on one or both sides. The noseband, which is often doubled and stitched leather about 1-inch wide, has a chin buckle so you can adjust it for the proper snug fit. However, Western-style rope nosebands have no buckles.

If you choose to add a noseband to your Western headstall, the noseband can be put on first, followed by the bridle. Sometimes a rider threads the noseband's crown piece through the browband loops on the headstall, making it part of the headstall. If you opt to do that, be sure to unbuckle the noseband's chin buckle before you put on and take off your bridle.

*A Western-style noseband typically is a separate piece of headgear although the cavesson, or noseband, often is built into an English-style bridle.* DARRELL DODDS

# 8
# Snaffle Bits

Browse through a tack catalog or Web site and you find bits galore. The options seem almost endless when it comes to designs, mouthpieces, rings, shanks and materials, not to mention prices. There might be more bits from which to choose today, but the bit itself is hardly new.

"Indeed, we put bits in horses' mouths that they may obey us, and we turn their whole body," writes James in what is likely the oldest book of the New Testament, written as early as A.D. 45. Yet bits were around long before James penned his letter.

Thousands of years ago, before metal was used, early horsemen fashioned bits using such materials as leather, bone, rope, horn and wood.

An exciting find in 2012 revealed the earliest known metal equestrian bit. Archaeologists from Ben Gurion University in Israel unearthed an equid burial site at Tel-Haror, and discovered the metal bit in a layer of material dated from 1750 B.C. to 1650 B.C. Found with the remains of a donkey, the bit had round plates at both ends with triangular spikes that put pressure on the animal's lips as the reins were used.

"I've seen snaffle bits in European museums that were thousands of years old, and they were sliding ring snaffles with a toggle ring in the middle. These bits measured more or less the same as ours today," notes horseman, trainer and clinician Les Vogt, who has 50 years as a trainer, and 30 years a premier bit-and spurmaker to his credit.

Vogt has won many world-championship reining and working-cow-horse titles; in addition, he and three horses he has shown and trained have been inducted into the National Reined Cow Horse Association Hall of Fame. His performance

experience, combined with the opportunity to design, fabricate and test bits, puts him in a unique position when it comes to understanding the principles of bitting. Vogt makes his home in Pismo Beach, Calif., but conducts clinics and lectures in several countries. The artisans who do the metalwork and silversmithing in Vogt's shop have a 400-year-old legacy in their craft since they trace back to Spanish bitmakers trained by Hernando Cortez.

"It's pretty amazing that these bits haven't really changed as far as basic fundamental design goes. That means a lot of thought went into it," says Vogt. "Thousands of years ago, the horse trainer was the 'rocket scientist' of the age. He was the one with that equipment, and horses were used to obtain or protect kingdoms. If one landowner or king had better horse trainers than the next, then he would surely out-battle the one with poorer trainers. Bits were even more important then than now because people lived or died by them."

## Basic Bit Function

Although bits vary greatly in shape and design, they address four parts of the horse's mouth, but not necessarily in the following order:

- the corners of the mouth

- the palate

- the tongue

- the bars, both the narrow ridge and the fatter, more cushioned outer edges

---

*Although the snaffle bit has been in existence for many years, the basic design has remained much the same.*

ROSS HECOX

*No matter a young horse's future career, a snaffle bit handled properly allows him to begin on-the-job training.*

DARRELL DODDS

The chin and/or lower jaw also are affected when riding in a leverage bit with a curb strap or chain.

Stories abound of horses whose mouths have been damaged by abusive handling of bits, resulting, for example, in severe lacerations to tongues. Yet, the tongue actually can take more abuse than any part of the horse's mouth, explains Idaho horseman, trainer and clinician Martin Black, whose ranching roots in the Great Basin region trace back five generations. Black has worked closely with top cutting, reining and racehorse trainers, and conducts horsemanship, colt-starting, cattle-working and ranch-roping clinics in Europe, South America, Australia and throughout North America. He also can be found competing in ranch-rodeo, ranch-roping, cow-horse and even camp-drafting events.

To demonstrate his observations about the horse's mouth, Black picks up a pencil.

"Take this pencil, lay it on your tongue, press it down as hard as you can, and note the amount of discomfort to your tongue," he says. "Now take the same pencil, place it on your gums below your teeth and apply that same amount of pressure. Your gums are the equivalent of the horse's bars, and you see how much more sensitive they are. Your tongue can actually take much more pressure.

"Next, take a teaspoon, which somewhat resembles a spade bit, and put it against your palate, which is the roof of your mouth. You find the palate also can take more pressure than your gums. Anything the horse eats passes over his tongue and palate, so both of these are more durable than the bars. The corners of the mouth are the most durable. The tissue on the bars is the easiest part of a mouth to damage.

"Sadly, you see a lot of swelling and bruising on the bars of the mouths in a lot of

2-year-olds that are being started," adds Black. "You can also see this in some older horses, but mostly in younger ones. In addition to being caused by riding, you also can damage a horse's mouth this way if you tie his head around while he's in a bit."

## Mouth Configuration

You and a friend might wear the same size boots, but your foot can be much narrower than your friend's. This concept also applies to horses' mouths. People often don't consider the fact that not all horses' mouths are built the same way, and this directly influences how the bit fits and functions. A bit that works beautifully with one horse might not be as effective—and can even be uncomfortable—for another horse, simply because of differences in mouth sizes and shapes. This concept applies to more than just the size of the mouthpiece.

"Some horses have high palates and some have low palates. Their tongues can also be wider, fatter or narrower," says Vogt. "Under the horse's tongue is a slot where the tongue rests, and some horses have very shallow slots. I've found horses that want to open their mouths a lot have shallow slots and/or very fat tongues. This is a reason to switch to a mouthpiece that accommodates that tongue."

For example, a horse with a low palate and fat tongue might be uncomfortable in an eggbutt snaffle with a fat, hollow mouthpiece, even though this is traditionally described as a mild bit.

Not only do horses' mouths vary, but so do riders' skills. In the wrong hands, even a plain snaffle can do serious damage. Horses known as hard-mouthed to handle aren't born that way. Hard mouths are a direct result of a rider's hard hands.

Some horses are more sensitive than others—not just physically, but emotionally and mentally—and this also can affect bit choice. As Vogt explains it, the durable "bully" who leans on the bit is much less responsive than the "Type A drama queen" who is overly sensitive and reactive.

"You might have a durable bully with a high pain tolerance. If he's not responding to the bit you're using, you might need to change to a bit that uses different pressure points to gain his respect. You can upgrade the response level of the mouthpiece by changing the pressure points that the bit affects," says Vogt.

"With the drama queen, you can get along fine as long as you know what you're doing, but if you're not careful, you get an overreaction. If you keep trying to correct this overreaction with different bits, the horse can have a 'breakdown' and you end up losing all your communication."

Horsemen talk about a bit being "warm" or having "bite," but the results can vary from horse to horse—according to how a particular bit is used.

"A warm bit for one horse may not be the same as for another," says Vogt. "If you put something mild in a horse's mouth that he doesn't acknowledge with respect and no fear, then he learns how to lean into or disregard this bit. In order to educate a horse, you need a bit that gets respect and gets the horse's attention, but doesn't create fear. Without respect, the horse doesn't communicate well. It's like the schoolteacher who demanded attention versus the teacher who let you do anything you wanted. You learned more from the one who made sure you paid attention."

## An Educational Tool

A snaffle bit is used by many horsemen for starting colts and taking the young horse through the stages of basic schooling. According to Vogt, the snaffle is a "fundamental education and fix-it tool. The varying weights of rings and lengths of mouthpieces are really popular these days to match up with your individual horse's performance needs," he notes. "This is the tool that you never quit using and rarely wear out."

Because it has no shanks, the snaffle is a nonleverage bit. The reins attach directly to the rings, and the snaffle works by applying direct pressure—not leverage—to different parts of the horse's mouth. With a snaffle, the amount of pressure applied to the reins is not "amped up" as it can be in a shanked bit. If you apply two ounces of pressure to the reins when riding in a snaffle, this translates to two ounces of pressure on the horse's mouth. That mouthpiece applies pressure to the tongue, the bars, and the corners of the mouth. The rings apply pressure to the sides of the mouth and, depending on design, to the sides of the face.

Many people think that a snaffle is always mild, simply because it has no leverage, but this is incorrect. Heavy, abrupt hands can turn even a smooth-mouth snaffle into a device that inflicts pain.

## Snaffle Mouthpieces

Mention the word "snaffle" and people tend to think of the loose ring, smooth-mouth version. Although this might be considered a classic snaffle, the truth is that scores of combinations of rings and mouthpieces can still be snaffle bits. There are a number of ring options, and mouthpieces come in a variety of designs, diameters, materials and textures.

Although all snaffles are hinged bits, they might have either two-piece or three-piece mouthpieces. This, along with the design of the mouthpiece, affects how and where a bit applies pressure:

- The straighter the mouthpiece, the more pressure it applies to the tongue.

- A curved mouthpiece puts the most pressure on the corners of the mouth.

- A three-piece snaffle rests on the tongue and offers a softer feel than a two-piece. The third and middle piece often is a spoon or roller, which gives the horse something to play with.

- In any mouthpiece design, the thinner the mouthpiece, the more potential for severity.

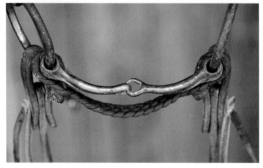

*The straight snaffle mouthpiece creates more tongue pressure than a curved one, which most affects the corners of the mouth.*

ROSS HECOX

*A textured mouthpiece, such as this one of twisted copper, typically provides increased contact and feel in a horse's mouth.*

ROSS HECOX

Mouthpiece shapes and designs vary greatly. Most are solid metal, but some riders like lightweight hollow mouthpieces. Smooth and textured mouthpieces might be twisted, ribbed or made with some texture other than a smooth finish.

"A textured bit provides more contact and feel with the horse. It doesn't need to be severe. Some people think a twisted bit allows them to ride even lighter," says bitmaker Tom Balding of Tom Balding Bits & Spurs in Sheridan, Wyo., who actually uses concrete rebar to manufacture some of his textured mouthpieces.

"I rode pretty intensely for several years, riding every day on ranches, but I didn't know a 'light' horse until I rode a nice pleasure horse down in Denver. For me it was like an epiphany and gave me a definition of light," recalls Balding, who started his business in 1984 and works with many of the equine industry's top trainers. "To one person, a light horse may be one he doesn't have to jerk around, but to someone else, it may be a horse that picks up on a cue if you just tip your hand.

"There are so many variables to bitting," he adds. "People ask if a bit is severe or mild, but I have to say, 'It all depends on how you ride, on your hands.' When a rider is pulling a horse around and trying to accomplish things through pressure, this creates a hard-mouthed horse, and it's hard to take a horse back from that to lightness. The sooner you can get on an extremely well-trained horse, the sooner you can appreciate this. If you're constantly pulling on the horse, he gets used to constant pressure, then you have to use more bit, more pressure to accomplish anything, and that's not where you want to go."

Although there are many variations of snaffle mouthpieces and diameters, construction options include:

- smooth mouthpieces that can be contoured or straight.

- textured mouthpieces of some form, such as ribbed or twisted metal.

- twisted-wire mouthpieces than can be tightly or loosely twisted and made of different diameters, with thinner mouthpieces having more potential for severity.

- half-and-half mouthpieces, which have twisted wire in the center hinged area with smooth metal on both ends.

## Materials

Bit material has a direct bearing on how well a horse tolerates the bit. There are several materials commonly used for mouthpieces, such as:

- **sweet iron,** which despite the warm and fuzzy term, is really just plain steel that rusts with time, even though most horses like the taste of a steel bit.

- **stainless steel,** which doesn't rust and stays shiny, but doesn't have the same taste or appeal to a horse as a regular steel mouthpiece.

- **copper,** which increases salivation and helps keep the horse's mouth moist and wet. Just adding some copper can accomplish that; the entire mouthpiece doesn't have to be copper.

- **combination** bits that use more than one type of metal in the mouthpieces, such as stainless steel or regular steel with copper inlay or coating.

- **plated metal,** a less expensive option, although the coating, often nickel, eventually flakes away, exposing the underlying metal.

- **rubber,** actually vulcanized rubber over a thin steel core, which is sometimes

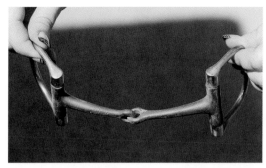
*Copper in a bit mouthpiece encourages effective communication by helping to keep the mouth moist and the jaw relaxed.*
ROSS HECOX

*A rusty-looking, well-used bit can have a far more appealing taste to a horse than a shiny bit of stainless steel.*
ROSS HECOX

used for early training or for sensitive-mouthed horses. A rubber bit can encourage chewing and wears faster than any type of metal bit.

- **plastic,** typically a mouthpiece of firm, nontoxic plastic with a stainless-steel core. This offers some flexibility and sometimes is flavored to encourage acceptance by the horse, but plastic also tends to encourage chewing and wears faster than metal.

- **aluminum,** another inexpensive option, is lightweight, but many horsemen think aluminum dries out the horse's mouth.

## Bit Rings

The size and weight of the bit rings impact the amount of pressure applied to the horse.

"When you pull laterally on a snaffle bit, depending on the type of ring, it can put pressure on the horse's cheek, making it rub against the molar," Black explains. "A small,

*Snaffle-bit rings are available in varying weights, sizes, and models, such as the D-ring design shown here.*

KATE BRADLEY

**Loose (sliding) rings** on a snaffle bit:

- move freely since they're not fixed.

- allow more play of the bit in the horse's mouth than do fixed rings.

**Fixed rings** on the bit:

- give more direct cue to the horse than loose rings.

- allow less play and movement of the bit than loose rings.

**Eggbutts** at the end of a mouthpiece:

- have fixed cheeks.

- create less bit movement in the mouth.

- give more contact on the sides of mouth.

- make it more difficult for the bit to pinch the corners of the mouth.

**D-rings** on a bit mouthpiece:

- can have either fixed or ball hinges.

- reinforce the rider's turning aids.

- help prevent the bit from being pulled through the horse's mouth.

round ring puts little or no pressure on the molar, but the corner of a D-ring often hits a horse in the molar. This can put a sore on the inside of the cheek because the cheek is pressed between the molar and the corner of the D-ring. This is another reason to make sure a young horse's teeth have been worked on so they're smooth and don't have sharp edges. Otherwise, even with light hands, you can end up with a sore mouth. With a young horse, you should always look at the mouth before you do anything with a bit."

A visit by the equine dentist always is in order before you start riding any young horse in a bit. If the horse has wolf teeth—and many young horses do—the wolf teeth easily can be removed. Doing so greatly improves the horse's ability to comfortably carry a bit.

**Full cheeks** are similar to D-rings, but with straight extensions above and below each D, which:

- reinforce the rider's turning aids.

- spread the bit pressure felt through the reins.

- usually prevent the bit from being pulled through the mouth, even without a curb strap, or bit hobble, attached.

- can be attached with keepers fastening the upper parts of the bit cheekpieces to a headstall, to make the mouthpiece fixed, if desired.

# GOTCHA?

## When It's Not About the Bit

When a horse has been handling nicely in a particular bit and then begins to have issues, those are red flags that something has changed. Horses communicate through body language, so if your horse gradually becomes unresponsive to the bit and/or develops such actions as head-tossing, grinding the teeth, mouthing the bit, an aversion to being bridled, or some other physical action he hasn't done before, listen up. He's trying to tell you something and it's likely related to his mouth—not his bit.

A rider might assume the problem lies with equipment or that the horse is just acting up or being stubborn, and switch to a different bit. But the sudden or gradual appearance of physical actions can indicate a problem with the horse's mouth.

"Horses can suffer dental problems, including sore teeth, or scrapes on the tongue or gums, which can cause head-tossing, fidgeting and acute discomfort," says California trainer and bitmaker Les Vogt. "Many bit problems are reduced or eliminated with proper dental care, so horses should have their teeth checked at least once a year, and more often as they age."

A horse's teeth continue to change, based on age, wear and the shape of the mouth. Horses have hypsodont teeth, which means they continue to erupt, anywhere from two to four millimeters a year. If opposing teeth don't come together and meet with equal pressure, they wear unevenly. When teeth are out of alignment, they can develop hooks, waves, ramps, and enamel points, seriously sharp edges that can cause ulcerations inside the mouth. Regular dental care by floating, also known as equilibrating, the teeth, can correct these problems.

Your equine dentist might finish the floating procedure by giving the teeth a bit seat, which just means he rounds the upper and lower second premolars to allow the bit to rest comfortably in the mouth without interference from these teeth.

A young horse always should have a dental exam before being introduced to a bit for the first time.

"This is something a lot of people miss," notes top reined cow horse trainer and competitor Ted Robinson, emphasizing the importance of dental care in the earliest phases of breaking and training. "We don't put bits in their mouths until their teeth have been floated. Those babies can have really sharp teeth."

*Often there is a direct correlation between bitting problems and the need for equine dental work.*

ROSS HECOX

## Curb Straps and Snaffles

On a leverage bit, the curb strap or chain helps the bit work properly and actually serves as part of the signaling process to the horse as the rider handles the reins. You see plenty of people, including many working cowboys, riding in snaffles with a curb strap, but for a completely different reason.

Because the snaffle doesn't work off leverage, the only purpose of a curb strap is to keep the bit rings from being pulled sideways through the horse's mouth. In effect, that strap serves as a "hobble" on the rings, so the adjustment of the strap should be loose.

*A bit hobble used on a snaffle looks much like a leather curb strap on a shanked bit although the purpose for one is entirely different than that of the other.*

COURTESY EQUIBRAND®

## Quality Workmanship

When shopping for bits, you quickly notice a wide range of prices. You can buy a snaffle bit for $30, and you also can buy one for $300. Why the big difference?

Part of the disparity can be attributed to materials, but most of it is due to how the bit is made. A handmade bit costs significantly more than a bit that is mass-produced in a factory. That's not to say there is anything wrong with the factory-made bit; you and your horse might get along just fine with that bit and with no complaints. But there's definitely a market for handmade bits, and the horsemen who use them swear by these individually made bits.

"With mass-produced bits, most parts are typically cast metal and then assembled by hand. With a hand-built bit, each different piece is cut and welded, and then put together for that particular bit," notes Balding. "The difference is in the choice of materials and attention to detail. We measure

everything within a few thousandths of an inch, so the bit is perfectly balanced and symmetrical, and the joints don't pinch or wear excessively. This is critical."

Balding explains that horses are very sensitive to a bit that is not centered and balanced.

"I've been in manufacturing since 1965, and having built airplane parts to exacting standards, I carried that over into building bits," says Balding. "When I started making these bits, I thought it would be easy compared to what I'd been doing, but it's extremely difficult. The reality is that it's very difficult to put 20 to 30 parts together and have the bit come out exactly centered and balanced. I built extensive tooling to cut, bend and make all the different pieces. During the whole assembly process, we use tooling to hold the parts in exactly the right positions while they're welded, to make sure everything is squared, centered and exact. That's how we get symmetry."

You might watch someone holding a bit's mouthpiece in his or her hand to see if the bit is balanced, but it's impossible to tell this way. As Vogt explains, "Balance is defined as where the bit seeks gravity. A snaffle bit only seeks gravity straight down. In order to create more balance, you want more weight in the rings, which creates more release."

"Balance and workmanship are more important to me than the type of steel used in a bit. Balance is so important! You see a bit that is just a hair off on one side or the other, and that affects how the horse works. The precision on a bit has to be totally correct,"

*This D-ring snaffle with copper inlay and ball hinges has been dressed up with silver spots and a custom concha.*

COURTESY TOM BALDING BITS & SPURS

# GOTCHA!

## Using Bit Hobbles

As previously explained in this chapter, a curb strap can be used to "hobble" a snaffle bit so that it cannot be pulled through a horse's mouth. The bit hobble for a shanked, or leverage, bit serves a different purpose.

In order to keep a bit's shanks from moving or swiveling excessively, you can add a hobble between the rein rings at the bottom of the shanks. The hobble shouldn't be tight or cause any tension between the shanks. Some horsemen and bitmakers use metal bars; others use sections of chain, nylon cord or even pieces of rawhide. The hobble doesn't have to be fancy in order to do its job.

Another benefit of the bit hobble: When you're roping, the hobble prevents the rope from accidentally getting between the shanks of the bit and burning a horse's nose. This could do serious damage to the horse's mouth and, at the very least, could cause a pretty good wreck. Cowboys riding in high brush also use bit hobbles.

So no matter if you ride with a snaffle or a shanked bit, be sure to hobble the bit so you have one less thing on your mind when you're horseback.

---

says Ted Robinson, who has seven National Reined Cow Horse Association Open Snaffle Bit Futurity championships and two World's Greatest Horseman titles to his credit. A former NRCHA president, he's also among the founders of the National Stock Horse Association.

## Young Horses in the Snaffle

Many horsemen like to start a colt in a halter or hackamore, so there's nothing in the horse's mouth for those all-important first rides. Then, once the colt has a little knowledge—even just a few days' worth—the trainer might switch to a mild snaffle to continue the horse's education.

At Ted Robinson's Working Cow Horses training facility in Oak View, Calif., he moves young horses into snaffles after about two days of riding. To start, he likes a smooth-mouth snaffle, but one with a mouthpiece that is fat and contoured.

"I don't want tongue pressure on the babies; I want pressure on the corners of the mouth, so that's why I use a contoured mouthpiece," explains Robinson, who has been training full-time since 1983 and became the first cow-horse trainer to win $2 million.

"Normally, I start with a loose-ring. I think with a fixed-ring you get more direction with left and right because of the way the ring comes against the cheek, so I usually save that for later. I show in a D-ring snaffle all the time; that's my favorite." (In fact, Tom Balding makes his Ted Robinson ball-hinge D-ring snaffle based on Robinson's design input and ideas.)

Robinson likes a mouthpiece to have a little copper, but not a lot. He's found that if the mouthpiece has a good deal of copper, horses tend to chew on it, and in time the bit can develop sharp edges.

His snaffles always have loose chin straps to keep the bits from pulling through the horses' mouths. Robinson adds that reins always should be attached to the bit above the chin strap, not below it.

As for the weight of the snaffle rings, he prefers rings with some weight, but not actually heavy rings.

"The reason I like some weight is because it signals the horse better," he notes. "A bit is supposed to be a signal. If it's too light, the horse tends to flip his nose up in the air and not take the signal."

One thing you don't find in Robinson's tack room is a three-piece snaffle, and he has definite reasons for not using that type of mouthpiece.

"A regular snaffle just collapses in the center, but I think a three-piece is too loose in the mouth and gives the horse too many signals. For me, it doesn't pinch the tongue but pushes on the tongue and makes it round out."

As the young horse progresses in his training, Robinson downsizes from the fat, contoured mouthpiece. "The further along a horse gets, the more I put him in a

# MAKE IT WORK FOR YOU

## Does that Bit Fit?

Whatever type of bit you're using, it needs to fit the horse's mouth. If you have to err on one side or the other, a mouthpiece a little too long from side to side is better than one too short. Although you don't want to see a lot of mouthpiece extending beyond the lips, on the other hand, if the bit is too narrow, the rings or cheekpieces can pinch the sides of the mouth. They also can press the cheek between the horse's molar and the corner of the mouthpiece, which is painful and can rub a sore spot.

"We used to sell a lot of 5-inch-mouth snaffles, but I haven't sold one in 10 years. Now everyone wants 5½ to 6 inches," says Vogt, who goes on to explain why. "When you pull the right ring, the lower jaw slides in the direction you're pulling. It may be only a quarter-inch, but that's enough that the ring of the snaffle is pulling on the outside of the horse's face, and the tender fatty tissue inside the cheek on that side is pulled against the shelf of the upper molar, which can literally turn the cheek to hamburger. So, a narrower mouthpiece engages the ring to the face faster and tends to cause inner cheek soreness.

"A slightly wider mouthpiece gives the horse a little more time to respond to the mouthpiece sliding through his mouth, as opposed to a narrow mouthpiece in which the ring engages the cheek more quickly and with less warning," he adds. "A wider mouthpiece gives the horse more time to react to the presignal of the bit starting to move in his mouth. A wider mouthpiece also offers more feel than a narrower mouthpiece because it gives more friction sliding through the mouth."

"If a horse has a really wide muzzle, you want to make sure you get a bit that is wider than usual," adds Robinson. "I have some 6-inch-wide snaffles because I don't want pinching on the corners of the mouth, especially with a round ring. The reason I like a ball hinge is because those never pinch."

The mouthpiece is measured from the inside of each ring or cheek piece. To get the correct width, when you shop for another bit, take along a bit that you know is the correct size. If you've never had a bit in the horse's mouth or think you need a different size, you can measure the width of the horse's mouth with a plastic sewing tape measure, or a piece of baling twine.

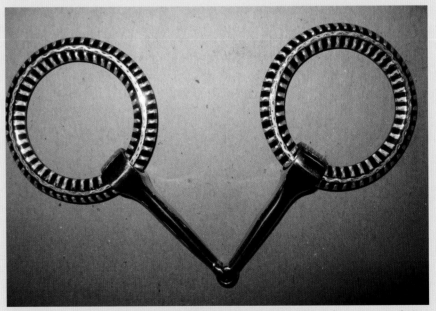

*A horseman understands that a snaffle mouthpiece that is too short can pinch or rub a horse and adversely affect how the horse responds.*

COURTESY LES VOGT

straight mouthpiece. I get away from the fatter snaffle, as I get closer to showing, and straighten out the mouthpiece. This works on the tongue and, at this point, the horse is giving his chin a lot more. A snaffle with a straight mouthpiece works the tongue and the corners of the mouth, where the regular snaffle works only the corners of the mouth. If I start having problems with a colt giving his nose, that's when I put the D-ring on the horse."

### Introducing a New Bit

When Robinson introduces a snaffle to a young horse for the first time, the trainer doesn't give the horse anything else to worry about. Robinson just wants to give the horse time to get used to carrying that bit around in his mouth.

"The first time I hang a snaffle on a 2-year-old, I do it with nothing else—no reins and no saddle. I just turn him loose in his pen wearing the bit and let him cruise around messing with it. I don't leave him in a regular 12-by-12-foot stall because I think that's too small, and he could get the bridle caught on something. For this one time, I just let him wear the bit for an hour or two, and then the next time I put it on him, I'm riding him in it."

Robinson adjusts the headstall so that the bit rests in the mouth with no wrinkles at those corners. "I don't pull it up in the mouth and 'make him smile.' I want him to learn to hold that bit with his tongue. I also make sure the chin strap is not too tight."

The trainer uses a browband headstall with a throatlatch when he rides in a snaffle,

"You see people using a split-ear [head-stall] with a snaffle, but it's not designed for that. It can slide back on the neck too far, which pulls on the horse's mouth, and then he's got his nose in the air."

Some riders change bits frequently, but Robinson cautions that there should be a reason for doing so.

"Before you change bits, you have to know what you're trying to accomplish," he notes. "The first thing I do is analyze and ask myself, 'Have I started with too much bit already or is this bit not enough? Is the horse reacting because this bit is too severe or is he

*When introducing a bit to a young horse, the snaffle often is attached to a headstall, but with no reins, but can be fastened to a halter as shown here.*

ROSS HECOX

pulling on this bit?' I have to figure out the problem before I change bits."

Black weighs in on the same topic.

"People often mistake an unwilling horse for an uneducated horse. A lazy—but educated—horse might be motivated by the more severe bit, but for the green horse, a severe bit makes things worse. He probably needs a milder bit and more direction, more education."

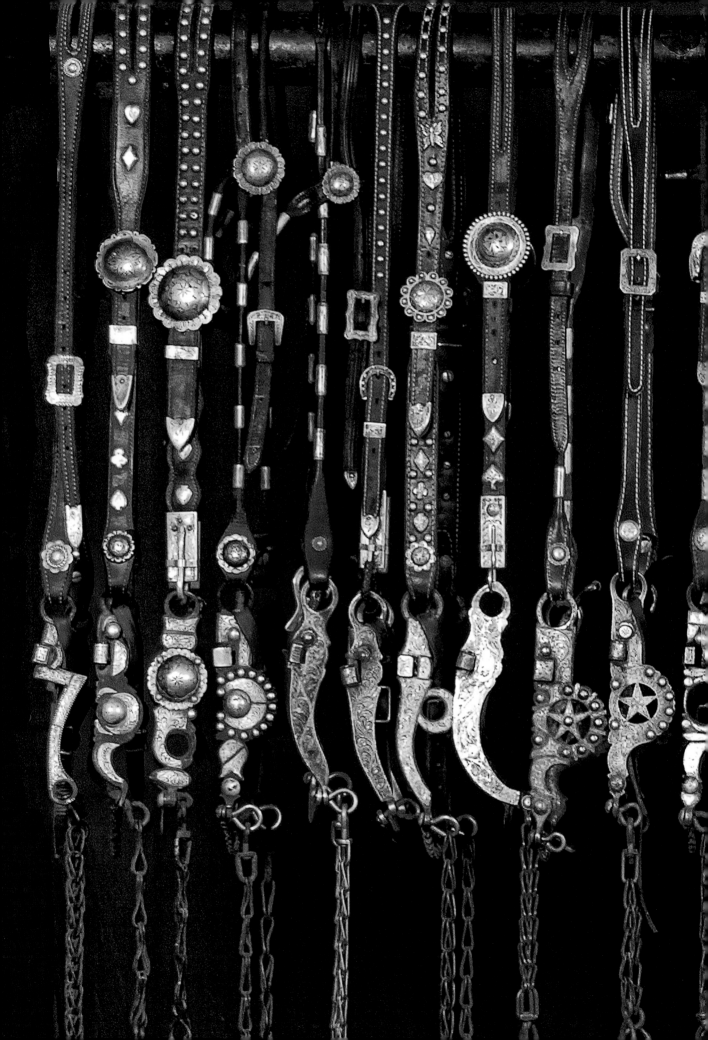

# 9

# Shanked Bits

Finely made, elaborate shanked bits have been used far longer than you might think. Relief carvings found in ancient Persia, now Iran, reveal bridled horses in bits with long cheekpieces used as early as the 6th century B.C. Early Greek and Roman horsemen also used various shanked options.

In some early bits the cheekpieces appear to be designed primarily for decorative purposes, as well as to keep the bit from sliding through the horse's mouth. Others, as with today's curb bits, are meant to be used with straps or chains under the horses' chins, and work off the principal of leverage.

"Many cheekpieces have been passed down for hundreds of years and derive from a very technical science that originated as many as thousands of years ago," says longtime trainer, clinician and bitmaker Les Vogt of Pismo Beach, California. "I have a bit from Sweden that is 2,000 years old. The mechanics, design and theory of leverage in that bit are exactly what we have today. It's pretty hard to design something new."

Although the snaffle is a nonleverage bit and operates off pressure, a shanked bit operates precisely on the principle of leverage.

"Leverage is powerful stuff. A bit with a high-leverage ratio, tugged at the wrong time by a 100-pound girl, can make a 1,000-pound horse lose his balance and fall over backwards," notes Vogt.

*Based on the amount of headgear hanging in their barns, few horsemen can deny an ongoing fascination with bits.*
DARRELL DODDS

## Understand Bit Mechanics

Two main things determine how the shanked bit functions. These include hardware, which is a combination of the cheekpieces, or shanks, and the mouthpiece, as well as action, which is a combination of the leverage, flexibility and balance of that hardware.

People generally think a bit with long shanks—whatever type mouthpiece it has—is more severe than a bit with shorter shanks. After all, long shanks can exert plenty of leverage, which increases the potential for severity, right? Not necessarily. Severity is all about proportion. For example, a bit with 10-inch shanks, but with the mouthpiece located precisely in the middle of those shanks, has a leverage ratio of 1-to-1 or neutral, the same as a plain snaffle bit.

"A leverage bit acts like a teeter-totter in your horse's mouth. On a teeter-totter, even a skinny kid can launch a chubby playmate into the air with a long enough plank [lever] and a

*Mouthpiece placement in relation to the total length of a bit is an important consideration in determining how a particular bit's leverage affects the horse.*

ROSS HECOX

log [fulcrum] placed strategically close to the heavier child," explains Vogt. "Likewise, that overall length of a bit is not as relevant as the placement of the pivot point [fulcrum], which is the mouthpiece.

"Leverage is about the position of the mouthpiece in relation to the total length of the cheekpiece. A benign-looking bit can pack quite a wallop when the placement of the mouthpiece is considered."

Vogt goes on to explain how to determine leverage by measuring from the center of the mouthpiece to the loop where the headstall attaches, not the exterior part of the loop, but the inside of the hole on top to the middle of a mouthpiece. This gives one measurement. Then measure from the middle of the mouthpiece down to the point of pull where the rein attaches, which is halfway down the loop or rein hook. That's the second measurement. To figure a bit's leverage, divide the bottom measurement by the top measurement.

Say you have 2 inches from the middle of the mouthpiece up to the headstall loop and 6 inches from the middle of the mouthpiece down to where the rein attaches. Divide 6, the bottom measurement, by 2, the top measurement. This tells you the bit has a 3-to-1 leverage ratio.

"The greater the difference between the top and bottom measurements [such as 4-to-1], the more efficiently the bit transfers that energy originally sent from your hands on the reins to the horse's mouth," says Vogt.

"Whether a rider is green or an expert, he has the same amount of leverage to use," Vogt notes. "The higher the leverage—whether the shank is long or short—the slower the mouthpiece rotates, and the slower it pulls on the curb strap, which gives the horse more time to respond to your signal. The lower the leverage, the quicker and more abrupt the signal and the less time the horse has to respond. If I was going to put a green rider on the best horse I ever had, I'd put a high-leverage bit on the horse because it has slower action before the curb strap engages, whereas a lower leverage bit is faster acting, so you need quiet hands."

A "quick" bit—one with low leverage—can put a sensitive horse on the defensive as soon as he feels the bit start to move. This is especially applicable if the rider's hands are abrupt. Instead of a light response, the horse starts to brace. His neck is the first thing to tighten, but that affects his spine, and then his whole body becomes tense—not what you want in either a performance or pleasure horse.

The weight of the shanks also plays a role. For example, a horse that is more fragile—in mouth and/or mind—might respond better if you use a bit with lighter shanks rather than heavier ones.

## Put Leverage to Use

"Why do we ride? It's about heart and soul communication," Vogt reflects. "We want the horse to be part of us, and we want to be part of him. This happens only through communication, which means developing an extension of myself through the horse. To me, the bridling process is one of the intricate parts of communication. In order to do this, I need the correct tools, which is where bits come into play. Even the rider who doesn't compete should still have pride in his or her horsemanship and want to get the most done with the least amount of effort on the part of the rider."

A skilled horseman or horsewoman puts thought into selecting a shanked bit because that person knows the amount of leverage directly affects how the horse responds and carries himself.

"A higher leverage, like 4-to-1, drops the whole horse's neck," says Vogt, who believes this is one of the biggest secrets in bitting horsemanship. "It gives you that pretty rounded top line, so he can use his loins and hindquarters properly. If the horse lifts his neck, that makes it difficult—if not impossible—to use his hindquarters properly."

Vogt finds that mid-range leverage, 3-to-1, causes the horse to break at the crest, in the middle of the neck, while low leverage, 2-to-1, makes the horse break farther up the neck toward the poll.

"A low-leverage bit is good for the horse that wants to drop his shoulders, carries too much weight on the front end, and/or has a tendency to distribute too much weight to the forehand," he says. "If you have a short-necked, low-withered, long-backed horse that is heavy in front, you want a low-leverage bit designed so the pressure points get more respect."

Both curb-strap adjustment and cheekpiece design affect how quickly a shanked bit engages.

"You hear that the design or shape of a cheekpiece has an influence on leverage, but

*An understanding of leverage allows a rider to use minimal effort for maximum communication with a horse, and the necessary tool can be both eye-catching and effective.*

COURTESY LES VOGT

what design or shape really affects is not leverage so much, but rather how far the bit has to rotate in the horse's mouth before the curb strap engages and the mouthpiece rotates to its most effective point," says Vogt.

"If a shanked bit has no curb strap and is allowed to rotate fully in the horse's mouth, there is no leverage. The curb strap stops rotation, which creates leverage," says trainer and clinician Martin Black, a lifelong horseman in Bruneau, Ida., who is well-versed in the vaquero tradition of developing a finely trained bridle horse.

"A straight-shanked bit has an optimum amount of leverage engagement when used with a tight curb strap. That leverage engagement is reduced when you use a bit with a curved shank, even with a similarly tight curb strap," explains Black. "If you want faster leverage engagement, use a straighter shank with a tighter curb strap. If you want slower leverage engagement, go with a curved shank and a looser curb strap."

As Black goes on to explain, more leverage means more pressure.

"Basically, leverage is created by a lever [from the mouthpiece to the rein attachment] and the fulcrum point [where the mouthpiece rotates in the mouth]. We also need to recognize the effects of the curb strap and headstall. The headstall creates lift as the bit rotates in the mouth. The curb strap stops that rotation, determining the angle and, therefore, the amount of lift and leverage. Lift means the bit is actually rising up in the mouth or on the lower jaw of the horse. Leverage means we are multiplying the amount of pressure from the reins to the fulcrum point.

"The rotation of the bit makes a difference as to where leverage starts and stops, and rotation is directly influenced by how tight the curb strap is," Black adds. "This explains why the curb strap is such a factor in leverage. It's all about both the bit ratio and the curb strap."

Black points out that it's important to understand these basics because many riders don't realize the importance of curb-strap adjustment and how that affects the bit's function.

## Flexibility and Signal

A loose-jawed shank swivels where the mouthpiece attaches. With some horses, you might want this extra flexibility in the shanks, and/or even in the mouthpiece, because such a bit isn't as quick to engage the pressure points of the mouth as a bit with fixed shanks and/or mouthpiece.

A bit with mouthpiece flexibility helps allow a green horse to more easily feel every movement of the reins well before that movement becomes actual pressure. As soon as the horse understands this presignal, he becomes educated that the mouthpiece is soon going to change to a position of more authority. A light touch is often all that is needed.

"Flexibility has a pacifying effect on horses that are afraid of a quick-handed rider," notes Vogt. "The more joints a mouthpiece has, the more slowly it engages, while a solid-bar mouthpiece is quicker to engage."

## How Mouthpieces Work

A shanked bit, depending on the mouthpiece, puts pressure on one or more of the following:

- corners of the mouth
- palate, or roof of the mouth
- tongue
- bars
- chin and lower jaw, due to curb strap or chain

If a bit affects multiple pressure points, or affects pressure points more forcefully, it's known as a "hot" mouthpiece, meaning it demands more respect, and requires more feel from the rider to use it properly. A "cold" mouthpiece lightly affects pressure points.

A horse that leans on the bit might benefit from a somewhat hotter mouthpiece, rather than from changing the leverage. On the other hand, a sensitive, nervous horse might do better in a bit that has higher leverage, but a cooler mouthpiece.

The tough campaigner competing at a high level, but starting to feel a bit dull might not need a hotter mouthpiece, but rather one affecting different pressure points. A horse can get familiar with the way a bit affects his mouth and in time grow less sensitive to those pressure points. That old saying, "Familiarity breeds contempt," certainly can apply in this case.

There are many variations in ported bit mouthpieces. A bit with a high port can engage the palate, or roof of the mouth, while one with a low port puts more pressure on the tongue and bars. Any bit with a port can be considered a signal bit because the portion of the bit on top of the mouthpiece bar is designed to send a presignal to the horse before the leverage takes effect.

A shanked snaffle, sometimes called an Argentine snaffle, is popular with many Western riders and is considered by some a good tool to transition a horse from a standard snaffle bit to a shanked bit. The loose shanks offer more movement and flexibility than fixed shanks, giving the horse more time to respond to the initial rein movement.

*Although its loose shanks and broken mouthpiece give a young horse, new to bit leverage, time to respond, the shanked snaffle affects a horse's mouth differently than an O- or D-ring snaffle.*

KATE BRADLEY

"A shanked snaffle usually doesn't have as much curb-strap effect as other shanked bits because there's much more give to this bit than with an unbroken mouthpiece," notes Black. "When a shanked snaffle begins to rotate because you put pressure on the reins, the mouthpiece starts to collapse and puts pressure on the bars and tongue, squeezing the lower jaw, which is totally different from a ring snaffle, which gets no effect from a curb strap, other than to keep the bit from pulling through the mouth."

## Spade Bits

Of all shanked bits, the spade is perhaps the most misunderstood. The decorative shanks feature elaborate and intricate designs, often named for a specific region, such as Santa Barbara, or bitmaker's locale, maybe Las Cruces. The spade comes directly from the vaquero horsemen and features a straight bar mouthpiece with a high, narrow port; spoon, the flat, partially-rounded plate

above the port; cricket and/or roller; and copper-covered braces, all designed in ways that encourage the horse to hold onto the bit and carry it in his mouth.

The cricket and the roller are both rounded parts that rotate inside the bit port. Some people refer to them interchangeably, but there is a definite difference between the two. Black explains that the cricket makes its signature cricket-like sound because it has notches on the inside and rolls against a peg. In addition to the noise, the cricket offers a slight vibrating sensation for the horse. The roller has a smooth center and rolls on a smooth peg, so it makes no chirping noise or vibration.

Even though the spade has a curb strap, the spade never was meant to function as other leverage bits, but rather only to signal a horse with the slightest movement of the reins. It takes several years to finish a horse to the point that he can graduate to the spade bit, and some horses, and riders, never achieve this degree of finely tuned precision.

*No matter how new or well-used, a spade bit functions primarily as a signal bit used only after a lengthy training process to develop a highly responsive full-bridle horse.*

ROSS HECOX

"Many people look at the old spade bits and think of them as torture devices, but they were actually designed as signal bits," notes Black. "Horses weren't trained in those bits, but rather trained through years, and the spade bit was the final step, not the beginning. The spade operates off signal—not off pressure or leverage. The straight-bar mouthpiece rests on the tongue, which, being a muscle, can flex and hold the bit off the lower jaw. The horse actually can carry the bit on his tongue. A good spade bit horse doesn't even need a curb strap because he's operating off the signal from the spade. He feels the signal to his palate before the curb strap ever tightens. He's that finely tuned. With really good spade bit men, the curb strap isn't even a consideration."

Vaquero tradition dictates that a horse always is started in a bosal. By the time he is moved into the bridle and eventually advanced to the spade bit, he is responsive to the most subtle touch of the rider's hand on those reins—no leverage or force required. Once "straight up in the bridle," a spade bit horse always is ridden on a loose rein. Horsemen tell

*The practical artistry of the spade bit rests in the hands of a skillful horseman and with a proficient horse, yet there can be aestheticly pleasing artistry in the bit itself.*

COURTESY LES VOGT

you that if the horse requires anything but a loose rein, he's not ready for the spade.

Montana trainer and clinician Curt Pate puts it succinctly: "When you ride a spade bit, your horse tells the world if you're a horseman—or not."

"The spade bit is the most artful mouthpiece bit you can possibly ride with, and until you've ridden a good spade-bit horse, you've never had the thrills you deserve as a horseman," observes Vogt. "He makes you laugh out loud when no one is around—and there aren't many things that give you that feeling. A good spade bit has intricate action to very subtle movement of the reins. The spade is not made to gouge the palate. A spade-bit horse is very responsive and responsible. He's educated so he knows that when the spade leaves his tongue, it's headed to his palate, and he's learned through education to avoid that by responding."

## Tongue Relief

You also find a number of leverage bits with tongue-relief mouthpieces, which might seem mild, but in reality can be just the opposite. A tongue-relief bit has a port high enough and wide enough that the horse can't use his tongue to press against the port. When pressure is applied to this bit, all the pressure goes to the bars of the mouth, meaning this type bit easily can be abusive when used with a heavy hand.

Given the chance, a horse typically uses his tongue to keep the bit from putting pressure on the bars of his mouth. A tongue-relief bit prevents him from doing this, which isn't necessarily a positive thing. The tongue-relief bit eliminates protection of the bars by the tongue at least in part, if not totally. In other words, a wider port means more pressure on the bars because the horse can't effectively lift the bit with his tongue.

"If you have a lazy kid's horse, he may lay against a straight-bar bit because it's not on the sensitive bars of his mouth and he can hold it with his tongue," notes Black. "With a tongue-relief bit, he can't use his tongue to protect the bars, so the mouthpiece puts pressure on the sensitive bars of his mouth. A horse is much more sensitive to a tongue-relief bit and a chain curb strap used in combination—much more so than, say, a straight-bar bit and a leather curb strap."

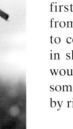

*Because the port in this popular grazing-bit design is more closed than opened wide, a horse can use his tongue to lift the bit and keep it from putting pressure on his bars.*

KATE BRADLEY

## Popular Mouthpieces

When choosing a mouthpiece, you must first know the kind of response you want from the horse. An entire book is necessary to cover all the many mouthpieces available in shanked bits and, even then, some likely would be overlooked. This chapter considers some of the most popular mouthpieces used by riders today:

- **high port:** about 2 inches in height; often favored by riders who think it encourages collection, proper head carriage and upright body position

- **cathedral port:** from about 2½ to 3¼ inches; with or without roller; a high, fairly narrow swept-back port for softer engagement in the mouth; a signal bit not to be used with force

- **medium port:** about 1½ inches; offers control and tongue relief without contacting the palate

- **medium-low port:** about 1⅛ inches; considered a useful all-around bit with a

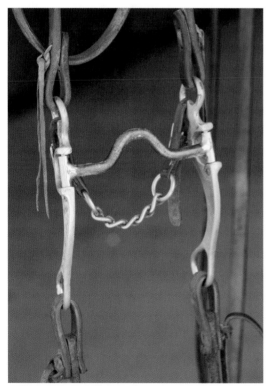

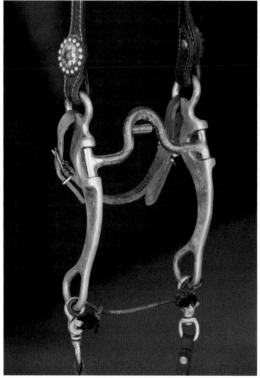

*Although both bits have been patterned from the same loose-cheek design, one bit has a low port and short shanks. A roller has been added to the other bit's higher port, and this bit's longer shanks have been hobbled.*

JOHN BRASSEAUX

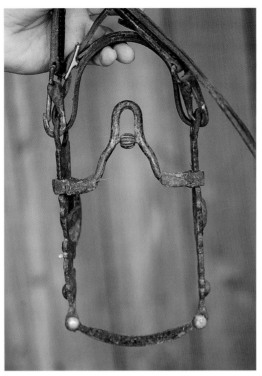

*This well-used cathedral port bit, so-named for its design, has a roller and is considered a signal bit best used on a well-educated horse.*

ROSS HECOX

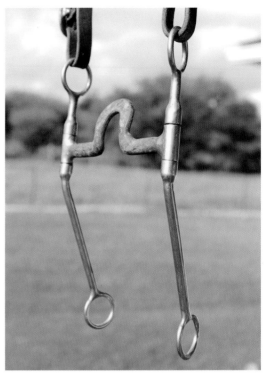

*Shiny stainless-steel bit shanks contrast sharply with the rusty, sweet-iron mouthpiece that horses seem to prefer.*

KATE BRADLEY

mild port exerting little pressure on the palate

- **low port:** about ¾-inch high; a mild bit putting no pressure on the palate, making it a comfortable choice for many horses

- **spade:** straight-bar mouthpiece with a high, narrow port, spoon, cricket, and copper-covered braces; often elaborate cheekpieces; intended to direct a properly educated horse by signal—not leverage

- **half-breed:** a high port, but typically not as high as a spade or cathedral; with roller(s); meant to operate off signal rather than leverage, much like the spade

## Mouthpiece Materials

Just as with snaffles, leverage bits use a variety of mouthpiece materials:

- sweet iron, plain steel that rusts with time and seems tasty to horses

- stainless steel

- silver, inlay or overlay

- copper, coating or inlay

- combinations of metals and alloys

- plated metal

- aluminum

## Mouthpiece Mounts

Mouthpieces are mounted in two ways on bits, and each method differently affects the way the bit functions.

A **front-mount** mouthpiece is one in which the mouthpiece is mounted on the front edge of the shanks, and:

- can have fixed shanks or shanks that swivel.

- can offer more lateral control than a center-mount mouthpiece if there's no bottom bar to stabilize the shanks.

- has more preload and counterbalance than a center-mount mouthpiece because the weight of the shanks is farther behind the mouthpiece. This helps prevent the bit from rocking back and forth, which might give confusing signals to the horse.

- unloads quicker than a center-mount mouthpiece when pressure is released, thereby rewarding the horse immediately.

A **center-mount** mouthpiece is one in which the mouthpiece is mounted in the center of the shanks, and:

- can have fixed shanks or shanks that swivel.

- has less lateral movement than a front-mount.

- with lateral pull, can pinch the corners of the mouth where the mouthpiece attaches to the shanks if there's no bottom bar stabilizing the shanks.

"A thoughtfully designed bit inherently has balance because it is made to hang from the headstall so that the mouthpiece rests

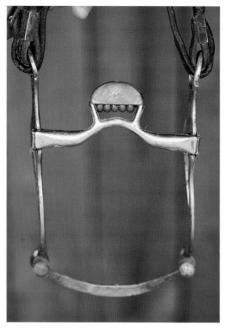

*Compare this mouthpiece mounted on the front edge of the bit cheeks with the center-mount on the grazing bit shown at upper left on page 121.*
ROSS HECOX

comfortably in the horse's mouth without rocking back and forth when he moves, thereby giving him false signals," Vogt explains.

"When a bit has more weight behind and below the mouthpiece, we call this 'preload' or 'counterbalance.' The more you pull back on the reins, the heavier this bit becomes. It 'loads' as you pull it back, and when you

# MAKE IT WORK FOR YOU

## Curb Strap and Chain Adjustment

If you remember only one thing about adjusting the curb strap or chain, it should be this: The tighter the chin strap, the sooner the bit engages.

You actually can make the same bit more or less severe according to how tightly or loosely you adjust your chin strap. With a tighter strap, the horse has very little chance to respond before the strap causes leverage. A somewhat looser strap or chain allows the horse to have more mouthpiece presignal—and, therefore, more chance to respond—before he feels pressure from the strap. Experiment to see what works best with your horse and the particular bits you're using.

As for whether you should use leather curb strap or a curb chain, this is mostly personal preference. Some associations don't allow chains in competition, but others do. The choice depends not only on association rules if you compete, but also on the respect—or lack of respect—you get from your horse.

*Chin-strap adjustment factors into how slowly or quickly a bit affects the horse and, thus, his response time.*
KATE BRADLEY

release, it's like a spring unloading, so it quickly rewards the horse when you give slack for his positive response. You have to be fair to the horse or it's meaningless to him. The quicker you answer and the quicker he responds, the better the communication."

## Q & A: Expert Advice

The subject of bitting is subjective and, in many ways, open to different interpretations. Two expert horsemen, traditional bridle horseman, trainer and clinician Martin Black of Idaho and Californian Les Vogt, longtime performance horseman, trainer and bitmaker, offer insights into their choices of bits and their uses.

### How do you decide which bit to use?

**Black:** "A lot of old ranchers got along with two or three types of bits, usually a snaffle and a Spanish-type bit, but now we have a wide variety of options. I have more than 100 bits, but my goal is always to get the most response with the signal—not pain—to get results. You can be effective with any type of bit with the right hands, while hard hands can make even a mild snaffle severe. I also have to look at the horse. An uneducated horse doesn't need more bit; he needs more education."

**Vogt:** "I used to think horses sometimes became angry with me during training sessions, but then I realized they weren't upset with me, but they were upset with the pressure points of my bit. Horses' mouths aren't all shaped the same, and their pain tolerance is not the same. I like to have three bits when I go out to ride. If something's not quite right or the horse starts to show some resistance, I change bits, and 100-percent of the time I get a fresh start either to make progress or to apologize for any mistakes I make today.

"If you ride and school a horse in the same bit you show in, this can develop too much familiarity. If your horse becomes dull in the bit you use now, that's because he's become too familiar with the pressure points and loses some sensitivity and respect. Even if you don't compete, having three bits for a horse is a great idea.

"I always have an 'A' bit, which is the bit I use in competition that gets me those magic results. It's a bit the horse is very respectful of, but I don't let him get familiar with it. Once I find a bit that gives me the best

communication with that horse, I make that my A bit.

"My 'B' bit is one that works off different pressure points than my A bit. The B has a different mouthpiece, and my choice of leverage is determined by the horse's performance. This gives me the tools to maximize the horse's performance, not just make him good.

"The 'C' bit is a downgrade from my A and B bits. I switch to this C bit if a horse becomes pushy or bullish. I've found this is better than upgrading to a stronger bit because that usually creates more anxiety in the horse and enhances the problem. Choosing progressively stronger bits is usually indicative of a training or communication problem, not a bitting problem. It's best to use the mildest bit that keeps a horse respectful, even if that's just a classic snaffle."

### Do straight shanks function differently from curved shanks?

**Black:** "If the shank has a 'C' shape and curves back, it's going to engage more slowly than straight shanks because, with the curved shanks, the bit doesn't even make contact until it's pulled at 45 degrees. This is why some horses are more relaxed in curved-shanked bits than those with straight shanks. But whether a bit has straight shanks or curved shanks, the curb-strap adjustment is also a very important factor in how quickly the bit engages."

**Vogt:** "The configuration of the cheekpieces can be totally different but have the same leverage. Say one bit has shanks that curve back and another bit has totally straight shanks, but they both have the same measurements and are 3-to-1 leverage. This means if I put one ounce of pull on the reins, this gives three ounces of pull through leverage on the curb strap. Regardless of the shank design—whether it's shaped like a lightning bolt or is straight up and down—the numbers are the numbers and the leverage is the same. The difference is that curved shanks potentially can engage the curb strap much more slowly than straight shanks."

### How do you adjust the curb strap when using a shanked bit?

**Black:** "The popular rule of thumb is to be able to slide two fingers between the horse's jaw and the curb strap. But there also can be other reasons to make it tighter or looser, depending on fine-tuning the direction you want to give with the bit. You want to adjust the curb strap to make sure it has the proper effect on the bit. If you have the curb strap overly tight with straight shanks, this really can make a horse overly reactive.

"When starting in a spade bit, I make the curb strap a bit tighter because I don't want the horse to experience too much pressure on the palate. The curb strap adjustment dictates the amount of gag and leverage, as well as the effects of gag and leverage. My goal is to be somewhere in the middle, with no extremes on either gag or leverage. Without a curb strap, there is no effect of leverage, and if the curb strap is too tight, the horse gets no presignal before the pressure from the bit is there."

**Vogt:** "As kids, we were told that you should be able to slide two fingers between the curb strap and chin. But if your curb strap is too loose with a high-leverage bit, the shanks over-rotate [to become parallel to the ground] and have zero leverage effect. Every mouthpiece has to rotate a certain amount in order to have a presignal sequence, whether it's tongue to palate, or to bars. Underrotating and/or over-rotating a bit's shanks and mouthpiece has extreme effects on the horse's responses.

"A good baseline is to adjust the curb strap so that it stops the bit at 50 percent of the swing of the shanks, or halfway, if with no curb strap you can pull the bit back and parallel to the ground. You might need to adjust the curb strap up or down a hole, depending on how the horse responds. Used properly, the curb strap is the final signal; it's the 'enforcer.' If the horse responds as he should—meaning he responds to the presignal of the bit moving in his mouth—the curb strap just touches or brushes his chin, but never gets really tight or causes pain."

*Despite the speed of the work, the horse appears responsive to and comfortable with the rider's choice of bit.*
DARRELL DODDS

## What about headstall adjustment?

**Black:** "I don't want to follow the English rule of tightening the headstall until I have two small wrinkles in the corners of mouth. The bit should rest on the tongue for the horse to carry it. Horses have plenty of feel on the tongue, palate and corners of the mouth. My philosophy about bitting is more about having the horse mentally prepared so he's educated and motivated to do what I ask. Then he can operate off the signal of the bit, not the pain from a rider having to abuse his mouth with the bit."

**Vogt:** "I want to adjust the headstall so that the bit is in the horse's mouth comfortably touching the corners, but not wrinkling them. During one ride, I might adjust the headstall up or down as much as two holes, and might lengthen or shorten the curb strap possibly one hole. Adjustment is not static; it never stays the same. If you're riding a lot and asking for a lot from your horse, changing the adjustment keeps the horse from becoming dull because he's too familiar with the pressure points of the bit."

# 10
# Hackamores

First things first: Is it a hackamore or a bosal? Many people refer to the same piece of equipment by both words, and use them interchangeably. When referring to this piece of braided rawhide or leather equipment, either word is widely accepted.

The word "hackamore" is actually a substitution—or corruption, depending on how you look at it—of the Spanish word *jaquima,* which means "headstall." The nosepiece, or bosal, is spelled *bozal* in Spanish and translates as "muzzle" or "halter."

## Rich History

The tradition of hackamore training arrived in the New World centuries ago, brought to this country from the Spanish conquistadors. Their methods eventually were passed along by the California vaqueros and remain popular with many horsemen to this day.

Early vaqueros started their horses' careers by riding them in hackamores, gradually changing in weight and diameter to lighter and smaller bosals as horses progressed in their training. It could take a year or longer for a horse to be ready to start in the two-rein phase, when he was fitted with a bridle bit, but initially still directed primarily by the mecate reins on a small bosal under the bridle. Only after several more years of training and fine-tuning was a horse considered finished. He was, at that point, in a full spade bit, complete with romal reins, and referred to as "straight up in the bridle," although tradition dictated that he still wear a thin "pencil" bosal, or *bosalito,* under the bridle, but without the mecate reins.

However, many modern horsemen, who train in the hackamore, like to start colts in snaffles first, and then follow the traditional progression.

*Hackamore training, as does the two-rein phase, reflects only a portion of the work required to develop the traditional full-bridle horse.*

ROBERT DAWSON

Because horses are individuals and not all respond the same, there's no exact science on choosing what weight and diameter hackamore to use. The mecate reins used also correspond in size to the bosal. For example, a colt ridden in a ⅝-inch bosal has a ⅝-inch mecate. The standard sequence is to use a thicker, heavier bosal for starting the horse, then to move

*The hackamore tradition continues, thanks to the vaqueros, who loved fine horses, horsemanship expertise, and artistically crafted gear.*

KATE BRADLEY

him into a medium-sized bosal, with the mecate also decreasing in size and weight, and finally to a thin, lightweight version as the horse makes the transition to a ported bit.

The hackamore operates off direct pressure—not leverage—and is ridden by using both hands. Those who train in a hackamore find it unparalleled for developing softness and flexion in the horse.

## Pieces and Parts

Let's break down the hackamore and look at the various pieces of the puzzle:

- **bosal:** consists of nose button, cheek buttons, cheeks and heel knot

- **hanger:** headstall or leather strap that adjusts to place the bosal higher or lower on the horse's nose

- **cheek string lash:** thin leather string running under the jaw and tied to both sides of hanger; used only to pull hanger slightly away from eyes

- **fiador:** rope throatlatch going over the poll, directly behind the ears, and attaching to bosal at the heel knot; stabilizes bosal and correctly positions it

- **browband:** addition to hackamore to hold fiador, or rope throatlatch, in place

- **forelock hanger:** narrow strip of leather to help support the bosal; attaches to the bosal nose button with other end tied to the horse's forelock; occasional use as not on all hackamores

- **mecate:** long one-piece rein attached above bosal heel knot and tied in one of several knot options to form a loop rein, with the tail being used as a lead; traditionally of mane hair, but also made of synthetic materials

Because the fiador and browband can limit the movement of the hackamore, some horsemen use these to support the bosal early in training, but remove them when the horse is

*Despite great variety in appearance, all hackamores share the same basic construction.*
DARRELL DODDS

further along. Most riders following California vaquero tradition remove the fiador when that support is no longer needed, but others leave the fiador as part of the complete hackamore rig. There is no right or wrong method, just personal preference and tradition.

"The fiador was originally used as a safety factor because when cowboys started riding broncs, the fiador kept the horse from pulling the hackamore off his head.

Also, if the cowboy came off, the hackamore would stay on and he'd still have control," explains Benny Guitron, longtime horseman and trainer, whose Benny Guitron Ranch is located in Merced, California. "As the horse became more gentle and was learning to work, the rider would take off the fiador because the hackamore doesn't release with the fiador. Then the rider could start developing the lightness and feel he wanted."

*The cheek string lash is tied to both sides of the hackamore hanger to pull it slightly away from the horse's eyes.*

DARRELL DODDS

## Materials and Construction

Granted, some hackamores are truly works of art, but you can't select one only for looks and craftsmanship. The materials used for a hackamore and the way it's made are important when deciding what to use, but the horse has a say in the matter. For example, a thin-skinned horse probably won't be able to tolerate a coarsely braided bosal with a stiff core although a horse with heavier bone and/or thicker skin might be fine in that type bosal. This is where good horsemanship comes into hackamore selection.

"There's no black-and-white method to training in any discipline, and this also applies to picking headgear for a horse. You have to look at the individual," notes Guitron. "With a really sensitive-skinned horse, a rawhide hackamore might be a little too much, even if you add a little electrician's tape to smooth out the rawhide braiding."

Depending on the material and construction, each hackamore has a different feel, weight and diameter. The higher the plait, the softer and smoother the finished surface, so a 12-plait bosal is coarser than a 32-plait bosal. Material options include:

- rawhide, the most traditional.

- leather, with latigo leather common. But cowhide is not the only choice; kangaroo and goat leather also are soft, but strong.

- rope of nylon or hemp, or even a horse-hair rope similar to that used in a mecate.

The core gives the bosal body and the ability to hold its shape through time and use. Some bosals are made with a nylon or cable core, but traditional horsemen insist on a rawhide core.

"The core is the most important part and no buts about it: A rawhide core is the best and holds its shape through use. It's also the traditional material," says Al Dunning, longtime horseman and trainer, who trains Quarter Horses at his Almosta Ranch in Scottsdale, Arizona.

"I like a rawhide core with a medium twist because it has a little flexibility and isn't too stiff, but isn't limp and without body.

"When you pull on a hackamore, it should have a little give and a little bite, and then

*Although hackamore cheeks typically are braided rawhide, such materials as rope or horsehair are sometimes used instead.*

ROBERT DAWSON

your hands do the rest of the work. When you release, it should spring back into shape. That's why you want a rawhide core, because a nylon or cable core can't do this the same way and doesn't have the same feel."

Some horsemen can tell by handling and flexing a bosal whether the core is rawhide or not. Dunning says the only way to ensure you're getting a good rawhide core is to buy from a reputable maker. He adds, "In the old days, the judges carried magnets to see if there was steel, cable or BBs in the cores, which were illegal."

There are times when you might want to vary the feel of the hackamore without changing to a different weight or diameter. For example, you might soften the potential severity of a hard or coarsely plaited bosal by wrapping it with sheepskin or electrical tape. Either option is a satisfactory temporary measure to change the feel of the nose button and/or cheeks.

## Fit and Adjustment

Each horse's head is different, so it's impossible to have a one-size-fits-all hackamore. Some horses have longer muzzles than others, so you must examine the horse's head structure before you can fit the hackamore.

"I like mine to rest midway between eye and muzzle," says Guitron. "I'll ride it up and down until I find the place that is most comfortable for that horse. Placement isn't cut and dried, although it would be nice if it was."

With your hand on the bridge of your horse's nose, notice the spot where bone ends and the cartilage and soft tissue begin. If you place the hackamore in this area, it's too low.

On the other hand, if the heel knot isn't touching the chin when your reins are slack, you have the hackamore too high and tight.

Correct placement is for the hackamore to rest on the bridge of the nose and for the heel knot and mecate wrap to rest at the chin when there is no tension on the reins. The shorter the noseband, the closer the headstall or hanger is to the eye and the more the heel knot drops.

You might fine-tune the adjustment for your particular horse, but if the nose button of the hackamore is about halfway between the horse's muzzle and eyes, this is considered standard fit.

"If you adjust the hackamore properly, when you pick up the reins, this gives the horse a signal because the nosepiece gradually tips down, and the back and side of the hackamore work on the whole face," Guitron

**131**

*General guidelines provide a starting point for hackamore adjustment, which can then be fine-tuned for a particular horse's head structure.*

JOHN BRASSEAUX

explains. "When you use a direct rein, the outside of the hackamore lays against a horse's face, on the outside, which is preparing him for the neck rein.

"The purpose of the heel knot is to provide weight to give the horse the release while you're developing lightness," he adds. "Heel knots vary in size, but I like to stay with a traditional size. Some people use weighted heel knots, but to me, a weighted knot is too heavy and doesn't let the horse have a real signal; it's just 'dead' and sits there. A hackamore has to be made so that it's balanced, or it doesn't function properly, and the horse doesn't learn the proper way of carrying it."

## Hackamore Care

With the proper care, a well-made hackamore easily can last your lifetime.

"I have hackamores I use today that were made in the 1940s," says Guitron. "The main thing is to keep the hackamore clean. If you put in a long day and your horse gets sweaty, you can clean your hackamore with saddle soap and put a little vaquero cream on it, but definitely do not put any oil on it. Oil rots the rawhide.

"With a leather bosal, just clean it like you would a saddle, but don't oil it. If it's made of nylon, you can wash it with water if you need to. You could pull a car with a nylon hackamore and nothing happens to this one."

## Q & A: More About Hackamore Use

Both tradition and mystique surround hackamore use. Many riders want to learn more about it, but aren't sure where to turn. Industry icons Al Dunning and Benny Guitron have made hackamore training an integral part of how they develop young horses. The men have collaborated on *The Art of Hackamore Training*, a *Western Horseman* book released in 2012, and also have kindly shared some of their experience and insights in this chapter. Guitron is a member of the National Reined Cow Horse Hall of Fame, and holds numerous American Quarter Horse Association world titles, as well as cow-horse snaffle-bit futurity and bridle-horse championships. Dunning has won AQHA world championships in reining, cutting, working cow horse and western riding, and has been a finalist in major National Cutting Horse Association events, as well as the NRCHA World's Greatest Horseman competition.

**Do you start all your young horses in a hackamore?**

**Guitron:** "There are plenty of guys who have a lot of success going from the snaffle to the bridle without using a hackamore. I showed my first hackamore horse when I was 14 in 1964, and I broke him in the hackamore. I was trained the old way of first riding in a hackamore and then going to the two-rein, and then the bridle. I think I make a better horse when I do this, rather than riding in a snaffle and then going to the bridle.

"If you want to train traditionally, I don't think there's any other way than starting with a hackamore. There's nothing wrong about staying in a hackamore, say, if you're going to trail ride and you're content doing that. I, personally, want to strive for more excellence, so I take the time it takes to advance the horse into the bridle. The discipline a horse learns by being ridden in the hackamore is crucial and so good for the end product."

**Dunning:** "My personal way is to start in a snaffle and get the horse where I want him, and then put him in a hackamore for a period of time, anywhere from 6 months to a year. I find it's a very important transition between direct-reining and neck-reining, because the hackamore teaches this as I ride with two

hands on the mecate and touch the neck with the reins as I guide the horse.

"With a snaffle, the horse gives the side of his mouth first, then his nose, then his ear, then his neck, then his shoulder. When you go to a bosal, you get all this, but with more flexion in the poll, because the bosal causes him to drop his nose more, follow his nose and also teaches him to neck-rein. Then when you go to the bridle, the horse is completely soft, so the transition is much easier.

"A lot of times we don't have the opportunity to ride for 6 months or more in a hackamore because people want to show their horses, so they want us to get them in a bridle sooner than that. Traditionally, if I can keep horses in a hackamore for a year or so, it really helps them. That puts the best feel on a horse of any equipment I can use."

### How do you know what size and type hackamore to use?

**Guitron:** "What you start with depends on the individual horse, and it also can depend on whether you're starting to break a horse in the hackamore or transitioning from a snaffle.

There's nothing cut in stone. Traditionally, you want a larger weight and diameter when starting out a horse in the hackamore, and then you work your way down to lighter weight and smaller diameter. It's an educated

*Traditionally, a hackamore of larger diameter is used when starting a horse, with a gradual progression to a smaller, lighter hackamore as the horse's training advances.*
ROBERT DAWSON

*A savvy hackamore horseman learns to "play" his horse into position, rather than pulling and tugging on the hackamore.*
ROBERT DAWSON

# MAKE IT WORK FOR YOU

## Tying the Mecate

There's more than one way to tie your mecate to the hackamore, although we look at only one here. (To learn additional methods, check out *The Art of Hackamore Training*.) In this method, which Benny Guitron prefers, the lead rope portion of the mecate extends from the back of the bosal and alongside the loop rein.

Before you start, uncoil the mecate and make sure it is smooth and has no kinks. When taking your wraps with the mecate, always go to the right.

*Place the tassel end of the mecate down through the V created by the heel knot, leaving a couple inches dangling below the knot, and bring the mecate over the right cheek.*

ROBERT DAWSON

*Start your first wrap, but before completing it, pull your rein loop through the V, as shown.*

ROBERT DAWSON

Cross the loop rein to reduce the risk of the rein feeding through this setup, which has fewer wraps than other methods.
ROBERT DAWSON

Make one or two wraps on top of the crossed rein to achieve the appropriate fit for your horse's muzzle.
ROBERT DAWSON

Complete the final wrap by bringing the mecate tail from the side, through the V and beneath the final wrap, so the tail extends through the back of your hackamore, next to the rein.
ROBERT DAWSON

Make sure the lead rope rests to the side of the loop rein, as shown here from the tassel side. When this hackamore is on your horse, with the tassel hanging down, the lead is on your horse's near side.
ROBERT DAWSON

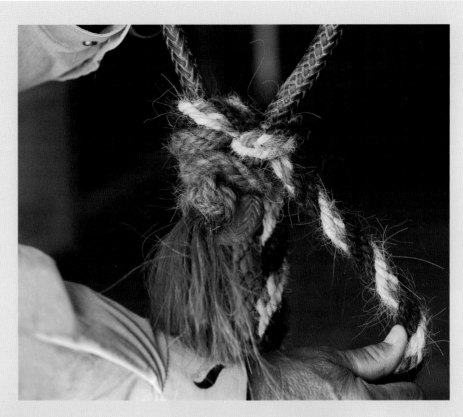

Pull everything snug, but not so snug that the hackamore becomes narrow or tight against your horse's lower jaw. Finally, open your hackamore by pulling the cheeks apart near the mecate.
ROBERT DAWSON

guess as to which you use first, and it's really trial-and-error as you find what makes each horse comfortable.

"Sometimes, a filly is more sensitive than a stud colt, and I start her in a ½-inch. A horse that is more coarsely made in the face can take a bigger hackamore. I don't have a favorite material, and I own 25 to 30 hackamores, but if I could only have two, then I'd have a ⅝-inch diameter and a ½-inch diameter, and the material would be rawhide."

**Dunning:** "What you pick, plait-wise and material-wise, depends on the horse. For example, a 12-plait is much rougher than a 32-plait. Most of mine are ⅝-inch, and I like a latigo or kangaroo braided bosal, but if I could have only one, it would be a ⅝-inch rawhide-braided Don Brown hackamore."

### Can you explain why you prefer different lengths of hackamores?

**Guitron:** "I like a shorter hackamore, 10- to 10½ inches [from nose button to bottom of heel knot]. I think it's a better fit for our smaller, modern horses. Also, I like to take fewer wraps with my mecate on the heel knot because I think this shorter hackamore doesn't bounce or move around excessively. That can cause irritation and confuse the horse about the rider's signals."

**Dunning:** "I prefer a longer hackamore, anywhere from 11 to 13 inches because I like to put on 3 or 4 wraps, a couple more than Benny does. I think the additional length and wraps add a little more weight to the bottom of the heel knot, which gives more of a distinct signal to the horse and falls away faster when I release."

### What are some insider tips you've learned when it comes to riding with a hackamore?

**Guitron:** "I think a common mistake people often make is that, instead of taking baby steps, a person rides a horse until he gets dull. The person lays into the hackamore until the horse pulls on him."

**Dunning:** "A hackamore isn't made to pull; it's made to rock. You need feel and rhythm to use it. You need to let the rocking of the hackamore do the work. Depending on a

rider's hands, the horse's jaw and/or nose can get scuffed up, but I like to say, 'It takes two to tango,' meaning the horse and rider both pulling. You want to 'play' the horse back into position—not pull him—and make it his idea to give. If you're bad with your hands, the horse can just stick his nose through and run off. You need educated hands. Riding in a hackamore teaches you to have soft and patient hands, where you play the horse rather than insist. The best way to learn is to ride with someone who's into the tradition of hackamore training."

## Mechanical Hackamores

The name says it all: This headgear works off the mechanics of leverage—putting pressure on the horse's nose, chin and poll—offering a way to stop the horse without having anything in his mouth. Far less sophisticated than a bosal, the mechanical hackamore is better for slowing and stopping a horse than it is for turning, encouraging flexion, or doing any type of precision riding. This headgear is not meant for training a horse or giving subtle signals. In fact, a horse should know how to neck-rein if you ride him in a mechanical hackamore, because it isn't designed for direct-reining.

*Although a mechanical hackamore might seem a mild piece of headgear to use, as always, severity depends on the rider's hands.*

COURTESY EQUIBRAND

Mechanical hackamores are favored by riders for different reasons, including convenience, control, and cases in which a horse's mouth or tongue has been injured. Some guest-ranch owners outfit their dude-string horses with hackamores so novices don't jerk and pull on the horses' mouths. Mechanical hackamores aren't limited to Western tack; they're even seen on horses competing on the international show-jumping circuit and, occasionally, on endurance horses.

Some advertisements for mechanical hackamores boast that they offer good "stopping action." That might be true—and it's probably their biggest selling point—but just because there is no bit doesn't mean this is a gentle way to control a horse. As with a bit, a mechanical hackamore is only as mild—or as severe—as the hands of the rider using it. Hard, heavy hands on this type of equipment can cause pain and injury, in extreme cases even damaging the nose or breaking the horse's jaw.

As with a traditional hackamore, a mechanical hackamore should rest on the bony bridge of the nose, never so low on any horse's face that the gear rests on the cartilage. To function properly, the mechanical hackamore requires a curb chain or strap. As with a curb bit, the adjustment of the curb chain or strap varies, depending on a horse's sensitivity, noseband construction and the rider's hands. The tighter the curb chain or strap, the quicker the horse feels pressure from the mechanical hackamore.

## Mechanical Hackamore Materials

The material of the noseband plays a significant role, as some materials have more potential for abuse than others. These materials include:

- rubber-covered bicycle chain, with the greatest potential for severity.

- braided rawhide.

- leather braiding.

- rounded, rolled leather.

- flat leather with fleece lining and the least potential for severity.

Shanks range from about 4 to 9 inches and usually are made of stainless steel or plated metal. They are typically—but not always—held together at the bottom with a hobble, which might be a thin metal bar, a piece of chain or cable.

## Sidepulls

When starting young horses, some riders like to use sidepulls, which really are just a form of bitless bridle. The sidepull also is used by some trail riders, who don't want to use a bit on older horses for any variety of reasons.

The sidepull does not work off leverage, but rather lateral signal and some nose pressure. Just as the name implies, this type of headgear directs the horse as the rider pulls on the reins attached to rings on either side. The noseband, made of rope or leather, comes in varying widths. Depending on the material and width, a noseband can be more harsh, as with a thin, single-rope noseband, or less harsh, as with a wide, padded leather noseband.

Unlike the heel knot on a bosal, there is no weight at the bottom of a sidepull. If you intend to put a colt in a bosal for part of his training, many trainers think using the sidepull is a waste of time.

"You can't put the finesse and feel on a horse with a sidepull that you can with the bosal or snaffle," observes Dunning.

However, if you aren't ever going to ride the horse in a bosal, a sidepull might be a useful tool in the early training stages, to teach the young horse to turn, give to pressure, and understand direct-reining—without carrying a bit in his mouth. Then he can graduate to a snaffle once he has mastered these basic lessons. In fact, you can buy a sidepull with a snaffle bit attached.

A sidepull should conform to the horse's head and fit like a regular bridle. The noseband shouldn't be so low that it rests on the nose cartilage, but if the noseband is too high, it loses much of its effect. The chin strap should be neither tight nor loose; you might have to try different adjustments on both noseband and chin strap to find the right amount of control and comfort.

Remember, too, that as with any type of headgear, the more constantly a rider pulls on it, the more likely a horse is to become insensitive to the sidepull.

*The sidepull works off lateral signal instead of leverage.*

COURTESY EQUIBRAND

## Sidepull Materials

The headstall portion of the sidepull is typically leather, ranging from harness to skirting or latigo leather. However, there are several variations when it comes to nosebands:

- single-rope noseband

- double-rope noseband

- rolled-leather noseband

- padded-leather noseband

- leather noseband encasing a cable or wire core

- single- or double-rope noseband with attached snaffle

Another sidepull option is the braided-rope sidepull, sometimes referred to as a "loping halter" or "training halter." Commonly made of polypropylene or similar material, this lightweight, inexpensive bitless option typically has four knots in the noseband and rings on the sides, where the reins attach. This option basically looks much like a standard rope halter, except for the additional knots in the noseband, and is meant to fit fairly snugly around the nose.

# 11
# Reins and Mecates

Whether you're riding a young colt in his first hackamore, exploring new territory on a good trail horse, or showing a finished horse straight up in the bridle, reins are among your most essential equipment. This holds true for someone riding with a custom bit worth hundreds of dollars or a simple snaffle that costs less than $50 at the neighborhood tack shop.

Although you don't find as wide a range of choices in reins as you do bits, there are still plenty of selections, whatever your style or riding interest. Unless you compete in disciplines or breed shows that have specific requirements in their rules, the type and length of reins are more about personal preference and comfort than anything else.

"In our area, we sell a lot of split reins, but we also sell a lot of reins and romals, and mecates, too. It really depends on what kind of rig you're riding," says Scott Grosskopf of Buckaroo Businesses in Billings, Mont., the company he and wife Staci started in 1998.

Grosskopf uses much of the gear he sells and also teaches ranch-roping clinics. "For the most part, the guys in this business have to know the gear to sell it; it's hard to sell it without knowing how it works," he says. "We try to keep up with the Great Basin and vaquero traditions with horsehair and rawhide gear, and we sell a lot of ranch rope."

## Split Reins

Preferred by many working cowboys and riders in different Western disciplines for both tradition and convenience, split reins:

- traditionally are made of leather, with harness leather considered top quality.

- also can be made of rawhide, nylon, horsehair and sometimes a combination of materials.

- commonly are found in 8-foot, as well as 8½-foot lengths.

- might have leather poppers on the ends.

Traditionalists don't opt for nylon, but plenty of riders like the durability of nylon and the fact that it's basically maintenance-free.

"We have guys who buy reins and romals from us to use when the weather is good, but they have split reins for regular use," notes Grosskopf. "Guys who ride in a lot of brush use these because they don't want to get their good reins and romals torn up, or when they ride in a heavy rain storm."

Split reins have a distinct advantage over a one-piece loop rein or a mecate when riding in thick brush. If a rein gets hung on brush, you just drop one rein and then lean down to catch it while a one-piece loop rein or a mecate can get hung on something and turn a horse around pretty quickly.

Available in single-ply leather, as well as doubled-and-stitched leather, split reins come in different diameters available in a variety of lengths. Some have leather poppers on the ends.

"Rein diameter is strictly personal preference. We split the reins from ⅜-, ½-, ⅝-, ¾- and 1-inch diameters. Some people like bigger diameters because those feel more secure and are less likely to run through their hands," says Grosskopf. "With split reins, we've found that ⅝-inch has been the most popular. That size is supple and feels good. It isn't too big in your hands, but it's not too light; it still has some weight and release."

*Enthusiasm for horsehair and rawhide headgear has spread far beyond such regions as the Great Basin, where buckaroos have long preferred traditional equipment.*

JENNIFER DENISON

*Split reins with water ties, a classic design, are available in several widths, lengths and weights at most tack shops.*

COURTESY EQUIBRAND

Although 8-foot split reins are probably the most common, you can also find 8½- and 9-foot lengths.

The type of leather used and the manner of construction affect the weight of the reins. For example, a single-ply leather rein can have a weighted, tapered end when cut with the heavy portion of the hide at the rein end. Grosskopf finds that heavier split reins are popular with snaffle bit-rigs.

"We also sell a lot of ½-inch and ⅝-inch doubled-and-stitched split reins that are heavily oiled," says Grosskopf. "Cutters really like to use these. They like the release in the reins so when they give the rein to the horse, he feels that drop. The oil helps make the rein very supple, but it also gives weight. If you don't oil these doubled-and-stitched reins, they can be a bit stiff."

## One-Piece Reins

Because they are frequently used by ropers, barrel racers and contestants in other speed events, one-piece reins, also referred to as sport, game or loop reins, are ideal for riders who don't want to worry about dropping their reins.

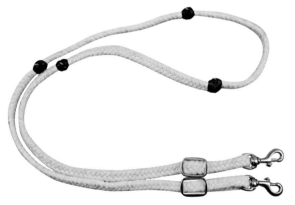

*Barrel racers and ropers typically use a one-piece loop rein, such as this mohair version that is soft in hand yet easy to grip.*

COURTESY EQUIBRAND

Depending on the rider, a one-piece rein might have a center section wrapped in suede, made of braided or plaited leather or rawhide, or even have a few evenly spaced grips or knots. All these designs are meant to offer a secure handhold in events where winning and losing is often determined by fractions of a second. Of course, you don't have to compete to appreciate the convenience of a one-piece rein; some trail riders also favor this style.

Length varies; speed event competitors often want a 7- or 7½-foot rein instead of one longer. Diameter also varies and depends on personal preference. A roper, for example, typically wants a smaller diameter rein in his or her hand while someone starting colts or trail riding might want a thicker diameter. There is no rule; it's just what feels best to the individual rider.

One-piece reins can be round or flat and are found in most all the same materials as split reins, including:

- leather, usually single-ply in widths from ⅜-inch to 1-inch.

- buttered nylon, which is extra soft and flexible, but strong and durable.

- hollow-braid nylon that's soft and supple, but durable, and has good weight.

- yacht braid that's durable, yet supple with good feel.

- horsehair, preferably mane hair, but of variable weights.

## Romal Reins

Those competing in reining, reined-cow-horse, trail and Western pleasure classes often ride with this closed style of rein. Vaquero tradition is obvious in romal reins, typically used only when a bit has shanks—never with a snaffle bit.

Unlike split reins, romal reins are a closed set of reins with a loop, which is attached to the romal, a long braided extension resembling a quirt with a leather popper on the end. Typically 4 to 5 feet long, the romal is flexible, but heavy, which keeps it from swinging around wildly. The closed loop rein

*The two-rein phase of traditional bridle-horse training makes use of both the mecate on the bosalito and a romal rein on the shanked bit.*

attaches to the bit, or rein chains if used, with rawhide or leather connectors.

The time and craftsmanship that go into creating a set of romal reins are apparent, and quality romal reins easily can run into hundreds of dollars. Romal reins:

- are made of braided rawhide or leather, and occasionally nylon.

- can be made in eight-, 12-, 16-, and up to 34-plaits.

- vary in diameter, generally from ⅜- to ⁵⁄₁₆-inch.

- tend to be softer and more pliable when thinner in diameter.

- have rawhide button patterns, a series of knots strategically placed to add weight and feel.

- can have silver ferrules that give extra weight and drape to the rein.

# EXPERT TIP

## The Rig and the Task at Hand

On a working ranch, equipment choice is typically based on practicality. At the Pate Ranch in Ryegate, Mont., clinicians and ranchers Curt and Tammy Pate choose reins for specific reasons.

"I like riding with heavy split reins," says Tammy Pate. "I like the feel of leather reins, and I prefer them, but I also ride with a mecate when we're branding or doctoring cattle and getting on and off. I use a mecate then, instead of split reins, just because this gives me a lead rope and, also, the horse won't step on the reins."

"I very seldom use split reins myself. All my snaffle bits have a mecate on them, but that's also because I ride outside all the time, not in an arena," says Curt Pate. "I do everything horseback, whether I'm checking fence, irrigating, or moving cattle. I ride with a snaffle bit a lot, because I'm training on most horses. With ranch work, I get off my horse a lot and the get-down—the lead rope part of the mecate—allows me to do that, yet still have a nice rein that is easy to manage. It's like split reins when it comes to weight and feel, but it's easy to manage when doing cowboy work or trail riding. I also think I get a little better feel with the mecate than with split leather reins because I have big hands and I like the thicker mecate rein."

Curt finds the slight additional weight of the slobber straps and mecate on his snaffle bit rig offers the horse a quick sort of "double release" when he releases pressure.

There's no rule about which side to have the get-down part of the mecate. That is all about personal preference.

"I put my mecate lead on the right side because I do a lot of things left-handed," Curt says. "I have heard negative comments about one side being a little heavier because the rein and lead rope part are on the same side, but I have never seen a horse different on the left or right side because of this."

Curt braids his own mecates out of parachute cord, using a 12-strand herringbone braid. He also has horsehair mecates, but young horses can be tough on equipment and the parachute cord can take a lot of punishment.

"I have one real nice hair setup and I'm pretty careful what I ride with that," he says. "I don't want the colts chewing on my hair mecate."

When he isn't working on a young colt, Curt often uses reins and romal.

"On a finished horse I love riding in reins and romal. I really like how the romal balances my reins, and I can also use it as a quirt, similar to a dressage whip," he notes. "A lot of the Californio and reined-cow-horse riding comes from dressage. I always keep my reins and romal in the same hand and if I need the romal, I split it off. Some people use the romal to slap their chaps and make a little noise, but I'm not really into noise when I'm working cattle."

Curt always uses rein chains with his reins and romal.

"I'm a traditionalist, and rein chains are the tradition. I also think they add to the balance and give a true proper release. When I pick up on my reins, the rein chains actually give the horse a presignal that the signal is coming, so I need very little actual movement of the bit itself.

"I also just like the tradition of the reins and romal," he adds. "With the rawhide work, it's almost like riding with a painting on your horse, or like a good tattoo. When you see someone with good gear, you know they either have a lot of money or know how to braid!"

- should never be oiled if made of rawhide, but kept dry, and can be wiped down with a soft cloth if dampened in a sudden rainstorm.

"We sell a lot of eight-plait reins and romals, but 12–plait are our biggest sellers," says Grosskopf. "The 12-plait are popular because they hold up and are pliable. They feel really good and have good suppleness, whether you're riding two-rein or straight up in the bridle."

The strands of rawhide usually are beveled on both sides to make an especially smooth rein and romal. The finer the braid, the smaller diameter the rein; the coarser the plait, the thicker the rein.

"With a heavy rein and romal, you can move your hand very little to send signal down that rein," Grosskopf notes. "The lighter the rein the more you have to move your hand."

Those braided rawhide buttons on reins and romals in a wide range of patterns do more than just look good.

"Buttons offer weight, balance and signal," explains Grosskopf. "If you have a decent set of rawhide reins with no buttons, they feel pretty flat and 'dead.' How the buttons are set and how far up the reins they go has a lot to do with balance and signal. You might want a heavier romal with a horse when he's straight up in the bridle than with a younger horse."

Grosskopf says that there are probably endless button patterns, but two of the most popular are the traditional Oklahoma and California styles.

"The traditional Oklahoma pattern has five round buttons up the reins, a long barrel knot and then five pineapple knots and another barrel knot, which adds a lot of weight to it, but they don't wear as much as a more ornate pattern. The California pattern has five small Spanish ring knots, a pineapple knot, five small Spanish ring knots and then a barrel knot. They're very ornate, very showy, but also very useful. Depending on the braider, these patterns can vary slightly, but those are the general descriptions. They are always rawhide or leather, and have a decorative weighted popper on the end that may have elaborate tooling or carving."

Grosskopf finds another popular choice is the Santa Ynez style, in which eight rawhide plaits are divided into two sets of four, then rejoined into eight. Not only does this look fancy, but it also adds life to the rein.

"For a really finished bridle horse, a lot of guys like a set of Santa Ynez reins. You'd probably ride only your best horse in these reins," he adds. "They lay flat in your hand and have a great feel. If you have 70 feet of reata in your hand, these [reins] lay really nicely in your hand."

## Connectors

Whichever style of reins you use, there are several ways to connect them to a bit, and choice depends on personal preference.

**Water ties,** leather loops that attach with leather laces or sometimes small buckles:

- can protect headstall and reins because they usually break before the rein does.

- provide additional length to protect reins from moisture, much like a slobber strap or rein chain.

- are inexpensive and easy to replace. "Your reins are only as good and as strong as your water ties," cautions Grosskopf. "Be sure to check their condition regularly because they can get worn out."

*Many rein attachments are designed for quickly changing the reins from one bit to another.*

COURTESY EQUIBRAND

**Buttons,** which fasten simply by passing through loops:

- are made of either leather or rawhide.

- usually break before the rein when a horse steps on a rein or during an emergency.

- are attractive, but inexpensive and easy to replace.

- often are used with rein chains.

**Slobber straps** are pieces of leather that loop around the snaffle bit rings and have a large hole in each end, so you push the mecate through the holes and attach it with an overhand knot. Slobber straps:

- can be plain or fancy with stitching, stamping or carving.

- also can be single-ply or doubled-and-stitched leather.

- range from 4 to 8 inches long.

- can add weight and signal to the snaffle.

- help keep reins in better condition by protecting them from moisture from the horse's mouth and from water if he drinks while bridled.

*Slobber straps used to attach a mecate not only protect the mecate from moisture, but also add weight and signal when cueing a horse.*

COURTESY EQUIBRAND

**Snaps** make it easy to change equipment quickly or to unsnap one rein end to lead the horse, but snaps:

- have moving parts, which can break, stick or fail.

- can interfere with signal because of the constant jiggle and rattle of the snap.

- can numb the horse's mouth, according to many horsemen, or, at the very least, make the horse less sensitive to your cues. If you want snaps for convenience, you can use rein chains attached to the bit and then attach rein snaps at the end of the chains.

**Rein chains** are intended to be used with romal reins, not split reins, and are a form of connector that adds weight, balance and feel, which helps with the bit signal. They also function as "slobber chains" to protect rawhide or leather parts of reins when the horse drinks or chews.

"Working cowboys, and those who are true traditionalists in the manner of bridle bits, want rein chains. Other riders, like reined-cow-horse guys, often want the reins connected straight to the bit," says Grosskopf. "An old-timer was telling me that rein chains go back to the era when knights rode into battle. They didn't want their leather reins to be cut by an opponent or by their own lances or swords, so they added chains. I'm not sure if that's true, but it makes sense."

He notes that riders usually select the color and style of chain based on the bit they're using. For example, someone using a fancy old German silver bit doesn't want bright, shiny stainless-steel rein chains because the colors of the two silvers clash. Rein chains:

- range from 4 to 12 inches long.

- usually are made of stainless steel, which doesn't rust, or carbon steel, which can.

- have different styles of chain-link designs.

- attach to the bit with round swivel rings.

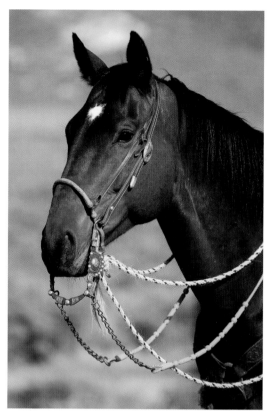

*Rein chains, which are used with romal reins, add weight, balance and feel to complement the bit signal.*

ROSS HECOX

- might have a swivel piece in the center.

- have an S hook at the rein end that is crimped so it can't come undone.

- attach to the reins at the S-hook end with either a rawhide or leather rein connector.

- protect the reins because the chains break first in a wreck or if the horse steps on the rein, especially when using leather rein connectors.

- help increase the life of leather reins since chains channel away moisture from slobber and water if the horse is allowed to drink while bridled.

## Mecates

Galloping full out in a thundering herd of buffalo—some of which easily weighed a ton—was risky business. Consider that Plains Indians hunted these massive animals from the backs of hardy mustangs that typically stood only about 14 hands and weighed around 700 pounds.

Since the hunt often took place over rugged, uneven ground, the odds were high that a running horse might stumble or a buffalo might even career into him. If a rider went down in such conditions, his only hope to avoid being trampled was to be pulled out of the melee by his horse. In addition to simple rawhide bridles looped around the lower jaw, these finely trained and highly valued buffalo ponies often had 15- to 20-foot ropes tied around their necks with the free ends dragging. A falling rider hoped to have enough time to grab hold of the rope and hang on while his horse veered out of the herd. Then the rider could mount again and continue the hunt.

A traditional mecate serves much the same purpose, in that it has saved many a cowboy a long walk home after he hit the ground, whatever the reason. With the tail tucked in his belt, a quick-thinking rider can take hold of his mecate and still have control of his horse, even when the reins are no longer in his grasp.

Who knows what culture made the first twisted hair ropes? While we already know the Plains Indians used them, archeologists also have discovered horsehair ropes at sites in Europe, as well as in North America. In the

*Typically, a mecate is about 22 feet long with a leather popper on one end and a horsehair tassel on the other.*

DARRELL DODDS

**147**

United States, we credit the early vaqueros with introducing the mecate to our cowboy culture. American cowboys often use the term "McCarty," which is simply a corruption of the Spanish word *mecate,* which literally translates as "rope."

The standard length is 22 feet—although mecates can be longer or shorter—with a leather popper on one end and a rawhide knot with horsehair tassel at the other end. This single rope is wrapped around the bosal, as described in Chapter 10, or attached with slobber straps to the snaffle bit, to form both the loop rein and the lead, sometimes referred to as the get-down rope. This free end allows the rider to step off and lead a horse without bringing the reins over the horse's head, a "no-no" for any true vaquero. The tail is either tucked through the mounted rider's belt loop (see tip box on page 144), tied to the saddle strings or hitched around the saddle horn.

Mecates are commonly round, but can be flat, and are available in a variety of diameters. Many horsemen like thicker mecates, ⅝-inch to 1-inch in diameter, when breaking colts, just to have more in their hands although a smaller diameter usually is preferred when roping or riding a horse more advanced in his training.

Early vaqueros used hair ropes on hackamores in the early stages of training bridle horses, and today hair ropes are used for that same purpose, as well as on snaffle-bit rigs. The heavier the mecate, the more signal it offers the horse.

"With a snaffle bit, we sell more mecates, whether nylon or mane hair, than leather reins, and also for a hackamore setup," says Grosskopf.

## Not Just Horsehair

Although purists like traditional horsehair mecates, other types of hair and synthetic materials also are utilized. Hair from angora goats, or mohair, and yak hair can be used, and even human hair although the latter isn't common.

Synthetic mecates are made from nylon parachute cord and also polyester rope. These choices are less expensive, extremely durable and come in a wide range of colors, but traditionalists still prefer real hair with its natural colors and gradations. In addition, real hair rope has feel and life to it that is hard to

*This synthetic mecate is tied with saddle strings, just one way of several to manage the mecate tail while riding.*

ROBERT DAWSON

describe, but preferred by many horsemen over synthetic materials. Material options include:

- **hollow-braid nylon,** which is soft, supple, of good weight, round and typically ¼-, ⅜-, ½-, or ⅝-inch in diameter.

- **solid-braid** nylon that is stiffer than hollow braid, round and typically ½- to ⅝-inch in diameter.

- **parachute cord,** which is supple and of good weight, but can be round or flat. Typically ½- to ⅝-inch in diameter, this type cord comes in almost endless color choices and variations.

- **yacht braid** that is more supple than tree line due to additional strands, yet the typical ½- to ⅝-inch rope has good feel in hand and is available in multiple color choices.

# GOTCHA!

## Tucking Your Tail

There's no written-in-stone rule on where to put your mecate tail. The main thing is to stay safe and to have the tail handy if you need to grab it. You can coil the end and tie it with your saddle strings, or, if you're not roping, take a half-hitch to secure the tail around the horn.

Many riders tuck mecates through their belts, which keeps their mecates right at hand. Just be sure to pull the mecate up through your belt, not down. If you push the mecate tail down through your belt, you can get hung up in an emergency.

"It's really personal preference, but I like to pull it up through my belt and on the right-hand side of my chinks or my chaps so that, when I get on, it's draped across my front," says Scott Grosskopf. "When I get off the horse, it's not across my body and I don't have to turn myself around to get out of the mecate."

*The tail of this horsehair mecate is half-hitched around the saddle horn, rather than fastened with the saddle strings.*

ROBERT DAWSON

*Depending on the day's work and weather, a rider might use a horsehair mecate or one of, for example, yacht-braid or tree-line rope.*

KATE BRADLEY

# MAKE IT WORK FOR YOU

## Caring for a Hair Mecate

For the longest life and to keep it in the best condition, a horsehair mecate should be untied from the hackamore after every use. If not, the rope can develop bends and kinks that might be impossible to remove. Coil and hang the rope separately from the bosal, which helps preserve the life of both mecate and bosal.

If the mecate is especially dirty or sweaty, rinse it with clean water and hang to dry out of direct sunlight.

"If it's really dirty, you can wet it in a sink with lukewarm water," says Scott Grosskopf of Buckaroo Businesses. "I've also taken a new, fairly stiff mecate and put it in warm water with a little Woolite®. I just rinse it and let it hang by its own weight to dry on a fence, and, boy, does it feel good when it's dry."

Grosskopf recommends that you never use strong detergent, saddle soap, leather conditioner or any kind of oil or hair polish on a hair mecate.

• **tree line,** also is known as arborist's rope, which is somewhat stiffer than yacht braid, but less apt to fray or snag as easily. Of good weight, round, and shape-retentive with little to no stretching, tree line usually is white or black with a ⅝-inch diameter.

• **horsehair,** which has natural life and feel, as opposed to synthetic materials, but very little stretch although it gets stiff in humid, wet climates. Typically ¼, ⅜, ½, ⅝, ¾, or 1 inch in diameter, horsehair mecates have various weights due to the cores, also of horsehair, and amount of hair used.

A new horsehair mecate is prickly because of the hair ends along the length of the rope. Unless it's made from tail hair, as the mecate is used, the "prickles" wear off, and then the color pattern looks sharper and more defined.

"We sell a lot of six-strand, twisted-horsehair mecates," says Grosskopf. "Some manufacturers make stuff out of tail hair, but you can hardly grab it with your bare hand. Everything we sell is mane hair."

Grosskopf sells mecates that vary from four- to eight-strand, but says six-strand is most popular and explains that the way strands are twisted affects the feel of the rope.

"If you twist the strands tight to start with, they are stiff and hard in more humid areas, but people in more dry, arid areas like mecates like this," he notes. "Any live fiber is going to stiffen in wet conditions and also can be 'sticky' in your hand until it's broken in. But the natural feel and signal are the plus."

Gone are the days when a real hair mecate was available only in the natural colors of the animal from which it came.

"We sell a lot of barber-pole black-and-white and sorrel-and-white mecates, but since 2010, we've started seeing the trend of people wanting more color variations," says Grosskopf. "We just bought a bunch of white mane hair, and we're dying it pink, green, purple, etc. People are going nontraditional and want bolder colors in their mecates."

Although mecates typically are chosen according to bosal size, it's important that the diameter is the same along the entire rope. The full length should feel consistent when you run your hand along it. Otherwise, once the mecate is tied to the bosal, you can end up with reins of uneven thickness and weight, which is obvious to both you and the horse— and not in a pleasant way.

# 12
# Martingales and Tie-Downs

When it comes to control, balance and collection, there are times when a rider wants to enhance what the bit offers. This is where tie-downs and martingales can come into play. Although commonly seen, these two types of equipment have very different purposes and are used for different reasons. It's important to realize that such gear isn't necessary for every horse, nor should it be standard gear every time you ride.

Someone might say, "I ride with a tie-down; otherwise my horse's head is too high." That might be the case, but that's not the correct reason to use a tie-down. There are a host of reasons why a horse tosses his head or holds it high, including teeth and mouth issues, heavy hands, poor saddle fit, improper training and more. Forcing a horse's head into position manually with a tie-down doesn't address any of those problems.

A tie-down or martingale should be used to accomplish something specific and, because of that, used only when needed—not every time you saddle up to ride.

Properly used, a tie-down helps control the horse's stride and achieve collection and balance, particularly when working at high speeds. Properly used, a martingale serves as a training device to help a horse learn to soften his resistance, give to pressure, and maintain proper body position to perfect athletic maneuvers in the training pen.

## Tie-Downs

What Western riders call a tie-down, English riders refer to as a standing martingale. It is basically the same piece of equipment although there tends to be slightly more slack with a standing martingale. Both styles have a strap attached to the noseband at one end and to the cinch, or girth, at the other. A standing martingale attaches to the noseband of the bridle and also has a neck strap. The tie-down lacks the neck strap and consists of a noseband with a single thin poll strap to hold the noseband in place, as well as the tie-down strap that snaps to the cinch D-ring. Unlike a running martingale with the rider's hands influencing the adjustment, tie-down or standing martingale adjustment is fixed.

"There are several different types of nosebands, depending on what a rider is trying to achieve with rate and feel. They range from a single-rope noseband with a braided-nylon cover, which is the most severe, to a one-inch flat leather noseband, which is the least severe," says Ken Bray, president of Equibrand, a group of manufacturing companies in Granbury, Texas, that includes Classic Rope, Classic Equine, Rattler Rope and Martin Saddlery.

"Think about choosing a noseband as you would a bit. You don't want to overdo it; you need only enough to do the job," notes Bray. "Tie-downs aren't intended to inflict pain, but nosebands are a lot like bits in that in the wrong hands, a bit deemed severe

*A tie-down can help a roping horse achieve and maintain collection and balance when working at top speeds.*
KATE BRADLEY

*Just as with a bit, the severity of a tie-down depends largely on the person using it.*

COURTESY EQUIBRAND

by one person can be really light in the hands of another rider.

"A severe noseband doesn't compensate for a lack of training. All too often, tie-downs are used to compensate for poor training. If a horse is properly broke, he doesn't need a tie-down to maintain a proper headset, unless it's during a high-speed competition, such as roping and barrel racing.

"In performance speed events like these, the noseband and tie-down serve the purpose of giving the horse a balance point when he's at a high rate of speed," he explains. "The horse actually pushes into the tie-down during the run."

## Tie-Down Materials

Some horses are more sensitive than others, so you must be careful in selecting the material for the tie-down noseband. For example, a nylon noseband cover is more

abrasive and rigid than one of smooth leather. A single-rope noseband has more bite than a wide noseband because the pressure is isolated on a smaller area.

When it comes to the tie-down strap, you want strength, but not stretch. Some straps have snaps at each end, making it quick and easy to attach to the noseband ring and the cinch D-ring. The Conway buckle is another common strap attachment option.

The most common options for tie-down nosebands include:

- single rope with braided nylon cover and the greatest potential for severity.

- single rope with no covering.

- a single rope with braided rawhide cover.

- single rope with leather cover.

- double rope with leather cover.

- an inch-wide, flat leather noseband and the least potential for severity.

Common options for tie-down strap materials include:

- harness leather.

- nylon.

- BioThane® over nylon core.

Leather, a traditional strap choice, absorbs sweat and moisture, so must be maintained or the strap becomes stiff and brittle. When exposed to sweat, nylon hardens and becomes stiff with time. BioThane® earns points as a tie-down strap because it can't absorb moisture, so remains flexible and doesn't stiffen with use.

## Adjust the Tie-Down

A tie-down is a static piece of equipment that doesn't fluctuate due to the rider's hand movement. When improperly adjusted and used, a tie-down can cause serious damage to a horse's nose and even destroy nerves. Properly adjusted, a tie-down should put no pressure on the horse when his head is in a normal position as he performs at all gaits.

# GOTCHA!

## Watch those Feet

It takes only a second for a wreck to happen. The last thing you want is for your horse to get a foot over his tie-down strap, yet it can happen in a heartbeat if a horse trips or drops his head low while traveling.

Eliminate this possibility completely and have one less thing to worry about by putting a keeper on your breast collar. The keeper can be as simple as a leather or rawhide loop. At the very least, use a piece of narrow nylon cord to secure the tie-down strap to the center ring of the breast collar. Set the loop loose enough that it doesn't interfere with the strap or its adjustment, but snug enough to prevent slack that could catch a foot.

For this reason alone, it's recommended always to use a breast collar when riding with a tie-down.

Downward pressure should be felt only when and if the horse raises or tosses his head above the normal level.

Set too loosely, a tie-down is completely useless, and when too tight, the tie-down forces a horse's head into an unnatural position, which can lead to muscle soreness. In addition, a too-short tie-down makes it hard for a horse to catch himself when he stumbles, as his first instinct is to raise his head to regain balance.

You might need to make further adjustments after seeing how your horse responds when you start riding him in a tie-down.

"The length of the tie-down strap directly affects how the tie-down functions," says Bray. "The strap should be adjusted so a horse can elevate his head, but not past the point that he loses his ability to become collected."

"The adjustment depends on each horse, but you have to be careful not to make it too tight or too loose," says Chris Cox, life-long horseman and trainer, whose Diamond Double C Ranch is located in Mineral Wells, Texas. "I like to adjust the strap so that when the horse is carrying his head naturally, there's no pressure pushing against him and, at the same time, not too much slack. When the tie-down strap is flopping, it can't be effective, just like a too-loose back cinch."

*A tie-down is similar to a running martingale in that neither interferes with the horse unless his head moves out of the appropriate position.*

KATE BRADLEY

# MAKE IT WORK FOR YOU

## Common Sense and Introducing a Tie-Down

A horse might panic or become reactive when he realizes his head movement is restricted. The first time you use a tie-down, make sure the horse is comfortable with it before you get in the saddle. As when introducing other equipment, spend a little time working with the horse on the ground in a round pen or other enclosed area so he's familiar with the feel of the tie-down before you swing a leg over him to ride.

"If the adjustment is too tight, the horse feels trapped or confined," says Ken Bray of Equibrand. "The first time you use a noseband and tie-down, adjust the strap length as long as you can, and then slowly and gradually shorten it. It's a good idea to let your horse get used to and move into the tie-down strap in a round pen. It's important to let the horse get accustomed to the feel and honor that pressure before you try to do anything on his back."

## Q & A: Ins and Outs of Tie-Down Use

Although the tie-down is a very popular piece of equipment, many riders have questions about when and why to use one. Ken Bray, president of Equibrand, has been riding since childhood. He trains team-roping and calf-roping horses, and competes in team-roping events. Chris Cox, three-time winner of the Road to the Horse colt-starting competition, travels the United States and beyond, conducting horsemanship clinics. Among the most popular clinics at his Diamond Double C Ranch are those held with such ropers as multiple world champions Speed Williams and Rick Skelton. Cox also ropes, and at the 2011 Reno Rodeo Invitational Team Roping, where he headed for partner Slick Robison, the pair took home $120,000 as reserve champions.

### When do you use a tie-down?

**Bray:** "I use a tie-down only when making a roping run. I don't use one when I'm exercising my horse or riding outside the arena. When I'm warming up my horse before competition and don't want the tie-down strap attached to the noseband, I just snap it to the center ring on my breast collar."

**Cox:** "I use a tie-down only for roping competition, no other time. I use one whether I'm heading or heeling, but I warm up and practice without it. I don't use a tie-down outside the arena because I think it's dangerous outside. If I'm working cattle, a branch could get caught in the tie-down which can cause a wreck, and a horse in a tie-down can drown when crossing water."

### What benefit do you get from using a tie-down?

**Bray:** "In roping events, with a steer or calf, a horse, a rider and a rope, there are a lot of things involved. The horse naturally becomes more elevated with speed, and he loses softness with speed, so the tie-down can help maintain proper headset and body position, establish rate and aid in collection and balance."

**Cox:** "When I rope faster and bigger steers, I use the tie-down so the horse can lean against it a little to absorb the jerk of the steer on the end of the rope. That's the only benefit I see for using a tie-down. I like to use a leather noseband, not anything with steel or anything that can create pain over the bridge of the horse's nose."

### Are there detriments to using a tie-down?

**Bray:** "You definitely don't want to have a tie-down on your horse if you're going up and down hills or crossing creeks. For safety reasons, you never want to have any type of tie-down or martingale on a horse when you ride in water. A horse can drown in a hurry if he can't get his head up."

*Although a tie-down is appropriate for arena work, one shouldn't be used when riding a horse through water because the horse can't lift his head to recover his balance if necessary.*

JOHN BRASSEAUX

*The neck strap is an integral part of a running martingale although the after-market add-on, the silver square, is not.*

JOHN BRASSEAUX

**Cox:** "A lot of people use it to correct a head-set, but that's not why a tie-down should be used. A problem I've seen with putting a tie-down on a young horse is that it doesn't teach him to collect and soften to the bridle. If you start using a tie-down before a horse has learned to be soft and collected in response to your hands, the horse starts leaning on the tie-down. Then the tie-down becomes like a Band-Aid®; when it's taken off, the horse becomes out of control or carries his head so high that it creates balance issues because he's learned to rely too much on the tie-down."

## Martingales

Used primarily for training, martingales are designed to help horses establish headset and develop collection by causing downward pressure on the reins, encouraging horses to carry their heads at designated levels.

Martingales are intended for use with snaffle bits—not shanked bits—and designed to attach to regular nosebands, not to figure-eight or dropped nosebands. Martingales not only can interfere with bit signals, but also can cause nose and/or jaw injury if used with these types of nosebands.

The **running martingale,** one of the most common types, consists of a forked strap that attaches to the cinch and is held in place by a strap around the horse's neck. Each end of the fork strap has a metal ring through which one rein runs. The running martingale's effect is directly influenced by the rider's hands, and how the rider tightens and releases the reins, in turn, dictates how much pressure the martingale creates.

A **training fork** has a design similar to that of the running martingale. A forked strap attaches to the cinch, but there is no neck strap. As with the running martingale, the rider's hands directly influence the results as the fork creates downward pressure on the reins when the horse raises his head higher than desired.

Running martingales and training forks are made of leather or nylon, and have snaps or Conway buckles for attachment to the cinch's center D-ring.

A **string martingale,** favored by some trainers when starting colts, operates like a standard running martingale. But the string martingale is a lightweight, inexpensive option made of soft, narrow nylon cord with stainless steel rings. Knots are used instead of buckles to make adjustments.

For safety's sake, when using these types of martingale, always use rein stops. These simple devices, usually made of rubber, slip

*Unlike a running martingale, the training fork has no neck strap to help hold the fork in position.*

JOHN BRASSEAUX

*Several rings provide adjustment options on a German martingale, which is somewhat similar to a running martingale.*

COURTESY EQUIBRAND

natural headset no matter where my hands are, and a martingale puts pressure against the reins in one particular area. If a horse has become used to a martingale and I were to lift my reins in a different way, the pull can be confusing to the horse. I also feel that a martingale can get in the way at times when I want to lift a horse's shoulder or poll."

Cox emphasizes the importance of not adjusting any type of martingale too short because this can make the horse overflex or overbend.

"The biggest downfall of a martingale is that by making it too tight, you restrict the horse's mobility. Sooner or later you have to take off the martingale—and then you see what you really have. I like to work on developing a headset and softness through feel and timing with my hands and seat. I don't want to rely on a piece of equipment as a tool to accomplish that."

## Adjust the Martingale

When properly adjusted, a running martingale or training fork creates downward

onto the reins between the bit and the martingale rings. The stops keep the rings back where they should be and prevent them from sliding too far down the reins, where the rings might catch on the bit. If a martingale ring hangs on a bit ring or rein connector, this can panic a horse and cause a wreck.

A **German martingale** is another training aid that functions much like a running martingale, but offers more leverage. As with a running martingale, a German martingale has a forked strap attached to the cinch. However, several rings sewn into each strap, typically four, allow the rider multiple options for rein adjustment.

A German martingale encourages a horse to give to bit pressure, flex at the poll, and maintain headset and collection. Although usually not seen in competition, some barrel racers use this style martingale to have more control during their runs.

## Need a Martingale?

It's easy to think some type of martingale is required when training a young horse, but this is not necessarily the case.

"A lot of great horsemen use martingales, but I personally don't use them," says Cox. "I like to teach my horses how to achieve that

*Initially adjust a running martingale so that the rings reach or almost reach the throatlatch; then fine-tune the adjustment as necessary.*

JOHN BRASSEAUX

pressure on the reins when a horse raises his head above the desired position. That pressure gives the rider leverage through the reins to the bit, which encourages the horse to lower his head to the point he finds relief.

The strap forks, properly adjusted, should have approximately an inch or so of slack when the horse holds his head in the desired position. The reins should form straight lines from bit to rider's hands with no tension on the reins from the martingale when the horse's head is held correctly. Make sure no downward pressure from the forked straps affect the horse's head when it's correctly positioned.

The key to proper martingale use: Release rein pressure as soon as the horse's head is in the desired position. By giving the horse relief, he learns to carry his head correctly.

If you adjust a running martingale or training fork too short, it interferes with lateral rein movement. A too-short martingale also increases bit severity by creating downward pressure on the bars of the mouth.

Bear in mind: If a horse starts bucking in a running martingale or training fork, you aren't able to bring his head up higher than the adjusted level.

*Ideally, a training fork or martingale is a bit slack unless a horse's head moves out of position. Note the straight line the rein makes from the bit to the rider's hand and elbow.*

JOHN BRASSEAUX

# 13
# Breast Collars

Today's versions come in numerous styles and materials, but breast collars have been a practical piece of equipment for thousands of years.

About 700 years B.C., Assyrian horsemen used breast collars and cruppers to help stabilize the saddle-like cloths or skins on which they rode. Early Roman riders relied on breast collars to keep their saddles in place. Primitive saddles uncovered in Siberian burial finds dating back to 500 to 400 B.C. included breast collars.

Although breast collars are an ancient concept, horsemen can appreciate the many centuries of history, yet choose from a variety of modern options to meet specific needs.

"Choosing a style of breast collar is as much regional as traditional. For example, in the northwestern portion of the United States—and anywhere else the Wade saddle is popular—it would be very common to see the martingale-style breast collar," notes Roger Allgeier of Brighton Feed & Saddlery in Brighton, Colorado.

"A style that really has gotten popular since around 2000 is the pulling collar," Allgeier adds. "In wheat-grass-area states, like the Oklahoma and Texas Panhandles, those cowboys might rope, then doctor 30 to 40 head of cattle a day, and this type breast collar is one of the most efficient styles for pulling livestock and doing heavier work. Not only does a pulling collar help hold the saddle in place well, the collar doesn't sore a horse, even when used for a long day's riding.

"That's because the collar follows the shoulder up and lays in that hollow between the neck and shoulder, where there's much less movement. A straight breast collar and some of the standard three-piece styles cut across and over the shoulders. As the horse's front legs move back and forth, the shoulders also move, and a breast collar laying over the shoulder can rub and sore a horse. That's one of the big issues you have to watch for, particularly if you're riding long distances or in the mountains."

## Types of Breast Collars

Materials and styles vary, but several standard types of breast collars are used with stock saddles.

**Straight** breast collars basically run straight across the horse's chest and typically have no center rings. Straight breast collars:

- are made of one long shaped piece and might have a slight dip, or scallop, where the horse's neck ties into the chest.

- generally are 3 to 4 inches wide.

- have a sturdy D-ring at each end.

- might have double tug straps at each end to attach the breast collar to both the rigging rings and the breast-collar D-rings in the saddle skirts on either side.

- are favored by many calf, team and steer ropers.

- can sore a horse because of how the collar lays across the shoulders.

**Three-piece** breast collars can run straight across the horse's chest, or have a noticeable contour. This style breast collar might have a pinch guard, a small leather piece behind the center ring, meant to

*Regional influences often affect equipment selection—and even the name by which a piece of horse gear is known.*
ROSS HECOX

*Not every three-piece breast collar has a pinch-guard behind the center ring, but many do.*
COURTESY BRIGHTON SADDLERY

*The width of this type breast collar disperses pressure well, and the two tugs fasten it securely to withstand a heavy load.*
ROSS HECOX

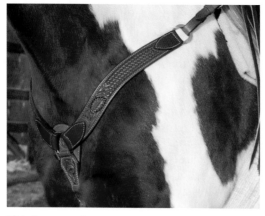

*This breast collar is contoured to accommodate the shape of a horse's shoulder and allows ample room at the base of the horse's neck.*
COURTESY BRIGHTON SADDLERY

prevent pinching and irritation. Some riders insist on the guard; others say it can sore the horse, so that's really a matter of personal preference. If the breast collar has a pinch guard, it should be lined with soft leather, felt or woolskin. Three-piece breast collars:

- are made of three separate pieces, whatever material is used, and have center rings.

- are anywhere from 1 to about 3 inches wide.

- usually have only one tug strap on each end.

- can sore a horse depending on how the collar lays across the shoulders.

- are used by a wide segment of riders, from working cowboys to trail enthusiasts and barrel racers.

**Martingale-style** breast collars take the name from the fact that they are designed to fit much like the straps on an English martingale. "With the popularity of the Wade saddle, most have breast collar D-rings set high near the front saddle strings," notes Allgeier. "Breast collars built for this saddle, such as the martingale-style, have more contour in the shoulders. Because these collars attach so high on saddles, the collars have to be shaped to accommodate the shoulders."

*Because a martingale-style breast collar often is attached to rings set high on the saddle, the collar is contoured to fit the shoulders.*
COURTESY BRIGHTON SADDLERY

*The high attachment of a pulling collar allows a horse to really lay into the collar and handle a load.*
ROSS HECOX

Martingale-style breast collars:

- typically are constructed of three pieces sewn together to make a one-piece collar, although some martingale collars do have center rings.

- usually are 2 to 3 inches at the widest tapering to about 1½ inches toward the top of the neck and saddle.

- are shaped somewhat like the horse collar used in a pulling harness.

- have adjustable neck straps, in addition to tug straps, to help hold the breast collar in place.

- tend not to sore a horse because of the contoured design.

- are known as "chokers" in some parts of the country, such as Wyoming and Montana.

- are popular with riders who like this traditional look, especially with Wade saddles.

**Pulling** collars have gained in popularity since around 2000 and are designed specifically for heavier work where the horse needs a stout collar. Pulling collars:

*The tug strap on a pulling collar goes through the saddle gullet and then wraps around to fasten the collar into an effective position for pulling.*
COURTESY BRIGHTON SADDLERY

- usually are three-piece designs with a center rings, but are shaped similarly to the martingale-style collar.

- are very efficient for working with large livestock in situations where the horse really must put his shoulders into the collar and pull.

- are designed so the tug straps go through the gullet and wrap around the saddle swells on either side of the horn to provide the right pulling position and strength.

- tend not to sore a horse because of the contoured design.

## Materials and Construction

Breast collars range from simple and practical to showy and detailed. Leather is commonly used, but as when shopping for cinches, you also find synthetic and corded materials. Hardware can be nickel-plated metal, brass or stainless steel.

Leather breast-collar construction can be single-ply, but it's more common to find doubled-and-stitched construction. The vast majority of breast collars are lined with a soft leather, such as latigo or chap leather, and some are lined with felt.

"The first two places a horse sweats are behind the ears and over the shoulders. Sweat is really hard on leather, so lining the breast collar helps it last longer," notes Allgeier. "In the past you used to find breast collars lined with woolskin or synthetic fleece, but those are not as popular any more. Those materials pack down in time with use and sweat, and they also pick up a lot of stickers, dirt and debris."

Some riders especially like the look of a corded, or string breast collar, which is

Depending on a region's climate, a synthetic or synthetic-blend breast collar can be easier to clean and maintain than one of leather.
JOHN BRASSEAUX

available in both straight and three-piece styles. They might or might not have a tie-down strap that attaches to the cinch D-ring. Because of the material, these collars require the same care and maintenance as a corded cinch.

Breast collar material options include:

- **harness leather,** which is thick, strong and most durable of leather options.

- **skirting leather,** which, despite a shinier finish, is strong, but less durable than harness leather.

- **latigo leather** that is soft and stretchy, but not as strong or durable as harness or skirting leather.

- **mohair,** which is soft, breathable, less durable than leather, available in numerous colors and patterns, and needs the same care as mohair cinch.

- **mohair-synthetic blends** that gain strength from synthetic materials, but aren't as soft or breathable as pure mohair.

A soft, flexible string breast collar might also be known as a cinch-style collar in another region of the country.
COURTESY BRIGHTON SADDLERY

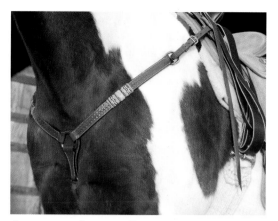

*A narrow-cut breast collar with rawhide trim functions the same as a breast collar that's several inches wide and of plain leather.*
COURTESY BRIGHTON SADDLERY

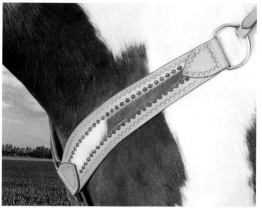

*The use of hair-on inlay and overlay on horse gear is popular with riders of all ages.*
COURTESY BRIGHTON SADDLERY

- **cotton-synthetic blends** with wide color and pattern options, but which, as a result of sweat and dirt, can get stiff and rough with use.

- **nylon,** a less expensive option than leather and an extremely durable material, which must be lined because edges can be sharp; however, nylon comes in a wide range of colors and can be embroidered.

- **BioThane®,** which has the look of leather, but the strength and low maintenance of synthetic material.

- **neoprene** with a nylon core, which, although strong and easy to clean, can be hot and might rub a horse.

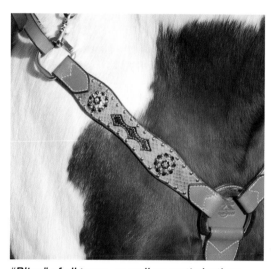

*"Bling" of all types, as well as exotic leathers, can now be found in tack rooms everywhere.*
COURTESY BRIGHTON SADDLERY

# GOTCHA!

## The Saddle Still Must Fit

"I think a common mistake is using a breast collar to hold an ill-fitting saddle in place," notes Roger Allgeier of Brighton Saddlery. "I have people come to trade a saddle and say, 'I have to use a breast collar to make this saddle work.' They need to come to the realization that they need better fitting saddles.

"A breast collar doesn't make a saddle fit better; it's just something to keep a saddle in the proper position, especially when traveling in rough country. I think anything you can do to keep a saddle in the right position and keep the ride more enjoyable—without having to stop and make adjustments—is good. The two things that help do that are a breast collar and a back cinch."

"You can dress up a breast collar in many ways, whether it's the shape (scalloped or contoured), or by adding conchas, rawhide, hair-on cowhide, inlay, overlay, or bling," says Allgeier. "It's also common to find leather breast collars that are handcarved, embossed or stamped with a geometric pattern, such as a basket."

## Q & A: Breast-Collar Use

Horsemen don't always use breast collars, but when they do, it's with good reason. Ted Robinson, the winningest rider in reined-cow-horse history, who has two World's Greatest Horseman championships to his credit, and multiple American Quarter Horse Association world champion Mike Major both weigh in with their thoughts on using this practical piece of equipment.

### When do you find yourself using a breast collar and why?

**Robinson:** "A lot of it depends on the individual horse. If a horse's back conformation doesn't allow the saddle to stay in place easily, I don't want to cut a horse in two with a cinch. So just putting on a breast collar really stabilizes things. A properly fit breast collar keeps a saddle from rolling left and right, besides slipping back. I use one when I'm working a cow up and down the fence because the horse takes big, deep breaths, which can let a saddle slide back.

"Also, if you have a latigo or billet accident when you're going down the fence, a breast collar keeps the saddle from turning so you can get the horse pulled up. That can keep you out of a jam, no doubt about it. I also use a breast collar when I'm team roping, and it's really a back-saver when I'm riding in the hills.

**Major:** "Our ranch in Colorado [the Flying A Ranch in Fowler], is mostly flat, so I don't use a breast collar there so much, but the country in New Mexico where we have our cow-calf operation is more rugged, so we use them there. If I'm dragging calves, I definitely use a breast collar. But when I'm training colts, I don't use one much. Some horses have really rounded backs and really sloping shoulders, where the shoulder blades can push the saddle back. So with a horse like that—whether you're riding flat terrain or up and down hills—you probably want to use a breast collar all the time."

*This breast collar design, which has no center ring, is cut in one piece shaped to fit a horse's shoulders.*

JOHN BRASSEAUX

### What style breast collar do you prefer?

**Robinson:** "I use a three-piece leather breast collar with a center ring. For showing, I like a 2-inch width, and when I'm roping, I use about a 6-inch width. We ride a lot of little horses today, and many breast collars are too big for them. From the center ring to the side rings, I've found just 10 to 11 inches long works best, so I often have my breast collars specially made. This is not so much the case with our roping horses, but for our show horses and young horses, they need the short sidepieces. Some breast collars have a strap over the neck, which keeps it in alignment with the neck and shoulders. When a horse has less prominent shoulders, this strap helps prevent the breast collar from dropping down, but it isn't allowed in cutting."

*An improperly adjusted breast collar can cut off a horse's air, and a too-tight strap between his front legs can soon chafe and rub the horse.*

DARRELL DODDS

*A narrow breast collar often is appropriate in the show ring although a wide breast collar is typical in a roping pen.*

DARRELL DODDS

*The type of breast collar used can vary among competitive arena events, as well as from the arena to the ranch.*

ROSS HECOX

**Major:** "I have used the straight breast collar, but when I'm dragging a big cow into a trailer and the horse is really pushing into the collar, a straight style actually can choke a horse. Because of that I like the one-piece [martingale-style] without a center ring so there's no movement or wear on the horse's chest. I mostly use leather breast collars. I've had a few braided rope breast collars I used on Smart Whiskey Doc [Major's multiple world champion versatility ranch horse]. People really noticed them, but I haven't found replacements that I really like."

**Can you share any adjustment tips you've learned?**

**Robinson:** "I don't want to hook the breast collar to the rigging rings of my saddles because I think that puts the breast collar too low on the horse's shoulders, which can interfere with shoulder movement. I hook a breast collar to the breast-collar D-ring in the skirt of the saddle, because this pulls the breast collar up into the proper position.

"If you look at the horse where his shoulders tie into the neck, the breast collar needs to come into this area as closely as possible. It shouldn't be tight, but it needs to be snug; if it's not making contact with the horse, it can't work properly.

"I also want to make sure the breast collar attaches to the cinch underneath, not just across the chest. If it's not attached to a cinch, the breast collar can move up on the shoulders because of the horse's movement. I want to have some slack in that strap between the front legs. I want to be able to put my fist—knuckles up—in between the leather strap and the horse's lower chest right in front of the girth. Any tighter than that and it can cause irritation and rub him, which can change his movement."

**Major:** "A lot of people try to put a breast collar on too tight and it pulls the saddle way up on the shoulder blades. You need to put the saddle in the correct position and then adjust the breast collar accordingly. You also need to make sure it's attached to the cinch where it can't ride up too high, because you don't want it to slip up and cut off your horse's wind.

"People don't often think about this, but the rigging of your saddle also makes a difference when it comes to using a breast collar. If you have a three-quarter or seven-eighths rigging, they have a tendency to keep the saddle more forward on the horse's back, so you're not as apt to need a breast collar when you're riding in flat country with those riggings."

*During a fast-paced event, the breast collar can help stabilize the saddle, which, in turn, helps the rider maintain a balanced position.*

JOHN BRASSEAUX

# MAKE IT WORK FOR YOU

## Check Your Adjustment

You can attach the breast collar to either the rigging rings on the saddle or to small D-rings set into the front of the skirts and specifically meant for a breast collar. These small rings usually are centered about halfway from the bottom of the skirt to the bottom of the swell.

"For most normal riding, attaching to the breast-collar D-ring in the skirt is fine, but the downside to this is that a really strong pull—or a wreck—is likely to pull that ring loose, although that would usually only happen under heavy-use conditions," notes Roger Allgeier of Brighton Saddlery.

"Some ropers use two tug straps on a breast collar and hook one to the rigging ring and the other to the breast collar D-ring in the skirt. This decreases the chance of that D-ring being pulled out of the skirt, but it also helps keep the center ring in the breast collar from moving up into the base of the neck and choking the horse, or interfering with his breathing in any way. Today, most custom Wade, association or other working-style saddles have the breast collar D-rings set up high at, or near, the front saddle strings."

If the breast collar has a tie strap that attaches to the cinch D-ring, this strap shouldn't be tight, which can irritate the horse, but it shouldn't have too much play in it either. If it's too loose, it can't do its job, which is to keep the breast collar from riding up the base of the neck and interfering with the horse's breathing. Use Ted Robinson's adjustment tip in the Q&A section on page 168 to make sure the strap isn't too tight or too loose.

*A breast collar can be fastened or, in this case, snapped into small d-rings set high on either side of the saddle.*

DARRELL DODDS

*This close-up shows the two tugs fastened with one high on the saddle and the other to the rigging.*

COURTESY BRIGHTON SADDLERY

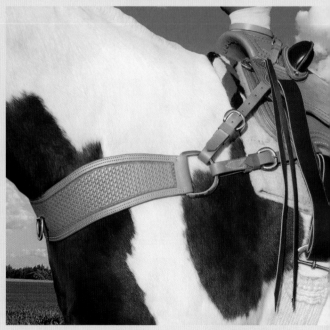

*Here, the collar tugs are fastened to the dee on the saddle and the cinch ring.*
DARRELL DODDS

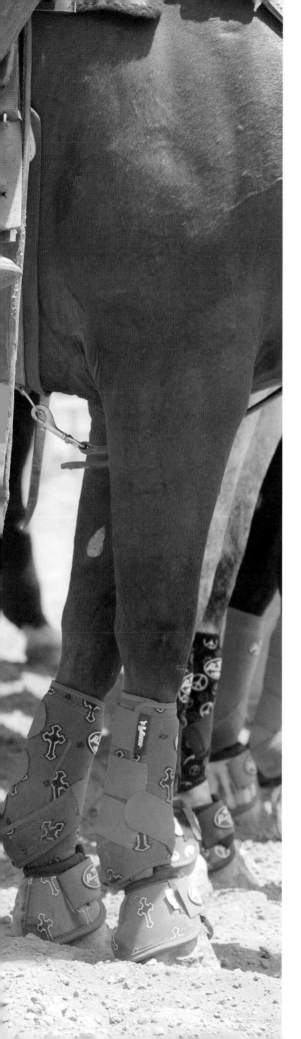

# 14
# Leg Protection

Plenty of horses never see a splint boot, bell boot or polo wrap, but still spend long days under saddle. Just because a horse is ridden for hours at the time doesn't mean he needs any sort of leg protection. On the other hand, a high-level competition horse can work hard only for a matter of minutes, but during that time might need the support and protection of a specific type of boot.

Your horse might need leg protection if:

- he forges, or interferes, striking himself with his own hooves.

- the horse needs tendon support and protection.

- he works hard and fast with plenty of stops and turns.

- you ask for a lot of hind-end engagement with the horse's hind legs reaching well forward.

- he's ridden in deep footing or in a small area, such as a round pen.

"Prevention ahead of time is the best reason for using leg protection," notes Erin Gross, marketing coordinator for Professional's Choice® in El Cajon, California. "For example, any time you ask a horse to come to a stop with his hind end engaged—whether it's reining, roping, cutting or barrel racing—you want to protect the back of the fetlocks from being burned by the [ground] surface. If stopping starts to hurt the animal, his performance decreases, so skid boots are a good preventive measure."

*Initially leg gear was available in minimal material, design and color choices; now a multitude of colors and technologically advanced options can be found.*

COURTESY PROFESSIONAL'S CHOICE

Tendon injuries are among the most common injuries experienced by competition horses. The lower leg in particular is vulnerable when a horse moves at top speed, turns sharply, or works in demanding conditions, such as deep sand or wet, sloppy surfaces.

Anyone who has gone through the time and effort of rehabilitating a serious leg problem can identify with the desire to protect the horse against injury. Although you can't package him in bubble wrap, you can select equipment that helps prevent problems. Still, you must choose leg protection wisely and use it judiciously.

## Types of Leg Gear

When a horse does need leg protection, there are plenty of options from which to choose. Choice all comes down to the type of riding you do, the conditions in which you ride, and the design and material of boot best suited for your particular horse's needs.

For example, a thick, fleece-lined neoprene boot can offer protection from impact and abrasion, but when used for too long a time, can create enough heat on the leg that it might cause problems. Depending on its material, a boot can absorb moisture and become heavy when a horse is ridden in wet conditions, or attract stickers and burrs when traveling through brush. In these cases, your horse might be better off without a boot, or with one of different construction and/or material.

Although styles and types of leg protection vary, an array of boots and wraps are designed:

- to protect against impact and abrasion.

- to absorb shock and concussion.

- to prevent injury from the horse's own hooves or other objects.

- to offer tendon and ligament support.

In no particular order, here's a look at various types of protection so you can decide what's needed and when.

**Splint boots** of different materials are intended to protect the inside of the front legs along the cannon bones and upper ankles. Splint boots:

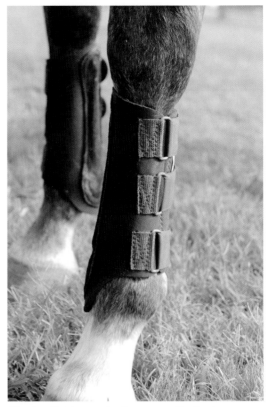

*Most splint boots, leather or synthetic, have additional padding in key areas to reinforce protection.*

KATE BRADLEY

- can be used when riding and for turnout to protect the horse from damage he might cause to the inside of the front legs by interfering, or hitting himself with his own hooves.

- are designed to protect the splint bones, as well as tendons, ligaments and the cannon bones.

- are meant to offer protection from surface injuries.

- are not intended to provide support for the suspensory ligaments.

- typically are made of leather or synthetic materials, such as neoprene, with thick, reinforced portions in the splint areas.

- are held in place by either buckles or hook-and-loop straps.

**All-purpose boots,** sometimes known as protection or exercise boots, also can be referred to as brushing boots. These boots:

- are used when riding and for turnout, and are similar to splint boots in offering padded protection to the insides of the ankles and front legs.

- help absorb impact.

- are typically lightweight and made of leather or synthetic materials, such as neoprene or PVC.

- can be lined with fleece or have gel inserts to absorb impact.

- are held in place by buckles or hook-and-loop straps.

**Skid boots** come in handy during hard stops and sharp turns. Routinely used by reiners, ropers, cutters and barrel racers, skid boots:

- have sturdy, shaped cups, which protect the rear fetlocks from abrasion when contacting the ground.

- come in varying heights, with taller boots meant to offer additional tendon and soft-tissue support.

- typically are made of leather or synthetic materials, such as neoprene.

- often are lined with foam for comfort.

- are held in place by buckles or hook-and-loop straps.

**Sport boots,** also known as support boots, have become popular among riders in many disciplines, who want supportive protection for the lower legs. Professional's Choice manufactured the first boots of this kind, Sports Medicine Boots. Just as people commonly refer to "Kleenex®" when talking about tissues, many horse people use the terms "sport boots" and "sports medicine boots" interchangeably. Features vary from company to company, but generally speaking, sport boots:

- are one-piece, user-friendly boots providing a snug fit.

- typically are made of lightweight synthetic materials, such as neoprene.

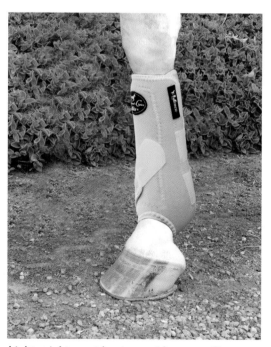

*The look of protective leg gear for has changed in recent years; compare this shot with that of the leather skid boot on page 182.*

*Lightweight sport boots provide a snug fit and shock-absorption, as well as additional suspensory support.*

- cover the lower legs from below the knees to underneath the ankles.

- help absorb shock.

- feature a strap designed to provide suspensory support and help prevent bowed tendons.

**Polo wraps,** used by many riders, offer support and protection for the horse's lower leg. As with any type of wrap or bandage, caution must be used as polo wraps can cause tendon damage if wrapped unevenly or too tightly. Polo wraps:

- usually are 9 to 10 feet long and about 4½ inches wide.

- typically are made of a stretchy, fairly thick fleece material.

- usually have hook-and-loop closures.

- can be "combo-style" with shorter fleece wraps and additional elastic wraps at the ends for additional protection and support.

*A polo wrap can support and protect a horse's leg, but can be harmful if wrapped too tightly.*

JOHN BRASSEAUX

**Standing bandages,** meant to be used over sheet cotton or quilted or pillow wraps, also are referred to as standing wraps. Standing bandages:

- generally are 12 feet long and about 6 inches wide.

- are meant for use on a horse when stalled to prevent swelling or for protection during shipping.

- are not intended for use when riding or competing.

- are thin and lightweight.

- generally are made of acrylic or polyester knit.

- might have hook-and-loop closures.

- can be used with medication on the legs.

**Leg wraps** are placed next to the leg, then covered and held in place with a standing bandage or self-adhesive disposable bandage or tape. Legs wraps:

- usually are made of cotton and/or polyester.

- can be quilted or have fluffy pillow construction that contains batting.

- can be used in place of sheet cotton.

- offer cushioning and protection, making them useful for shipping.

- help decrease swelling.

- often are used when applying medication, such as liniment or poultice, to the leg.

- also are known as "no-bow" wraps when made so that seams prevent creasing, which can irritate or damage the legs.

- can be infused with ceramic powder to help create soothing heat.

# GOTCHA!

## Introducing Leg Protection

It's hard to know how a horse might react the first time you put on a boot or bandage. Some horses pick up their feet and prance with those strange things on their legs. Other horses might kick or even panic and try to bolt. For your own safety, always give the horse time to get accustomed to leg protection before you mount.

Apply the leg protection first, then lead the horse around or take him to the round pen for a few minutes. The main thing: Give him a chance to work through any reaction he might have to the sensation of something attached to his legs—without you on his back.

**Shipping boots** are made specifically to protect a horse during travel when you use something other than leg wraps and standing bandages. Shipping boots protect when a horse scrambles and hits his own legs, or is kicked or stepped on by the horse next to him in the trailer. Shipping boots:

- typically have nylon outer coverings, dense interior padding and thick fleece interiors to provide cushioning and protection from impact.

- fully cover the lower legs.

- usually flare to cover the ankle and even the hoof.

- can extend upward to cover the knees.

- generally have hook-and-loop closures.

**Bell boots,** also known as overreach boots, are meant to protect the horse when a hind foot comes forward and hits a front hoof or heel. Both Western and English riders in many disciplines use these boots. Early models were one-piece rubber bells that were notoriously challenging to pull over hooves. Now considered fashion accessories, bell boots come in a huge variety of colors and patterns—everything from leopard and zebra prints to butterflies. Such colorful boots come in handy when a horse loses one now and then, as it's easier to find a brightly colored boot in the field than a plain black one. Protective bell boots:

- are used for riding and turnout.

- are useful when the horse works hard and/or is in deep footing.

- protect the coronet bands and bulbs of the hooves, as well as cover the entire backs of the front feet.

- also can provide shock absorption, depending on material.

- help keep a horse from catching on and pulling off a front shoe.

- come in a variety of materials and combinations, including neoprene, nylon, vinyl exterior, and rubber.

- can be lined with fleece or padded material for horses with sensitive skin.

*Although early pull-on bell boots were somewhat difficult to use, contemporary styles have hook-and-loop closures.*

COURTESY PROFESSIONAL'S CHOICE

- can have rolled, padded pastern designs to reduce rubbing and irritation.

- attach with buckles or hook-and-loop closures.

- come in no-turn styles designed to stay in position.

- are available in a wrap-around style.

**Fly boots** are lifesavers for horses especially sensitive to biting and annoying insects. Just as with other leg protection, it's important to buy the correct size because when these boots sag and gap, they don't do the intended job. Fly boots:

- are made of the same polyester mesh vinyl-coated material as fly masks.

- attach with hook-and-loop closures.

- aren't hot since the material is airy and breathable.

- protect the lower legs and pastern areas.

- also help protect against ultraviolet rays, much like fly sheets.

- typically are used for turnout, not riding.

- usually have padding around the edges so they're comfortable for long use.

- might collect burrs and stickers, depending on additional padding material.

## Materials Vary

In addition to choosing the style of leg gear your horse needs, you have choices of materials when shopping for leg protection. Consider the following pros and cons:

**Leather** leg gear protection:

- breathes, so doesn't get as hot as synthetic materials.

- is more expensive than synthetic.

- requires stitching, which can rot in time.

- must be cleaned and oiled, or becomes hard and stiff.

- can rub and irritate horse if sand or debris gets underneath the boot.

*Many horsemen use boots to protect and support the suspensories and tendons of their performance horses.*

JOHN BRASSEAUX

# MAKE IT WORK FOR YOU

## Watch that Fit

Boots don't work properly—and can cause problems—when they don't fit properly. When a boot is too tight, it rubs and is uncomfortable for the horse. Adjusted too loosely, a boot provides inadequate protection and can even slip or interfere with the horse's movement.

Unfortunately, there's no universal fit chart, and sizes vary among manufacturers. For example, one company's sizing can be based on the height and approximate weight of the horse, while another company determines size by the circumference of the cannon bone midway between fetlock and knee. How fine-boned or big-boned the horse also can play a role in sizing.

"People often buy the wrong sizes in leg protection," notes Erin Goss of Professional's Choice. "A lot of the boots are ballpark sizes and based on how many hands the horse is, but you might have a short horse with really stocky legs or a tall horse with thin legs. You always should follow the sizing chart for a particular boot and company. Sizes can vary from company to company in the same type of boots. Just as with buying a pair of shoes, there are differences from one company to another company."

Boots should have a snug—but not restrictive—fit. You don't want them to shift or turn on the legs, but you still should be able to slide a finger beneath the boots.

As with your own shoes, equine boots are made to fit left and right feet. If this isn't noted on the boots, you can use an indelible marker to identify which is which. Also, boots typically are designed so that the straps point backward when boots are positioned correctly. Just remember: The end of the strap should point to the end of the horse.

Bear in mind that some leather boots need a break-in period, just as with leather footwear for humans. Stiff, new leather can rub and cause sensitivity, especially if a horse is thin-skinned. You can accelerate the break-in time by using a good conditioner to soften the leather. The first few times you use any type of leg or hoof protection, after removing the boots, inspect the affected areas closely for irritation or rub marks.

When it comes to wrapping legs, be aware that you can cause serious tendon damage when a bandage is wrapped too tightly or incorrectly. The best bet: Ask your veterinarian or a trusted trainer to show you how to wrap a leg correctly, and then practice with that person watching.

"There are so many variables, including the angles at which you wrap the leg and how tightly you wrap it," says Goss. "If you educate yourself, you can protect against causing damage. There are plenty of how-to videos on wrapping legs. Be proactive about seeking out proper information."

*The use of leg gear is a matter of judgment and can depend on such factors as the type of work being done or how prone a horse might be to strike himself.*
KATE BRADLEY

*Dirt might get underneath a leather skid boot, but the open design generally allows the dirt to fall free of the boot.*

JOHN BRASSEAUX

**Synthetic** leg gear, typically made of neoprene:

- has a forgiving fit.

- is lightweight and fairly inexpensive.

- can be cleaned easily, usually by rinsing.

- doesn't breathe, so can allow heat to build underneath.

- shouldn't be used for extended periods of time.

- can rub and irritate horse if sand or debris gets underneath.

- doesn't absorb water.

## Boot and Wrap Care

It's important to use clean boots and wraps to avoid irritating the horse's skin. Before putting on boots or wraps, always make sure they are free of any mud, dirt or debris.

Avoid using wet or dirty boots, as these can cause irritation and skin infections. When working multiple horses and using leg protection, have more than one set of boots so you don't have to put a damp or muddy boot on the next horse.

As with any other equipment, leg protection lasts longer when cared for properly. Follow manufacturer's recommendations.

Leather boots should be cleaned, oiled and conditioned just as with any piece of leather tack. Synthetic boots usually need nothing more than a good hosing. If you have to use any soap, always rinse thoroughly so no residue remains. Hang equipment to air-dry out of direct sunlight.

"All manufacturers have care information on the packaging and on their Web sites," notes Goss. "Most boots made of synthetic materials should be hand-washed with mild soap. Wraps and bandages usually can go in the washing machine, but check the recommendations to make sure."

Wraps and bandages are machine-washable, unless otherwise noted. Brush off dirt and debris first. You might toss bandages into a mesh laundry bag before washing, just to keep them from becoming tangled. Don't use a dryer. Instead, hang wraps and bandages to air-dry. To store bandages, roll them, starting with the end with the closure.

*With routine cleaning and care, protective leg gear of any kind lasts longer than it would otherwise.*

KATE BRADLEY

# EXPERT TIP

## Judgment and Leg Protection

"I do use leg protection—both boots and wraps—and am a big fan of them at the competition level. When I'm in the arena cutting or roping, I definitely use leg protection, but if I'm riding outside or just riding ranch horses, I don't use any," notes lifelong horseman Chris Cox, whose Diamond Double C Ranch is located in Mineral Wells, Texas. An avid competitor in team roping, reined cow horse and cutting, Cox is a three-time undefeated Road to the Horse champion and Equine Experience colt-starting champion. Cox uses boots to protect and support suspensories and tendons, and to keep a horse from burning the back of the heels when stopping. If he thinks a team-roping or competitive cow-horse might overreach when working at top speed, Cox uses bell boots, but very seldom puts them on cutting horses. However, just being in the arena doesn't mean he always uses leg protection on his horses.

"I work my 2-year-olds a bit without boots when they're not going very fast," he says. "About midway through the 2-year-old year, when they're stopping and turning harder, I put on leg protection, and certainly on my more advanced horses. I use leg gear as insurance on my performance horses."

For support boots, Cox prefers styles with buckles, but also uses some with hook-and-loop closures. For suspensory support, he sometimes uses polo wraps on the lower legs and then puts boots on top.

"The problem with wraps is that few people know how to put them on correctly, and you can create more damage wrapping a leg incorrectly than by leaving it unprotected," he cautions.

Many riders feel pressure to use some sort of leg protection, simply because they see other riders using the well-advertised products, but that doesn't necessarily mean a horse needs boots or wraps.

"Not to say you can't use them, but Buster Welch is one of the greatest trainers of all time, and he never puts a boot on a horse," notes Cox.

"If you just walk, trot, and lope, boots can be more of a hindrance and aggravation to the horse than a benefit," he adds. "It's like a football player putting on full pads when he's only going out for a jog."

Some trail riders use leg boots on a horse, but Cox doesn't recommend this. "Many boots are made of synthetic materials, which tend to create heat and friction on the legs when you're on the trail. Also, sand, moisture, stickers, and burrs can get between the boots and the horse's legs, which can cause damage and irritation.

"There are a lot of good boots on the market, but when you do use boots, you need to make sure the ones you use fit your horse. They also need to be put on correctly so that they stay in the correct position with even pressure. Otherwise, using them can be worse than not using boots at all. Don't leave them on all day, and don't leave them on if they get wet, because that increases friction against the horse's skin. Always take off boots as soon as a workout is over so the legs can cool down."

*Although some trail riders use protective leg gear, not everyone does as burrs and briars can get underneath boots and irritate a horse's legs.*

JOHN BRASSEAUX

# Glossary

(Author's note: Please understand that words and terminologies can vary from region to region. That doesn't necessarily mean one is wrong and the other is right, but it does mean a cowboy in south Texas might refer to the same piece of equipment differently than, for example, a buckaroo in Montana.)

**A-fork**: stock saddle with no swells; also known as a slick fork.

**Argentine snaffle:** a loose-shanked bit with a snaffle mouthpiece.

**bosal:** Spanish for "muzzle" and often used interchangeably with the word "hackamore."

**bridging:** an undesirable result when the front and back parts of the saddletree bars make contact with the horse's back, but without any contact in the centers of the bars.

**cantle:** the back portion of a saddle behind the seat; varies in height and shape according to saddle style and/or use.

**cavesson:** a noseband designed to keep a horse's mouth closed.

**centerfire rigging:** the saddle rigging position located halfway between the fork and cantle, basically in the center of the saddle.

**cheek string lash:** a thin leather string added to a hackamore when necessary to keep the hanger slightly away from the horse's eyes; runs under the jaw and ties to both sides of hanger.

**Cheyenne roll:** the cantle style with a wide, rolled back edge; debuted in Frank Meanea's saddle shop in Cheyenne, Wyoming.

**chrome tanning:** a leather-tanning process utilizing chemicals.

**cinch hobble:** a short leather piece connecting the back cinch to the back D-ring on the front cinch; keeps back cinch from moving too far back and into the horse's flank area.

**double-rigged:** a saddle with riggings for both front and back cinches.

**fender:** the leather section of saddle that keeps the rider's legs from touching horse's sides; sometimes referred to by the slang term "sweat leather" for this reason.

**fiador:** a type of rope throatlatch sometimes added to a hackamore to help stabilize and correctly position the bosal; goes over the poll, directly behind the ears, and attaches to bosal at the heel knot.

**fiador knot:** a decorative, yet practical knot made from a single piece of rope; on a rope halter, used to create the loop where the lead rope attaches; on a hackamore, used to attach the fiador to the heel knot; sometimes referred to as a "Theodore" knot after President Roosevelt.

**flat-plate rigging:** rigging style in which both front and back rings attach to one large single piece of leather that wraps around the whole side of the saddle and all the way back to the cantle; also referred to as drop-plate rigging.

**forelock hanger:** a narrow strip of leather sometimes used with the bosal to offer support; attaches to the nose button with other end tied to the horse's forelock.

**forging:** when a horse strikes himself with his own hooves; also known as interfering.

**fork:** the front portion of saddletree that attaches to both bars; also referred to as the saddle swell.

**full rigging:** the most forward of all rigging positions with front rigging ring under center of saddle fork or swell; also known as full-double rigging.

**futurity brow:** popular browband-style headstall featuring two leather pieces knotted together in the center of the horse's forehead.

**gullet:** the tunnel portion under the fork of a saddle; bridge between saddletree bars that is positioned over the horse's wither area.

**hackamore:** American cowboy corruption of the Spanish word *jaquima*, a type of bitless headgear used for foundation training according to vaquero tradition; typically made of braided rawhide or leather; operates off direct pressure instead of leverage; ridden by using both hands.

**hanger:** the headstall or leather strap that adjusts to place a hackamore higher or lower on the horse's nose.

**half-breed:** shanked bit with a high port and roller(s); designed to operate off signal rather than leverage, much like the spade bit.

**headstall:** the portion of the bridle that surrounds the horse's head and to which the bit is attached.

**in-skirt rigging:** style in which rigging rings or plates attach directly to the saddle skirts; either built into or onto the skirts.

**mecate:** a long, single-piece braided or twisted rein with the tail end used as a "get-down" or lead rope, the end of which tucks into the rider's belt or is tied to the saddle strings or hitched around the horn, if not roping; commonly made from horsehair, but can be made of synthetic materials; used on hackamores and snaffle-bit rigs; also known by the cowboy slang term "McCarty."

**mohair:** hair of angora goats; traditionally used to make string cinches and corded breast collars.

**off-billet:** short, heavy piece of doubled leather or nylon with holes punched along the length; attaches to off-side or right cinch ring to the saddle.

**pulling collar:** practical style of breast collar that lays in the hollow between horse's neck and shoulder; designed for heavy work and pulling livestock.

**rigging:** the arrangement of rings and hardware that provide the method by which the saddle is secured to the horse; typically ring, flat-plate or in-skirt design.

**ring rigging:** style in which rings attach to leather plates screwed directly into the saddletree; front and rear rings attached with separate pieces of leather; sometimes can be referred to as a double rigging, but also can refer to the single-ring rigging in the center-fire rigging position.

**romal:** braided extension, typically 4 to 5 feet long, attached to a closed set of braided rawhide reins used on shanked bits; heavy, but flexible; resembles a quirt with a leather popper.

**seven-eighths rigging:** rigging position half-way between full and three-quarter positions, approximately seven-eighths of the way from saddle cantle to fork.

**shu-fly:** a horsehair tassel meant to attach to headstall or bottom of cinch; of varying sizes; can be practical or merely decorative, depending on size and design; also known as a shoo-fly.

**sidepull:** a bitless bridle that works off lateral signal and nose pressure; so named because reins attach to rings on either side of muzzle.

**single-rigged:** a saddle with rigging for front cinch only.

**slick-fork:** a stock saddle with very small, sloping swells; also known as an A-fork.

**slick horn:** a saddle horn that hasn't been wrapped with rubber or other material that grips the rope; allows rope to slide when the rider dallies.

**slobber straps:** leather loops with holes in the ends to connect snaffle bit rings to a mecate.

**spade:** a signal bit that originated with the vaquero tradition; features decorative shanks and straight-bar mouthpiece with a high, narrow port; also has a spoon, cricket and/or roller with copper-covered braces.

**spoon:** the flat, partially rounded plate above the port in a spade bit.

**sport rein:** a one-piece rein frequently used by ropers, barrel racers and contestants in other speed events; also referred to as a game, loop or roping rein.

**swell:** the front portion of a saddletree that holds the two bars together; can be referred to as saddle fork.

**sweet iron:** plain steel that rusts with time; popular bit material.

**tapadero:** protective leather covering that attaches to front of stirrup; prevents brush from poking through stirrup; keeps rider's feet warmer than open stirrup; prevents rider's foot from going through stirrup; also referred to as "tap" or plural "taps."

**three-quarter rigging:** rigging position half the distance between the forward full position and centerfire position halfway between the fork and cantle; approximately three-quarters of the way from saddle cantle to fork.

**vegetable-tanning:** leather-tanning process utilizing natural tannin found in tree bark; significantly longer process than chrome, or chemical, tanning process.

**Wade:** a type of stock saddle with distinctive shape and features built on a Wade tree; thinner, wider fork than other slick-fork saddles and with more bar contact over the surface of the horse's back; readily identified by its slick-fork design and large, low-set horn; first popular with buckaroos in the Northwest and later widely introduced to working cowboys and Western riders in general, thanks to Ray Hunt and Tom Dorrance.

**water ties:** small leather loops with leather laces, or sometimes small buckles, used to attach reins to the bit.

# Resource Guide

Almosta Ranch
Al Dunning
www.aldunning.com
480-471-4600

Animal Dynamics
Don Doran
www.animaldynamics.com
352-591-6025

Australian Stock Saddle Co.
Colin Dangaard
www.aussiesaddle.com
818-889-6988

Benny Guitron Ranch
Benny Guitron
www.bennyguitron.com
209-723-9087

Big Bend Saddlery
Bret Collier
www.bigbendsaddlery.com
432-837-5551

Brighton Saddlery
Roger Allgeier
www.brightonsaddlery.com
303-659-0721

Buckaroo Businesses
Scott Grosskopf
www.buckaroobusinesses.net
406-252-5000

Buckaroo Country
Mary Williams Hyde
www.buckaroocountry.com
541-883-7456

Cactus Saddlery
Webb Fortenberry
www.cactussaddlery.com
903-441-0700

Chris Cox Horsemanship Company
Chris Cox
www.chris-cox.com
940-327-8113

Circle Y
Robb Thomas
www.circley.com
800-882-5375

Craig Cameron Horsemanship
Craig Cameron
www.craigcameron.com
800-274-0077

Cow Horse Supply
Brad Loesch
www.cowhorsesupply.com
817-220-8200

Diamond S Ranch
Lee Smith
www.leesmithdiamonds.com
602-684-3884

Double Diamond Halter Co. Inc.
Pete Melniker
www.doublediamondhalters.com
406-582-0706

Equibrand
Ken Bray
www.equibrand.com
817-573-1884

Hansen Silver
Tim Hansen
www.hansensilver.com
209-847-7390

Haverty Ranch
Clint Haverty
www.havertyranch.com
940-482-6223

Les Vogt Bits & Spurs
Les Vogt
www.lesvogt.com
805-343-9205

LJ's Saddlery
John Willemsma
www.ljsaddlery.com
405-282-5336

Martin Black
www.martinblack.net
y6martinblack@gmail.com

Martin Saddlery
Brad Vance
www.martinsaddlery.com
972-481-8104

Major Cattle Company
Mike Major
www.majorcattleco.com
719-263-5540

Professional's Choice
Erin Goss
www.profchoice.com
619-873-1100

Smith Brothers
www.smithbrothers.com
940-566-9007

Ted Robinson Cow Horses
Ted Robinson
www.tedrobinsoncowhorses.com
805-649-9028

Teskey's Saddle Shop
www.teskeys.com
817-599-3400

Tip's Saddlery
Ken Tipton
www.tipswestern.com
775-623-3300

Tom Balding Bits & Spurs
Tom Balding
www.tombalding.com
307-672-8459

Watt Bros. Saddles
Jeremiah Watt
www.ranch2arena.com
559-935-2172

Weaver Leather
Molly Wagner
www.weaverleather.com
330-674-1782

Weber Stirrups
Trina Weber
www.weberstirrups.com
208-466-2870
208-899-0270

# Author Profile: Cynthia McFarland

Cynthia McFarland was raised in Tucson, Ariz., where she spent countless hours exploring desert and mountain trails on the back of her sorrel Quarter Horse gelding, Yuma, who was small in stature, but willing and huge in heart.

A horse owner for going on 40 years, Cynthia is a fulltime writer and contributes regularly to a number of national equine publications. She is the author of nine books, including two other *Western Horseman* books, *Ride the Journey,* written with Chris Cox, and *Cow-Horse Confidence: A Time-Honored Approach to Stockmanship,* written with Martin Black. Her writing has earned numerous regional and national awards, including a prestigious Steel Dust Award from the American Quarter Horse Association. In addition to books and articles, Cynthia puts her writing skills to use penning copy for advertising campaigns, brochures and websites, and she has taught creative writing workshops for both children and adults.

When not at the computer writing, Cynthia can be found riding the trails of north-central Florida on her good Paint horse, Ben. She and her four-legged family—Ben, Butler the donkey, beef cows and cats—live on a small farm in the heart of horse country near Ocala, Florida.

STEVE FLOETHE

# *Western Horseman* Books: Something for Everyone

What's your favorite aspect of the stock-horse industry—horsemanship clinics, training, trail riding, competition, ranching, raising well-bred horses or simply enjoying the Western lifestyle?

Whatever your involvement in the horse world, you likely can find something of interest on the **Western Horseman** bookshelf. After 75-plus years, we've had time to cover a few topics, from the amusing to the instructional, with a whole lot of the informative and entertaining in between.

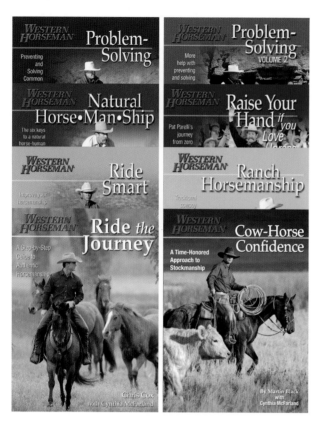

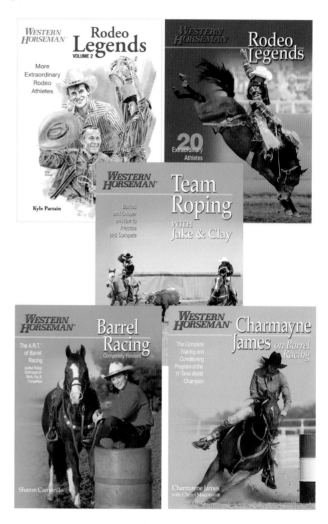

If you constantly strive to improve your **horsemanship**, equine clinicians provide take-it-to-the-barn training tips to help you partner up with your horse. *Western Horseman* book sources include many of today's top hands, and each professional considers hands-on horsemanship skills in his own unique way. **Martin Black** brings both horsemanship and stockmanship skills to *Cow-Horse Confidence*; **Craig Cameron** explains not only how to *Ride Smart*, but also how to *Ride Smarter* in his forthcoming second volume; and **Chris Cox** shows you how to put horsemanship theory into practice in *Ride the Journey*. **Marty Marten** addresses groundwork and riding issues in *Problem-Solving, Volumes 1 and 2*, and in *Ranch Horsemanship* **Curt Pate** describes how you can develop a reliable mount just as a working cowboy does—no matter the size of your spread. **Pat Parelli's** *Natural Horse-Man-Ship* is a classic, and *Raise Your Hand if You Love Horses* chronicles the first 50 years of his life.

If **rodeo** is your No. 1 sport, read about 40 of the sports' finest in *Rodeo Legends* and *Rodeo Legends, Volume 2*. Each chapter tells of a world champion's road to the top—his background, mentors, roughstock draws and/or riding horses, career milestones and more. Or hone your barrel–racing skills with multiple world-champion **Charmayne James**, who set and broke many of the sport's records, and **Sharon Camarillo**, who continues to encourage competitors to reach new levels of horsemanship expertise. *Team Roping With Jake and Clay*, of course, refers to longtime, record-setting partners **Jake Barnes** and **Clay O'Brien Cooper**, who provide sound advice for fast times.

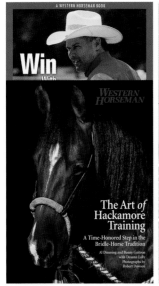

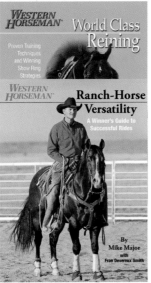

If you're a recreational rider who likes nothing better than hitting the trail, **Backcountry Basics** by **Mike Kinsey** shows you how to prepare your horse to be the best traveling partner ever, no matter the terrain or situation you encounter. In **Trail Riding,** author **Jeanine Wilder** shares her knowledge of riding throughout the country and even considers travel logistics, such as finding a great place to stay, from a wilderness horse camp to a roadside equine facility.

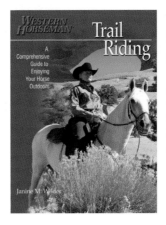

If your favorite event involves **reining** and/or **cattle, Al Dunning** brings his expertise as a multiple world champion to **Reining** and, with co-author **Benny Guitron,** to **The Art of Hackamore Training**. Likewise, **Mike Major,** also a multiple world champion, shares his insights on dry work and cattle-handling in **Ranch-Horse Versatility**. In **World Class Reining**, Shawn Flarida and Craig Schmersal describe their methods for winning championships at national and international events. To help achieve your **riding goals**—as you define them—nobody does it better than **Bob Avila**, with his many world titles.

If **ranching** rates high on your list of interests, various authors in **Legendary Ranches** tell compelling stories about enduring outfits—their histories, traditions, horses and cattle—and the strong, decisive people behind each ranch's success. To learn about regional differences in the ranching industry, read **Cowboys & Buckaroos** by **Tim O'Byrne** for an inside look at how these icons ply their trades, the similarities and differences in their gear and in their approaches to handling horses and cattle.

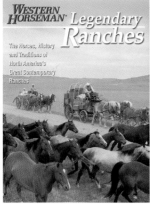

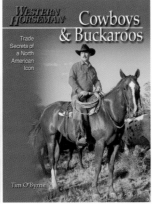

If you've just entered the horse world or have come back to riding after a long layoff since childhood, you might want **basic information** about horses and horse ownership. **First Horse** provides fundamentals of horsemanship and animal husbandry so your transition to horse ownership is a positive experience. Likewise, industry icon **Robert M. Miller, D.V.M.,** guides you through the foal-handling experience in **Imprint Training**, which details the techniques he has popularized worldwide. When your young horse is ready to ride, the **Mike Kevil** classic, **Starting Colts**, guides you step-by-step through the process of developing a solid mount.

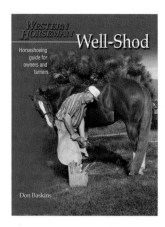

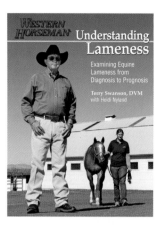

If equine leg and hoof care are a concern, these two books should be on your shelf. *Understanding Lameness*, by veterinarian **Dr. Terry Swanson**, takes a common-sense approach to preventive maintenance and treatment, considering injury and/or disease management not only from his perspective, but also from your perspective as horse owner. Even if you don't plan to shoe horses, *Well-Shod* by farrier **Don Baskins** provides a basic understanding of hoof care that serves any horseman well, from routine maintenance to event-specific and corrective shoeing.

If you like great **gear and equipment** or just want your daily barn routine to go smoothly, have a look at *The Revised Horseman's Scrapbook* and *Helpful Hints for Horsemen*. Both include tips, shortcuts and ideas from knowledgeable *Western Horseman* readers and staff with decades of horse-handling experience. *The Horseman's Guide for Tack and Equipment*, by longtime *Western Horseman* contributor **Cynthia McFarland**, compiles sound advice from industry professionals about how the gear must fit the horse's form to function best.

If **equine pedigrees and performance** are of interest, *Legends, Volumes 1 through 8*, are sure to please. Each chapters focuses on an influential stock-horse sire or dam, as well as the human personalities who made that horse a part of history. Pedigree, performance and production records, and vintage and contemporary photos are included.

If you love the Western **lifestyle**, you're bound to enjoy **Baxter Black**'s entertaining perspective of the West, *The Back Page*. It features many of his columns appearing in *Western Horseman*—on each issue's back page. For mouthwatering recipes, take a look at the wonderful **Stella Hughes'** classic cookbook *Bacon & Beans*. "Sides" include entertaining commentary about ranch life from the world-class cook and award-winning author.

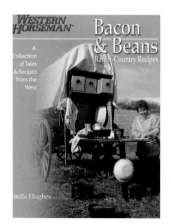